D1168250

Daily Gifts of Grace

Daily Gifts of Grace

devotions for each day of your year

NASHVILLE DALLAS MEXICO CITY RIO DE JANEIRO

© 2012 by Thomas Nelson, Inc.

All rights reserved. No portion of this book may be reproduced, stored in a retrieval system, or transmitted in any form or by any means—electronic, mechanical, photocopy, recording, scanning, or other—except for brief quotations in critical reviews or articles, without the prior written permission of the publisher.

Published in Nashville, Tennessee, by Thomas Nelson. Thomas Nelson is a registered trademark of Thomas Nelson, Inc.

Thomas Nelson, Inc., titles may be purchased in bulk for educational, business, fund-raising, or sales promotional use. For information, please e-mail SpecialMarkets@ThomasNelson.com.

Scripture quotations are taken from THE NEW KING JAMES VERSION (NKJV). © 1982 by Thomas Nelson, Inc. Used by permission. All rights reserved. Other Scripture quotations are taken from the following sources: The KING JAMES VERSION (KJV) of the Bible. *The Message* (MSG) by Eugene H. Peterson. © 1993, 1994, 1995, 1996, 2000. Used by permission of NavPress Publishing Group. All rights reserved. New Century Version® (NCV). © 2005 by Thomas Nelson, Inc. Used by permission. All rights reserved. The Holy Bible, New International Version®, NIV®. Copyright © 1973, 1978, 1984, 2011 by Biblica, Inc.™ Used by permission of Zondervan. All rights reserved worldwide. www.zondervan.com. The *Holy Bible*, New Living Translation (NLT). © 1996. Used by permission of Tyndale House Publishers, Inc., Wheaton, Illinois 60189. All rights reserved.

Some selections are from *A Perfect Mess: Why You Don't Have to Worry About Being Good Enough for God* by Lisa Harper, © 2009 by Lisa Harper. Used by permission of WaterBrook Multnomah, an imprint of the Crown Publishing Group, a division of Random House, Inc.

Compiled by Sue Ann Jones

Library of Congress Cataloging-in-Publication Data

Daily gifts of grace : devotions for each day of your year.
p. cm.
Includes bibliographical references and index.
ISBN 978-1-4002-0364-2 (alk. paper)
1. Devotional calendars.
BV4810.D2525 2012
242'.2--dc23

2011024268

Printed in Malaysia

12 13 14 15 16 TWP 6 5 4 3 2 1

Introduction

Each day comes with its own challenges—endless opportunities for worry, stress, guilt, regret, heartache. We could easily give in to despair just by checking the morning headlines, considering our overflowing to-do lists, or wondering how we'll fill the empty hours.

But sometimes with a change of perspective, a moment of reflection, those worries can become platforms for blessings and joys as they push us closer to the heart of our loving God and his plan for our future. That transformation—from fear to confidence, from despair to hope—is a daily gift of grace, available to us constantly: new every morning, fresh every evening, present every moment of the day as we reconnect with the loving Savior whose sacrifice made the gift possible.

This collection of daily readings expresses 366 ways that daily gift of grace has played out in the lives of the women whose words are shared here: in a kind comment from a stranger, a sunbeam streaking through storm clouds, a child's innocent insight, a revelation birthed in a moment of heartache, a laugh-out-loud moment that transformed pain to pleasure.

These Women of Faith speakers and writers have touched thousands of hearts over the years with their powerful presentations in arenas around the country. But in these pages they share, with poignancy, experience, and humor, how God's grace has touched them *personally*. We hope their stories and lessons will help you see that same gift in every moment of *your* day as well.

January 1

Not the *How* but the *Who*

> For I know that this will turn out for my deliverance through your prayer and the supply of the Spirit of Jesus Christ.
>
> —Philippians 1:19

One morning recently I felt discouraged and bone weary. Many things in my life were going very well, but there were a few areas where I felt very hopeless.

As I looked at my reflection in the mirror, I heard God speak four words to me: *I will deliver you!*

I didn't hear an audible voice, but in my spirit God's voice was unmistakable. I was startled by the clarity of the message.

I thought, *How will God deliver me from this*?

Looking back, I realize the *how* was ridiculous in light of the *who.*

All God was asking me to do was receive his promise and trust him. Nothing more.

He was offering much more than a quick fix or rescue; he was offering me a whole new way to live. But I wasn't sure if I was ready or even had the stamina for the journey that might lie ahead. Even so, the choices were painfully clear. I could continue to struggle all alone, pushing myself through one more day, or I could take God at his word—and let go.

Perhaps you, too, are experiencing a level of hopelessness. As you look at your circumstances, you despair of anything ever changing. Maybe you're wondering if God can deliver you even before your circumstances change.

He can deliver us into the grace and peace that are our birthright as his children so that we can be free—truly free.

—Sheila Walsh

Jazzed About Valley Living

> The pastures are clothed with flocks; the valleys also are covered with grain; they shout for joy, they also sing.
>
> —Psalm 65:13

On a cross-country flight recently, my plane flew over a range of snowy mountains. My eyes traced the trails up the rocky sides to see if any of them would take a car to the summit. None of them did. Isn't that just like life? It's never easy to get to the top.

When we do manage to get there, we seem to think we can shake off the valley dust of routine and hardships. And maybe even get closer to God.

But here is the breath-stopping truth: we are called to live most of our lives in the valley. And who volunteers to don a kilt and do the "Highland Fling" to that news?

That would be me. Yup, I'm jazzed about valley living (well, most of the time). From the mountaintop I can see an eagle soar, but in the valley I can hear a sparrow sing. On the mountain I see trees like canopies, but in the valley I can sit in their shade and eat of their fruit. On the mountain I see lakes like small mirrors, but in the valley I can ladle the water to my parched lips. On the summit I see people like walking sticks, but in the valley I can trace a child's face and dab away tears.

The mountaintop is distant and dangerous. The valley is fruitful and dangerous. Life is like that too: bone-drying hard and wildly wondrous.

—Patsy Clairmont

January 3

A Craving for Comfort

> O God, You are my God; early will I seek You; my soul thirsts for You; my flesh longs for You in a dry and thirsty land Where there is no water.
>
> —Psalm 63:1

The editor of a sophisticated food magazine links the recent rise in the popularity of cupcakes to our nation's longing for comfort and security. People want to be transported out of this era of modern-day threats and back to a time of greater innocence.

I understand that possible explanation, but the truth is, our desire for security is as old as Adam and Eve. There has never been a time when we were not fearful about something.

During my childhood, I was fearful about math. And yes, that little devil's food cupcake purchased after school from Boehm's grocery store did make me feel good, momentarily distracting me from the bewilderment of math class and the teacher who found me annoyingly unteachable. But reality forced me to recognize that the cupcake treated the symptom without providing the cure.

In today's world we still want to retreat into simple pleasures and believe that tomorrow's math class has been canceled, along with other demanding requirements beyond our capabilities. I believe it's possible to have our cupcake and eat it too. We can feel secure in this life without worrying that our security will be yanked from us, as it was for me as math class started at 10:00 a.m. each day. God has clearly stated promises in the Bible that are intended to produce security in us in spite of our circumstances.

For example, Psalm 9:10 states, "Those who know Your name will put their trust in You; for You, O Lord, have not forsaken those who seek You."

That truth, sweet baby, is reason to celebrate. May I suggest a cupcake?

—Marilyn Meberg

Permeating Our World with God's Glory

LORD, our LORD, how majestic is your name in all the earth!
—PSALM 8:9 NIV

Sometimes I think about the sorry state of our world and feel the burden of being responsible for others. The appalling smut passed off as entertainment, the horror of women and children sold for their bodies, the uncertainty of how best to care for the planet—I can't decide whether to build a bunker in the backyard or race out in full battle regalia. Perhaps you, too, have felt overwhelmed by the sight of hungry faces on the evening news or have been moved to anger by the casual attitude others have toward God's gift of life.

The good news is that a little bit of elbow grease on our part goes a long way when coupled with our heavenly Father's compassion for humanity. Just a smidgen of love will often sweeten a bitter relationship. A morsel of mercy can soften the most callous criminal. And a teaspoon of biblical truth, seasoned with grace, has the power to enlighten those who've been duped.

We must not forget that when God handed humanity the authority to manage his creation, he didn't intend for us to govern with an iron fist. We won't change society for good through autocratic bullying, scowling in disapproval, or waving protest placards. Instead we can permeate our world with God's glory by engaging our culture—by sharing microwave popcorn with a Muslim co-worker; by voluntarily cleaning up an abandoned lot in town; by chatting with the lonely, blue-haired ladies in church; or by simply dropping off a casserole to a frazzled single mom who works two jobs to support her family.

We will lead the way God intended when we love well the other messy image-bearers he weaves into our stories.

—Lisa Harper

January 5

The Judas Kiss

He who was called Judas, one of the twelve, went before them and drew near to Jesus to kiss Him.
—Luke 22:47

Yes, it is true. If we ask to be like Jesus, we will experience some of the things he experienced. We will have those who do not care for us because of our faith, and we will have those who hurt us even within the household of faith. There may be acts of betrayal. These acts can be deeply painful.

Forgiving them is the first step toward walking out the heart of God in these hurtful situations. In the past, when I have felt this type of pain (I call it the Judas kiss), it has taken me a little while to come to the place of forgiveness. Probably because I don't expect to feel betrayed by one who follows Christ, much less one I have known and trusted for many years. Jesus certainly knew and loved Judas, didn't he? Judas saw the miracles and felt the wonder of who Jesus was, and yet Judas still kissed him, betraying him to his enemies.

For a time I felt that simply forgiving the deep hurt that came with a Judas kiss was enough. Then one day, I felt the Lord wanting me to go deeper. I felt him impressing my heart that, after forgiving, I was to go out of my way to do something special or to give something special to that person.

I began to do that very thing. I gave a special gift, or I did some special deed or invited that person for a special meal. I was amazed at the results. Doing something kind that cost me something, either in finances or time expended, ushered me right into gratitude; and hidden between the letters of the word *gratitude,* I found (in the Spirit) the word *freedom*. I suddenly found myself set truly free of all that had taken place.

—Lana Bateman

Becoming a Safe Person

Whenever you stand praying, if you have anything against anyone, forgive him, that your Father in heaven may also forgive you your trespasses.
—Mark 11:25

While filming a *Facts of Life* reunion movie a few years ago, I reverted to teenage behavior and took up old junior-high-girls-gossiping activities with cast-member friends.

We didn't dislike the ones we were gossiping about. It was just a way of bonding. One of us might say to the other, "Can you believe _______ did _________?"

The night after the gossiping began, I felt the Lord whisper to my heart, *Lisa, you don't know why ______ does what you were gossiping about. You don't have a clue what she's going through.*

I felt terrible. Thankfully, God let me realize my wrong so I could change. During the rest of that month of filming, if someone started talking to me about someone else, I would say, "I've noticed she does that, but have you seen how much she's grown in other areas?" Or, "I can't believe she did that either. But I find myself doing the same thing sometimes. I wonder if we'll ever grow up!"

An interesting thing happened. I was soon perceived as a safe person. The cast and crew drew close to me, and when filming ended, some told me, "You just don't carry any baggage, do you? You're different now."

What I learned through this experience is that people are hungry for safe havens, places of grace, where they can be themselves without judgment, fear of exposure, or betrayal.

Despite what we think we see on the outside, everyone is hurting in some way on the inside. If we have allowed God to bring love and healing to our own hurting places, we can share with others the grace we've been given that shows we know what it feels like to be hurt and healed.

—Lisa Whelchel

January 7

Fresh from the Fall

> Your words have upheld him who was stumbling,
> and you have strengthened the feeble knees.
> —Job 4:4

At a concert in Iowa a few years ago, I fell off the stage.

Yes, you read that correctly. *I fell off the stage!* I don't know exactly what happened, but somehow I lost my balance, flipped through an Olympic-caliber aerial movement, and tumbled into the crowd.

Fortunately, people standing against the stage caught me and pushed me back up on the stage, where I lay curled up in the fetal position, thinking, *Lord, is there any chance you misunderstood earlier tonight when I asked that you would be* glorified *through my performance tonight? Maybe you thought I said* horrified?

I lay there on the stage another moment, lost in the darkness, ready to burst into both tears and laughter at the same time.

Girl, you've got two choices, I told myself: *Get off the stage while it's still dark and never show your face in this town again, or get up and keep going.*

I got up, and although I was embarrassed, humiliated, insecure, and unsure of myself, I finished my show.

I have not always been strong enough to make a fool of myself in front of thousands of people then blink back tears, regain my composure, share a laugh, and carry on with the show. The old Natalie would have run off that stage straight into the bathroom.

But the old Natalie's self-image was one of deception, shame, and failure. Now, as the new Natalie, I'm learning what it means to be real. I'm working each day to recognize and appreciate the unique person God created me to be. And I'm learning to see that person, that Natalie, through God's eyes. The difference has been life changing.

—Natalie Grant

The Power of Forgiveness

If you forgive men their trespasses, your heavenly Father will also forgive you.
—Matthew 6:14

We live on a fallen planet where terrible injustices can sometimes rain down on us. When the wound comes from the hand of someone we trusted, the pain and resulting anger can be crippling.

But holding on to those feelings of unforgiveness can become a prison. The other person goes free while we, encumbered by resentment and anger, are trapped. When we are unable to forgive or refuse to forgive, we become hostages to the pain of the past. The resulting bitterness can ruin our lives, poisoning the soul and making it hard for us to know where we end and where the bitter unforgiveness begins. That overpowering negativity warps our sense of self.

That's why unforgiveness is one of the most difficult things to let go of. Let's be honest: it's human nature to want to hurt the one who hurts us. But God claims vengeance for himself (see Deuteronomy 32:35). As hard as it is to admit, it's not really up to us to expect a feel-good ending for all our woes. We simply have to trust that justice will take its God-ordained course.

Forgiveness is one of the most powerful spiritual weapons God has tucked into our arsenal. From Genesis to Revelation, the golden thread of forgiveness is woven through the Word of God as the key to deliverance.

When we learn by God's grace to let go of revenge and to embrace forgiveness, the freedom that results is outrageous.

—Sheila Walsh

January 9

Dancing by Faith

> He sends the springs into the valleys;
> they flow among the hills.
> —Psalm 104:10

Jesus Christ came from the high places but lived out his thirty-three years among us in the valley. He began his human life in a lowly manger and completed his work on a barren hillside that became divinely lush with his holy sacrifice. Hope spilled out of his pierced side and into the valley. In that valley, birds sang inspired arias, leaves pirouetted to the earth with elegance, and breezes carried the grace melody throughout the lowlands. You still can hear the music in a bee's buzz, smell it in the lilac's sweetness, and see it in a snowflake's dance. Listen carefully.... There, did you hear it? If you didn't, you will.

We won't always hear the music, but even during those dark times, we can keep dancing by faith.

By studying his Word and listening to others who have spent time dancing in the valley, we can learn what it means to survive—and thrive—in the everyday muddle of our fast-paced existence. We can gain a fresh perspective to maintain and, if necessary, resuscitate our verve. We *can* learn to dance in the valley.

—Patsy Clairmont

The Gift of Stability

Jesus Christ is the same yesterday, today, and forever.
—Hebrews 13:8

There's no better way to provide stability and security for your children than to let them see you and your spouse showing sincere and affectionate devotion to each other. When children see their parents loving each other and making their relationship a priority, they come to feel that their household situation will be the same tomorrow as it is today. They can go to sleep at night knowing that they'll wake up in the morning and the adults who are in charge of their life will still be there, watching over them and maintaining a stable home for them.

For children whose parents are in second marriages, this kind of stability helps them slowly regain the trust that may have been damaged when their original parents divorced or even when one of their parents died. Knowing that the foundation of their blended family is strong, children develop confidence that helps them venture out, believing their family will still be there for them, steady and sure, when they come back home.

As an analogy, think of a toddler and his mother going to a park. The toddler finds himself in a new, unfamiliar place, and at first he clings warily to his mother, watching wide-eyed as the other children play. Then maybe he turns loose of Mom's hand for a moment and ventures toward the playmates-to-be. In an instant he's back, needing that touch of Mom's security.

In a moment he heads out again, and soon he's happily playing with his new friends. But as he plays, he's constantly checking in with Mom, looking for her. He needs to be able to count on her, and when she proves herself to be steady and dependable, he gradually gains the trust and confidence he needs to venture out and try new things.

—Sandi Patty

January 11

An Open Door

> The King will reply, "Truly I tell you, whatever you did for one of the least of these brothers and sisters of mine, you did for me."
>
> —Matthew 25:40 NIV

Visiting our local homeless shelter women's center recently, I was led into a big room filled with bunk beds. "People never get out of this room without crying," the director said.

Really? Who cries over bunk beds?

Open cubbies stood at the end of each bed. "Some of the mothers have four children, and all of their things have to fit inside this," she said. Five people. One cubbie. One story of abuse or violence after another. I stood there and cried.

God comes to us in such quiet ways: the homeless man seeking food at the shelter, the abuse victim who flees with her children, the addict who stumbles through the homeless shelter's chapel door. We like to water down the harsh realities of life, but the words of Christ bang away at our hearts: "Whatever you do for the least of these, you do unto me."

We realize that *not* doing anything *is* doing something. That's a hard truth to swallow.

God is here. Among us. Disguised as a battered mother, a scared child in a homeless shelter, or a homeless addict standing beside the road with outstretched hand. God doesn't speak, but we know what he's saying. "Will you help me?"

We are here to clothe, to feed, to love, to serve. May we all be an open door through which truth enters. For the sake of the least of these.

—Donna VanLiere

God Will Take Care of Us

Away with you, Satan! For it is written, "You shall worship the Lord your God, and Him only you shall serve."

—Matthew 4:10

When Satan tempted Jesus to jump off the pinnacle of the temple in Jerusalem to prove that Jesus was the Son of God, Satan played on the human fear of feeling insignificant.

Do you ever feel like a nobody? Do you wonder if anyone sees all that you do or if anyone cares? Do you ever fear your voice will simply never be heard? Our culture and, at times, our churches seem more impressed with charisma than character. We make heroes out of very flawed people and then wonder why they come crashing to the ground.

It has always been one of Satan's most powerful tools to tempt us to try to be "somebody." In the garden of Eden, he told Eve, "God knows that the moment you eat from that tree, you'll see what's really going on. You'll be just like God" (Genesis 3:4 MSG). The appeal was too much for Eve to resist; she took from the only tree in the garden forbidden to her.

To Jesus, standing on the top of the temple, Satan's approach was the same: *Show your stuff! Show them who you really are!* Perhaps Satan hoped Christ would plunge to his death.

How many times has Satan tripped us up by tempting us to grab it all? Power is a heady drug. Satan's whisper is, *You'll get away with it.*

But Jesus said, "It is written again, 'You shall not tempt the Lord your God'" (Matthew 4:7). It is to God, and God alone, that all glory goes. We are to enjoy his provision.

We need not fear anything. God has shown us again and again that he has our best interests at heart. He will provide for us. He will comfort us. He will reveal himself to us.

—Sheila Walsh

January 13

A Unique Life Journey Begins

> There is neither Jew nor Gentile, neither slave nor free, nor is there male and female, for you are all one in Christ Jesus.
>
> —GALATIANS 3:28 NIV

When I was about twelve, my folks gave me elocution lessons, and those lessons impacted my thinking about the future.

One day our teacher asked us to say, "Oh," in the manner she specified. When she said, "Lucille, please say 'oh' as though you're in pain," I let out a cry as though I were dying. She smiled then said, "Now, say 'oh' as if you were handed the baby to whom you had just given birth."

I let out the same cry.

Miss Little laughed, as did the rest of the class. The exercise continued with each of us saying "oh" in various ways: "Oh, how beautiful." "Oh, you can't mean it." "Oh, no, not again."

Somewhere in the recesses of my mind that day, I must have envisioned giving birth and disliked the idea. It just seemed clear that getting married and having children—a most natural longing and certainly the course "expected" from girls of my generation—was simply not on my radar.

I don't want to follow the traditional path, I thought. *I want to do life differently.*

Of course, it was too early to know exactly what I wanted in place of what most girls my age were aiming for. But I believe the seed-thought my daddy had planted in me years earlier began to grow heartily during those days: you are never alone . . . God is with you.

Unwittingly, I had already left the dock on a unique journey the Lord had charted especially for me.

—Luci Swindoll

Friends Needed

The sweetness of a man's friend gives
delight by hearty counsel.
—PROVERBS 27:9

A few years ago, I suffered a breakdown of sorts and went to a counselor for help. The treatment and cure surprised me, and I think it will surprise you too. Pure and simple, the medicine I needed was friends. That's right: friendship. Who knew?

Certainly not me. I had barely been seeing a therapist for a month when she remarked, "Lisa, you have the most elaborate defense mechanisms I've ever encountered. Your mind has created backup protections for just about any direction I attempt to reach your heart."

She suggested that we concentrate on creating a superstructure of supportive friends, specifically, grown-up, female friendships.

Mostly, my counselor and I explored why it was difficult for me to allow friends to get close to me. We talked about how to identify safe people and how to implement boundaries. Through authentic conversation with my professional friend, I was learning how to be more honest and vulnerable and, thus, make a two-way connection possible.

We started by taking a good long look at my oldest friendships. They definitely reflected my head and heart split. But I learned never to underestimate the power of tears, need, brokenness, desire, grace, and love. I gingerly practiced vulnerability with my old friends and then tiptoed into opening myself up to the possibility of new friends.

I'm happy to report that, within the context of those relationships, I began to experience deep healing and to grow healthier.

—Lisa Whelchel

January 15

Making Choices Align with Priorities

> I'm on the edge of losing it—the pain in my gut keeps burning. I'm ready to tell my story of failure.
>
> —Psalm 38:17 MSG

A dictionary defines the word *edge* in several ways, but my favorite is "the point at which something is likely to begin." Throughout each day, we encounter edges, points at which something is likely to begin. Sometimes those edges seem insignificant, presenting simple choices: should I eat the cake? But they can have disastrous consequences or powerful potential. For example, alcoholics know they're always one little drink away from disaster.

Conversely, many of us have seen how a simple word of kindness or the smallest gesture of friendship has had a big impact on someone's troubled heart.

Sometimes big decisions start with small choices: During the invitation hymn at the end of a church service, we may choose to cross a divine edge as we step into the aisle. Then we take a step forward, then another, and the next thing we know, we're committing our lives to Christ.

But here's the thing: an edge is the point at which something is *likely* to begin. It may not happen automatically. The edge may be a choice.

My top priority is to love and serve God. In the last few years I've gone through some health challenges. Through them I've learned that to be able to work toward my number one priority, I need to choose actions that honor and care for the body he has given me so I'm able to use it in his service and also use it to cherish and support the wonderful husband, family, and friends he has given me.

—Sandi Patty

Lord, Show Me Where to Start

How shall they believe in Him of whom they have not heard? And how shall they hear without a preacher?
—Romans 10:14

When Vesta Sauter, founder of Deaf Opportunity Out Reach (Door), first arrived in Romania to minister to the Deaf, she had a real problem. (Because Deaf communities function like cultural and language groups, Deaf Americans prefer a capital *D*.) How could she *find* Deaf people? Bucharest is a huge city, and no one seemed able to help Vesta.

If God wants me to minister, she thought, *he'll have to show me where to start.*

In a taxi she searched the streets, looking for anyone . . . anything . . . that might be a clue. As the cab passed an overgrown, trash-strewn city park, she saw a man standing on the corner—signing to another man! In a flash, Vesta was introducing herself.

That night, the two men took her to their Deaf club's meeting, where Vesta signed to the group, "I want to tell you about Jesus. He is alive, and he wants a relationship with you, the Deaf people!"

From that first encounter, an amazing ministry developed. In the next several years, DOOR sent more than thirty mission teams to Romania and saw five Deaf churches planted. Those church members then coordinated an outreach to the Deaf in thirty-plus Romanian cities!

Imagine what can happen when you pray to God, "Show me where to start."

—Joni Eareckson Tada

January 17

Our Greatest (Often Unknown) Fear

My people will dwell in a peaceful habitation, in secure dwellings, and in quiet resting places.
—Isaiah 32:18

I suggest that the greatest fear each of us struggles with is *abandonment*. We've all been left, one way or another, by someone somewhere. Abandonment feelings can come from a husband who is too busy to listen, a child who leaves home and rarely calls, a body no longer able to fight disease, dreams that do not come true, and even a God who seems not to hear.

Maybe you're not aware of any abandonment experiences in your life. That's probably why you're sometimes left wondering *What was that*? when the event's residual sadness or insecurity sweeps over you at an unexpected time or place.

That sometimes overwhelming emotion can suddenly appear and leave you hanging on to your sanity for dear life, wondering, *What's wrong with me*?

The good news is that God-assisted enlightenment makes it possible to understand these weird and unexpected rip currents and keep from getting knocked down by them. We do that by figuring out what we're feeling and then tracing the feelings back to their roots. Clarity leads to light, and light leads us to the Light of the world and the God of the universe, who pushes back the darkness, restores broken lives, and ties our hearts to his with inseparable bonds of love.

—Marilyn Meberg

Waiting on God

The LORD is good to those who wait for Him, to the soul who seeks Him.
—LAMENTATIONS 3:25

I came to a conclusion recently. As much as I would like it to be so, "waiting on God" will never end this side of heaven. It seems as soon as I rejoice at seeing a prayer answered, something else is thrown out of reach, the prayers begin anew, and I'm waiting—again.

And actually, when I think about it, it's not *one* thing after another. It's several things overlapping one another, some taking years to play out, others weeks or months. But no matter the length of time, somehow it's never easy.

Funny how God knew our flesh would find it hard. Thus he reminds us over and over in his Word that it's part of our walk with him. "Wait for the LORD; be strong and take heart and wait for the LORD" (Psalm 27:14 NIV). "Rest in the Lord and wait patiently for Him" (Psalm 37:7). "My soul, wait silently for God alone, for my expectation is from Him. He only is my rock and my salvation; He is my defense; I shall not be moved" (Psalm 62:5–6).

But he does more than charge us to wait. He gives us promises to hang onto: "The LORD takes pleasure in those who fear Him, in those who hope in His mercy" (Psalm 147:11). And I love that God "acts on behalf of those who wait for him" (Isaiah 64:4 NIV).

As much as my flesh cries out when it's forced to wait, my spirit rejoices. When I'm waiting, I'm praying more. I wake up seeking God and lie in bed at night pondering His ways. I search the Scriptures for answers. When I'm waiting, I'm keenly aware of my need for Him, that apart from Him I can do nothing.

Are you waiting on the Lord? I'm not here to tell you it's easy. But I've learned—yes, painfully at times—that one word goes hand in hand with waiting: *trust*.

—Kim Cash Tate

January 19

True Success

> They love the Lord's teachings, and they think about those teachings day and night. . . . Everything they do will succeed.
> —Psalm 1:2–3 NCV

At first glance the words "everything they do will succeed" at the end of Psalm 1:3 seems about as truthful as the weight listed on my driver's license until our government chose to omit that data (maybe because most people fudged on the number).

How can the psalmist label broken relationships or rebellious children or infertility or crippling depression a success? How can he sincerely sing, "Everything they do will succeed," when all of God's children experience failure of some kind or another? Has he been guzzling cough syrup, or is he just wearing overly optimistic blinders?

Neither. Because this promise of prosperity is preceded by the context "everything they do"—which in this passage is defined by spiritual obedience—"succeed" in verse 3 is in reference to walking closely with God. It's essentially an Old Testament version of Romans 8:28: "And we know that all things work together for good to those who love God, to those who are the called according to his purpose."

It doesn't mean we'll get everything we want exactly how and when we want it. And it sure doesn't mean everything we do will be judged successful by human standards. What it means is that ultimately our sovereign Redeemer will work *everything* out for our good and his glory because we are his people and he loves us. It means that being in a real, redemptive relationship with the Creator of the universe is the true measure of success.

—Lisa Harper

God's Truth Transforms

For the word of God is living and powerful, and sharper than any two-edged sword.

—Hebrews 4:12

Chuck Swindoll has taught me more about the grace of God than anyone. He has been my pastor, teacher, and friend for thirty years. About twenty years ago, I joined the board at Insight for Living, his radio and audio Bible teaching ministry. I love that Chuck's grace-based biblical teaching is heard all over the world every day in almost every language.

The Bible-teaching ministry of Chuck is unparalleled in my view, and the thought that his messages are delivered to a radio audience on virtually every continent is astounding to me. I am so grateful.

Many years ago, I was driving down the freeway in California with my niece Mary, who was then in high school. The radio was playing in the background, and I was singing along with Stevie Nicks. The lyrics were, "Tell me lies, tell me sweet little lies." Without even realizing it, I knew all the words. Little Mary said to me, "Mimi, why would you sing those words or even have them in your head?" (Out of the mouths of babes!)

A week later I was in Australia with Insight for Living. I was having breakfast in the hotel dining room, and that exact song was playing. I thought about what America exports to the world and my conversation with Mary. I felt sad. Suddenly after the song, I heard the Insight for Living theme song, and Chuck's voice as he began teaching. I was overwhelmed with gratitude that we export this message.

God doesn't tell us sweet little lies or any lies. He teaches us truth. And God's truth transforms the lies in our heads that the world has taught us to believe.

—Mary Graham

January 21

Healing for the Busy but Lonely

> We do not lose heart. Even though our outward man is perishing, yet the inward man is being renewed day by day.
> —2 CORINTHIANS 4:16

Many of us live busy, lonely lives. We can be surrounded by people, even family, and still feel isolated and alone.

How is that possible? It happens because it's risky to be known. It happens because we imagine that, in a moment of finally stepping out of our cocoon ready to spread our wings and fly, someone will laugh at us—or worse still, simply turn her back and continue with her conversation.

When a child is born and the very first face she focuses her eyes on is the face of her adoring mother, part of the rip of Eden is healed. When that love and acceptance are further strengthened through the years by her father and by family and friends, it will be hard to convince this little one that she is not worth loving. The trouble with the human experience of many of us is that the love we needed and craved as children was withheld, and the tear of separation that began in Eden has gotten bigger.

One of the greatest spiritual gifts of rebirth when we give our lives to Christ is that we have fresh eyes to look into and see how much we are treasured. You have a Father who adores you, who delights in your laugh, who celebrates your gifts, and who catches every tear that falls from your eyes. His love will give you the courage to leave the cocoon behind and fly.

—Sheila Walsh

God Readies Our Path

Make me walk in the path of Your commandments, for I delight in it.
—Psalm 119:35

I grew up with an innate love for school, even though I wasn't a crackerjack student. I had a lot of fun though, and that was more important in my way of thinking. Learn something new while having a good time—this was my mantra. *If I can do this all my life*, I thought, *I've got it made.*

What turned my crank most was figuring out how things work—gadgets, the world, my mind, problems, ideas. I spent a lot of time thinking about what I read or drew, investigated or discovered.

My daddy had told me that I am never alone, that God is always with me. I took Daddy at his word, and that made me think I could accomplish anything. So I tried it all. I built model airplanes and boats, played the cello, swam in competition, dissected frogs, made up games, took calculus. (Got a rotten grade in that last one, but at least I tried.)

I decorated my little bedroom bulletin board with magazine cutouts of faraway places with strange-sounding names that I dreamed of seeing one day. I sometimes imagined myself in another world, another time or place. I was an inventor. Explorer. Naturalist. Musician. Artist. Anthropologist. Singer. On and on. I saw myself as free to roam the world without any attachments, meeting people from everywhere.

As I write today, I see again how God had his hand on my future from the very beginning. I can't tell you what primary ingredient made me who I am. The only thing I can say is that God creates each of us uniquely by his design and for his purpose. He readies the path that beckons us in the direction he has in mind. And when we step onto the path, the adventure begins.

—Luci Swindoll

January 23

Learning to Connect

> Go home to your friends, and tell them what great things the Lord has done for you, and how He has had compassion on you.
>
> —Mark 5:19

I am learning how to connect with friends on an intimate level. On a good day, I would say that I'm in the middle of the messy, mysterious part of a journey into friendship. That's okay. I have a sneaking suspicion that the mess and the mystery are essential to friendship for grown-ups—that friendship this side of heaven may not get any cleaner or clearer.

At one time or another, and all at the same time, friendship feels scary, hopeful, overwhelming, life-giving, aching, enriching, stretching, and oxymoronically like a deeply satisfying hunger. Relationships can cause us to feel off balance and out of control, which makes it so much easier to give up our clutching for self-sufficiency and to grasp onto the Lord in utter dependence. He knows exactly who I am and what I need and who can best meet my needs.

Your process won't look exactly like mine, but three things I do know for sure: God will lead you very personally and gently, the path won't be anything like you expect, and the walking out of his plan will take longer than anticipated.

And I am here to say it is worth it. For me, learning about grown-up friendship has been difficult and painful, but I have so much growth to show for those friendships. My heart has been broken, but that was a severe mercy. Without the brokenness, I couldn't have known my need. Without realizing my need, I wouldn't have risked reaching out to others. Without entering into relationship with others, I would have missed authentic connection.

—Lisa Whelchel

He Chose Us

If we confess our sins, He is faithful and just to forgive us our sins and to cleanse us from all unrighteousness.

—1 John 1:9

My first boyfriend, John Pitter, was an eleven-year-old foster kid who lived temporarily in my neighborhood.

One day Pitter-Patter, as I called him, suggested we sneak into the church and snack on the communion crackers. I was horrified but soon found myself sitting beside Pitter-Patter on the church floor munching away. Feeling nauseated, I trudged home later carrying a huge load of guilt and shame.

When I confessed my sin of stealing to my father, the church's pastor, he kindly assured me God would forgive me. We prayed together, and I thought I'd feel better.

But I didn't. I persistently sensed that I was bad. I believed God wouldn't forgive me and would surely reject me.

Soon after that, Pitter-Patter abruptly disappeared from my life. His foster mom said he had been adopted.

I believed it was only a matter of time before I would be removed from my home, too, especially when my parents figured out that God had ditched me. My fears were completely illogical, of course, but emotions lack logic. They have no common sense!

Perhaps you, too, in some way have felt like you got ditched.

Honey, if that's the case, you're not alone. But I've got great news for you. The Bible assures us that the moment we confess our sin and receive the forgiveness for which Jesus died, God promises he will *never* abandon us. He *chose* us. He loves us and will never leave us.

I know that now. I wish I could tell Pitter-Patter.

—Marilyn Meberg

January 25

Time for a Divine Picnic!

> A merry heart has a continual feast.
> —Proverbs 15:15

When was the last time you went on a picnic? Last week? Last year? Perhaps it's been so long you can't remember. Well, don't put it off a moment longer. Pick up a few goodies, pull out a basket, and get ready for some fun. If the weather isn't agreeable, spread a cloth on the family room floor and see life and lunch from a new view.

I suggest attending your picnic via bicycle. By the time you arrive, the aromas emitting from your lunch will stimulate your saliva glands. You could motor to a mountaintop, but I suggest a fertile valley, even if it's your backyard vegetable garden. What could compare to a vine-ripened tomato or a freshly pulled carrot? Give it a healthy squirt under a hose, and you're good to go. A picnic menu doesn't have to be complicated.

In fact, part of the joy of picnicking is imbibing in the simple pleasures of life: slurping chilled watermelon while being serenaded by the brown thrasher on yonder limb. Just make sure you're not sitting under the feathered songster, lest some of the notes he hits cause an unseemly splash.

You might want to bring a friend, a journal, and a New Testament. Jot down inspirations and ponder valley life and the Shepherd who walks with us there. A meaningful conversation makes a meal a memory.

We may live in the valley, but we can find myriad ways to make mealtime divine. Bon appetit!

—Patsy Clairmont

At the Cliff Edge of Doom

Indeed these are the mere edges of His ways, and how small a whisper we hear of Him!

—Job 26:14

When I was looking at ways the word *edge* was used in Scripture, I found great encouragement in Jesus' words to his disciples in Luke 21:34–36. He was urging them to keep their enthusiasm for the coming return of God's kingdom, but those same words could apply to so many things in our lives today.

He said, "Be on your guard. Don't let the sharp edge of your expectation get dulled by parties and drinking and shopping. . . . Pray constantly that you will have the strength and wits to make it through everything that's coming and end up on your feet before the Son of Man" (MSG). (Don't you just love *The Message* paraphrase of the Bible? "Parties and drinking and shopping"? You'd think those words were directed at women as well as men. Oh! I guess they were.)

When making the right choices feels like stepping over the edge of a cliff into the unknown, it's a scary situation. With experience we learn to take that scary step, make that right choice. We can't know exactly how things will turn out, but we know that God is right there with us and he'll make even the worst things work for our good. When we believe that, we can "stand fearless at the cliff-edge of doom, courageous in seastorm and earthquake, before the rush and roar of oceans, the tremors that shift mountains. . . . God-of-Angel-Armies protects us" (Psalm 46:2–3 MSG).

—Sandi Patty

January 27

Set Free

Bear one another's burdens, and so fulfill the law of Christ.
—GALATIANS 6:2

I will never forget the first time I told my story from the stage. I was terrified. To stand before a large crowd of Christian women and admit that the shame and despair in my life sent me to a psychiatric hospital before I could be set free went against everything I grew up believing. I gave my life to Jesus at eleven, but I kept my shame. I believed if anyone knew what a worthless person I was, I would be exposed and shunned.

Believe it or not, I still struggle with this at times. Even though I work with a team of wonderful women who love me and who are my friends, there are moments when the old beliefs float to the surface. Satan whispers, "You don't belong here. People don't really like you. Everyone can see there is something wrong with you."

When this happens, I have to make an intentional choice to resist the lies of the enemy. I have to remember that, although my childhood painted a lot of shame on my heart, as a woman of God I was given a blank canvas. The picture now coloring my innermost being is a beautiful thing. I may not be spared the disappointments and frustrations we all face as adults, but I am changed. God whispers, "You are beautiful. You are loved. You are worth loving."

The glorious thing about healing from the crushing weight of shame is the hope it can offer to others. When you have been set free, your life becomes an open door showing others the way.

—Sheila Walsh

The Blessing of an Accepting Dad

I know that You can do everything, and that no purpose of Yours can be withheld from You.

—Job 42:2

Being reared in a home like mine had its challenges. We were a loving, upstanding, Christian family, but patterns and mores governed the thinking of my parents (especially Mother), and one didn't deviate from those without unpleasant consequences. It was 1950 when I graduated from high school and time for me to consider college and, of course, marriage.

I talked to my dad about college and my dreams for the future, which didn't include a wedding. I felt his support, but it was hard to escape the overriding, petulant moods of my mother when I mentioned these things to her.

Bowing to pressure from friends and Mother, I began dating and eventually was given an engagement ring the summer before college began. I didn't love this young man as one should when considering marriage, but I so wanted to please Mother that I accepted the ring and went away to college, engaged and insecure.

On campus, it was obvious to me that my dreams were very different from "settling down," as Mother used to say. I called off the engagement. Once again, Daddy came to my rescue, but Mother's disappointment lasted a very long time.

I was the first person in my extended family who chose to remain single. I've often wondered where I would be now had it not been for the allegiance and love of my father. He never criticized me for choosing the path I did.

Would that every girl had a dad like mine.

—Luci Swindoll

January 29

How Will You Respond?

> It's in Christ that we find out who we are and what we are living for.
>
> —Ephesians 1:11 MSG

At some point, most of us will encounter a challenging situation that will permanently alter the rest of our lives. A knock at the door, a middle-of-the-night phone call, or a diagnosis from the doctor that changes the future as you envisioned it.

The question is, how will you respond to your new normal? Will you withdraw from society and close the blinds on communication with other people, focusing only on your personal pain and deep grief?

Or will you choose to live a meaningful and vibrant life, even if it's different from the life you always wanted? Will you make choices based on unshakable truth that will not only enhance the quality of your own life but also bring renewed hope and fresh courage to people in your sphere of influence?

It usually takes a long time to find meaning and purpose when you are living in the middle of devastating circumstances. If you are up to writing the story of how God is helping you to find "redemption" in the midst of a heartbreaking, dream-shattering experience, you can journal about how he used the "shards" in your tragedy as the raw material for a renewed ability to choose life. That may not be the life you expected but the "redemptive life" you now have.

If it's too early in your journey to chronicle what happened, that's okay. For now, decide to move in the direction of life instead of slipping into self-pity, debilitating doubt, and the stranglehold of fear.

Choosing life is the first step in getting a foothold in your own new kind of normal.

—Carol Kent

Casting the First Stone

He who is without sin among you, let him throw a stone at her first.
—John 8:7

I never met the woman, but I connected with her many years ago. She had made a mistake so terrible the elders of her village decreed that she was too loathsome to live; they sentenced her to be stoned to death.

They brought her before Jesus, named her sin, and reminded him of Moses' law. Then they asked him to confirm her death sentence.

Jesus took his time answering them, but eventually he must have nodded. "Go ahead," he told them. "The sinless one among you, you go first; you throw the first stone."

You know her story, the one told so powerfully in John 8:1–8. Actually, it could be *my* story, in a way; maybe it could be yours too.

With Jesus' words ringing in their ears, the scholars and Pharisees turned one by one and walked away. Apparently they had made mistakes too.

Then it was just Jesus and the sin-scarred woman. She must have trembled as she waited for him to speak again. When he did, he asked her where her accusers were.

In my mind, I see her shrug, maybe wondering fearfully if this was a trick question. "Th-th-they're gone, Lord," I hear her answer.

"You go too," he told her. "Go and sin no more."

I'm paraphrasing here, but those of you who know *my* story know that several years ago I had good reason to identify with this woman. I *was* that woman! So many times, I've reconnected with her in entirely different ways.

I stood there with her, looking up at Jesus in total amazement, whispering, "You mean I get a second chance?"

—Sandi Patty

January 31

The Gift of Life

> He was wounded for our transgressions, He was bruised for our iniquities; The chastisement for our peace was upon Him, And by His stripes we are healed.
> —Isaiah 53:5

When I was a young girl, I had a recurring nightmare. In this terrible dream, I was about to be executed for a crime I didn't commit, but I couldn't get anyone to listen to me. Two prison guards were taking me down a long corridor that had a closed door at the end. I knew when I reached that door I was to be executed.

We passed people I knew, but they didn't even stop their conversations or turn toward me. I could feel my heart beat so fast I thought it would burst out of my chest.

Just before we got to the execution chamber, I would wake up in a cold sweat with tears pouring down my face. The dream was so real and vivid it always took me a few moments to convince myself it was just a nightmare and I was actually safe in my bedroom with my sister fast asleep beside me.

Now when I think back on that nightmare, I know it's a perfect example of the reality Christ spared each one of us from. For those of us who love him and have been forgiven by him, he turned the nightmare that would have been ours into the gift of life.

Most of us would not be guilty of crimes any human court might convict us of, but in the eyes of a holy God, we all stand condemned for the sin we were born into and the choices we have made. Jesus took the shame and judgment that was on us, and he heaped it upon himself.

—Sheila Walsh

A Difficult Admission

She calls her friends and neighbors together, saying, "Rejoice with me . . . !"
—Luke 15:9

The truth is I need friends. There, I said it. That was hard. I don't like needing anything because to need feels dangerous and *is* dangerous. But the reward is nothing less than the possibility of intimacy with God, yourself, and others. In my opinion, that is the closest thing to heaven on earth.

Intimacy requires me to become vulnerable to others as I share my true self. That vulnerability helps establish the honest connection that creates strong friendships.

As I have worked on finding friends, I've learned the importance of identifying safe people who can cushion me with love and courage—resources I need to face conflict for the things that matter rather than choosing peace at any price, which I'm prone to doing.

That's why learning conflict-resolution skills was a step I needed to take in order to make way for intimacy in my life. The intimate friendships that followed created an atmosphere of grace.

And grace, of course, ushered in self-acceptance. Embracing myself helped me believe and receive God's love. Resting in his delight changed me forever.

For years, I tried to get to an understanding of God's grace and love all by myself. But God had a different plan. He created us for relationship—not only with himself but also with others.

If God the Father, Son, and Holy Spirit need each other, then where in the world did I get the impression that he was impressed by my Lone Ranger exploits? Thank you, Lord, for teaching me otherwise!

—Lisa Whelchel

February 2

Eternally Connected

> Let everyone who trusts you be happy; let them sing glad songs forever. Protect those who love you and who are happy because of you.
>
> —Psalm 5:11 NCV

In the earlier days of the space program, space-walking astronauts had to have a tether that connected them to the spaceship. Imagine what it was like for those astronauts, completely dependent on that tether. If it broke, the astronaut might float off helplessly with no hope of re-tethering, no hope of ever reconnecting with the mothership—or the earth.

The fear the astronaut would have experienced at being disconnected from the spaceship is what all of us feel when we experience emotional disconnection. When abandonment occurs, the tether breaks, and we float about, lost in space, panicky and fearful as we scramble wildly to reconnect.

When a baby is born, the loss of the womb's security-producing amenities creates a nameless panic. One way Mama quells the panic is to hold the baby close to the familiar sound of her heartbeat in the warmth of her encircling arms. There are, of course, other possible causes for a newborn's tears, but the origin of those first tears is the disconnect from Mama's womb.

Psalm 68:19 reminds us that even though we may disconnect from Mama, we have a perpetual connection with our Creator: "Blessed be the Lord—day after day he carries us along" (MSG).

That image, of being carried daily next to God's heart, imparts an overwhelming promise of nurturance. Being held next to our mother's beating heart of love and connection has its root in the reality of God's consistent expression of love for us, his children.

—Marilyn Meberg

Buoyed by Hope, Saved by Christ

I wait in hope for your salvation, God.
—Genesis 49:18 MSG

When Ms. Reality Check comes rapping at my heart's door, I find her too blunt. ("Yes, that does make your butt look big!") What she says is truth, which is sometimes brutal and hard to bear. (It might do her—and us—good if she would dip her insights into mercy's pool before wrapping us up in them.)

Some of us answer, "I knew life wouldn't be perfect, but I thought it would be easier than *this*." We're told repeatedly in Scripture to prepare for hardships, so why do we believe our lives should be characterized by ease? Do you think it might be the hope of heaven within us that makes us willing to risk expecting the best? Or is it fantasy? Or denial? My best guess is that we flutter about like a butterfly to the flowers of hope, fantasy, and denial, depending on the situation and our ability to bear it.

Hope is a buoy to help keep our heads above the waterline of reality. Yet when we depend on it to be our protection against difficulties, we deflate it, and hope becomes a weighted sinker that drags down our faith. Hope doesn't announce that life is safe and therefore we will be safe; instead, it whispers that Christ is our safety in the midst of harsh reality, heartbreak, and disappointment. In his presence, we experience his tender mercies and care for our bruised emotions.

—Patsy Clairmont

February 4

Creating a Whole New Look

> I will praise You, for I am fearfully
> and wonderfully made.
> —Psalm 139:14

When I went to college, I met a girl who radiated confidence. Melanie loved everyone, and everyone loved her. She was a natural leader who had a lot of friends. Every time I ran into her, she took time out of her day to listen to my problems, encourage me, and make me smile.

She never wore the trendiest clothes. Come to think of it, I never even saw her put on makeup. But she had a look that said, "I am comfortable with who I am. I am secure and confident." That confidence was a beauty I hadn't seen in teens my age or in magazines or on the Style Network, but it was a look I wanted.

How can we get Melanie's look? How can we feel so secure in our skin that our slouching shoulders straighten, our darting eyes focus, our fears disappear, and our insecurities about men and friends give way to unwavering confidence?

We begin by cleaning up our hearts a little bit to make room for a new, fresh look. We have to get rid of the bad stuff that prevents us from radiating joy and sparkling with confidence so we can take on a whole new look that says, "I am beautifully and wonderfully made."

—Jenna Lucado

Making a Friend

I have loved you with an everlasting love;
Therefore with lovingkindness I have drawn you.
—Jeremiah 31:3

I met Heather while helping with a fund-raising event for our homeschooling group. She was extremely bright, organized, and creative and also funny, caring, and sincerely sweet.

As we became acquainted, I learned that she was struggling with a difficult assortment of hard knocks. Yet she always had a word of affirmation to offer. In contrast, I was living in *c'est la vie* mode, hiding my emotions.

Somehow Heather got behind my wall of defense mechanisms and next to my heart. I started to care about her and realized I wanted to be her friend. But that thought terrified me. What if she discovered that I wasn't really the strong and confident woman I pretended to be and she rejected me? I hated feeling so vulnerable.

In a brave moment, I confessed to her, "I'm scared to death to enter into this friendship."

She reassured me, "Well, I'm not scared. Trust me."

I began to open up and risk being vulnerable and needy with her. Then, one afternoon while I was working on a writing project at home, I was sinking under waves of emotion that threatened to pull me under. I cried out to God and felt him urging me to read Jeremiah 31:3. And in that verse, I found assurance that he was with me in the middle of that storm.

I was so happy that God had met me in my need that my first thought was that I wanted to call Heather and tell her about it. That felt odd to me. Why did I want to share that with her?

I called her, and she was accepting and affirming and said just the right thing: she said it sounded just like the kind of thing God would do for a daughter he adored.

—Lisa Whelchel

February 6

Seeing God in Everything

> He has made everything beautiful in its time. Also He has put eternity in their hearts, except that no one can find out the work that God does from beginning to end.
> —Ecclesiastes 3:11

Nineteenth-century theologian Charles Finney said, "A state of mind that sees God in *everything* is evidence of growth in grace and a thankful heart." When I came across that statement, I wrote it in my notebook, and it became a daily challenge for me.

Like me, do you also acknowledge that God *is* in everything but struggle to see God's hand in *everything* that is happening right now, in your daily life?

What are you dealing with right now that you don't remember signing up for? I think of those waiting for medical test results—for themselves or a loved one, maybe even a child—that may well determine the path their lives will follow. I think of a female soldier during the war in Iraq who wrote to say that listening to Women of Faith audiotapes was sometimes the only thing that kept her sane when she saw friends die.

Harsh realities that intrude into our lives can make it hard to recognize the fact that our God is always present. But some of the greatest surprises to me on this spiritual journey are those moments when it becomes clear that God has been faithfully cultivating my heart—those times when things don't go as planned but I *do* see God is in control.

These moments don't have to be extreme, life-and-death situations. Often it's in the little things that we see God's work. That is grace, and it is a gift.

—Sheila Walsh

The Great Deaf Bible Riot

For the word of God is living and powerful . . . and is a discerner of the thoughts and intents of the heart.

—Hebrews 4:12

On an outreach trip to minister to the Deaf in Romania, Vesta Sauter and Camille Beckham took many boxes of illustrated Romanian New Testaments to a Deaf club meeting in Bucharest. When the people saw the Bibles, they rushed forward, struggling to grab a copy.

"Don't worry," Camille quickly signed. "There are plenty of Bibles for everyone." But that wasn't what experience had told them. After decades of lining up for bread and nearly every other essential during the Communist regime, the Romanians couldn't believe there would be enough of anything.

I can just picture it—the Great Deaf Bible Riot! People pushing their way to the front, hitting, kicking, yanking on Vesta's and Camille's clothes to grab Bibles out of their hands. Each person seemed ready to fight to get a copy of the precious Book.

"When I saw their desperation to have a Bible, I was so convicted," Camille told me later. "Have I ever grasped my Bible as tightly as they did? Do I rush to open it and see what it has to say to me? Do I really, truly comprehend the incredible value of God's Word?"

She didn't answer her own questions. Neither did I. But I've never forgotten the image she painted, as she described the hunger those desperate Romanians had for the gospel.

God, give me that appetite too!

—Joni Eareckson Tada

February 8

The Simplest Things Speak Profoundly

> Return to your rest, my soul, for the Lord has been good to you.
>
> —Psalm 116:7 niv

The chair in the living room felt particularly comfortable that morning as I was settling into my devotional time. Although I had been feeling harassed by some difficult circumstances, I was trying to calm my heart and to focus. It was in the midst of that inner struggle that I felt the Lord nudging my heart.

He drew my attention to the amazing cat sitting before me. I was filled with the wonder of that exquisite beauty when I felt the Lord move in my thoughts: *Do you see how this creature rests in the warmth and safety of your lap? He has no fears, no concerns. He simply trusts you and knows that nothing can alarm him when you are holding him. He is not anxious or uneasy. He is not nervous or agitated. He is at peace because the one who loves him most holds him close. Oh that you would trust me, as this animal trusts you. All of your cares would slip away like the sun that sets so quickly. The warmth of my embrace would quiet your heart and ease your racing thoughts.*

When the struggle of the day seems overwhelming, when the demands seem more than you can handle, try curling up in my arms like that little one sleeping peacefully before you. What I ask is not difficult. It doesn't require a brilliant mind or a staggering bank account or years of profound theology. Just look at the sleeping cat you love and trust me the way he trusts you.

—Lana Bateman

You There, with the Scissors!

Even to your old age and gray hairs I am he, I am he who will sustain you.
—Isaiah 46:4 NIV

Things that used to be funny when I was younger aren't all that hilarious anymore. For instance, my sister, Janet, used to play the piano at a nursing home to entertain the residents, and we laughed about the old lady who bragged, "I wake up every morning and I know who I am, and I say, 'Praise the Lord!'"

Yes, that *used* to be funny. These days, however, it's losing a bit of its punch. Oh, I know who *I* am most of the time. It's *your* name I can't remember.

Sometimes I'll have to run through my entire mental Rolodex, calling a friend by every name that comes to mind—from former pets and automobiles to present-day helpers and relatives—before I finally arrive at the right one.

I have to admit this isn't really a *new* problem. Our boys used to roll their eyes as I was reciting roll call, trying to get the right name in the emergency lecture: "Bill! Steven! Whumphie! Tim! Barney! Spot! David! . . . You there, chasing your brother with the scissors! Stop it right now!"

As I've grown older, the problem has gotten worse, especially with all the abbreviations and acronyms used in modern life. I might mean to report on a friend's female problems requiring hormone replacement therapy that worried her about someday needing life-saving intervention but instead say that she had frequent parcel deliveries along with worries about the war in Iraq and hoped she would never need an accountant.

So it comes out as, "She had such bad UPS, she thought she needed to take WMD but worried it might affect her heart and cause her to need CPA."

—Barbara Johnson

February 10

Finding True Focus

> Truly my soul silently waits for God; from Him comes my salvation.
> —Psalm 62:1

The psalms remind us to trust in God's power not our own puny attempts to live righteously. Consider the opening words of Psalm 62, written by King David: "from Him comes my salvation."

In other words, wearing a happy face and hose to church doesn't make us good girls any more than painting racing stripes on a Yugo makes it a sports car. Walking in faith means trusting in God alone, not in what we say or do or wear. It means being honest about the fact that each of us is a mess and we need God's mercy. It means recognizing our complete dependence on his protection, provision, and providence.

When we focus all our energy on trying to be in control, we forget our innate sinfulness and our desperate need for God. We succumb to *moralism,* the false belief that somewhere in our hearts resides the aptitude for perfection and the ability to fix everything that's wrong with our world. Then we jump on the hamster wheel of working increasingly harder to be both holy and in control until we can't imagine living one more day under the tyranny of "need tos" and "shoulds."

Working so hard to pretend that we have our lives totally together—and therefore should be in charge of everybody else's—makes me want to say bad words and gobble chocolate. But there is hope beyond cussing and carbohydrates. There is a path that veers away from the exhausting effort of self-reliance and back to the security we have in divine redemption.

And we'll find the trailhead when we take our eyes off ourselves and instead focus on *who God is.*

—Lisa Harper

It's Okay to Be Needy

For this is God, our God forever and ever; He will be our guide even to death.
—Psalm 48:14

During a Bible study one day, I sensed God's love in such a visceral way that I asked him to let me understand his love in a way that would settle into my very being and flow outward to others.

I felt him respond: *The problem is, that wall you have built around your heart to protect yourself from getting hurt is the same wall that will prevent my love from flowing out of you and onto others.*

I answered, *Then tear that wall down!* In answer to my prayer, God orchestrated the perfect storm, and soon I was facing an abundance of mental, emotional, physical, and spiritual challenges. Looking back, I see how God had to hit me from every angle to crack my wall of elaborate defense mechanisms.

Ironically, his most effective battering ram appeared during a tender moment of vulnerability from a friend.

One evening my friend and I talked about what God was teaching us during that season of life. Angela said, with tears in her eyes, "I am learning it is okay to be needy, that God isn't surprised at me for wanting someone to love me and care for me. That these wants and needs are part of his design."

Her words shook the foundation of my heart. What? It was okay to be needy? That thought had never crossed my mind. I wasn't even aware that I had needs. I had carefully avoided wanting and needing in order to spare myself the inevitable disappointment when those desires wouldn't be met. It hurt less not to need.

I believe I began to grow in that moment of realization when I dared to humbly acknowledge my needs, beginning with my longing for connection.

—Lisa Whelchel

February 12

God's Fresh-Baked Grace

> By God's special gift of grace given to me through his power, I became a servant to tell that Good News.
> —Ephesians 3:7 NCV

As a believer for forty-plus years (I gave my life to Christ when I was eleven), when I am faced with life's crises, I usually know enough to turn to God for strength, grace, and guidance.

It's the small stuff that gets me. It's the moment when my plans are messed up and no one seems to care or when something upsetting happens and disappointment threatens to overwhelm me. Those are the times I must learn the lesson over again—to trust God.

I'm thankful God promises to help me through it. I don't have to be strong. I don't have to endure the situation on my own. I don't need to follow any rules or live up to any expectations. When my plans fall apart and my life takes an unexpected, unpleasant turn, I simply need to be honest and real and ask God to blanket me in his amazing, miraculous gift of grace.

As I look back over my life, I remember many times when challenges occurred, and although God's grace was right there, I didn't always reach out and receive it. Instead, I desperately hung on to my own agenda.

When I could let go of it, I found God's grace waiting for me, fresh every morning. Yesterday's grace is stale. It was baked fresh by God for the events of yesterday, but today there is a whole new supply for everything you and I will walk through today.

—Sheila Walsh

At Peace with Myself

I will praise You, for I am fearfully and wonderfully made.
—Psalm 139:14

It's always been hard to be me. When I was little I wanted to be Emma Lou, who was an only child as opposed to living in my family of eight children. When I was in high school, I wanted to be Jeanie, whose parents (as far as I could tell) were richer than anyone in the world. When I was in college, I wanted to be anyone who was born in California. I'd grown up in Oklahoma and was attending school in California. I barely spoke the language and was way over my head in most of my classes. If I'd been *them* instead of *me*, it would have been so much easier.

Even now I want to be a better me than I am. I want to always do the right thing, say the right thing, wear the right thing, and be with the people who make me feel better about me. I could think of many reasons how I got here, but it doesn't matter.

It's the Word of God that takes me to a place of not only acceptance of myself but also peace with the quarrel. I am a child of God. I have been made *in his image*. I'm not defined by my family of origin, my background, my strengths, my weaknesses, my friendships, my work, my gifts, or my skills. I am a child of God. He loves me just as I am. God's love is perfect. Complete. Whole. And I am the recipient of that great love not because of who I am but rather because of who God is. All of us should remember that when we think that maybe we want to be someone else.

—Mary Graham

February 14

Motivated by Love

> I ate the fruit and honey, I drank the nectar and wine.
> Celebrate with me, friends!
> Raise your glasses—"To life! To love!"
> —Song of Solomon 5:1 msg

"Life ain't no picnic!" How many times have you heard Ms. Reality Check spout that one? Or how about, "If life gives you lemons, make lemonade"? I pucker at the thought.

Yes, we've all been told that the "school of hard knocks" is part of life, but if you're like me, crushing blows still catch you off guard, leave you speechless, and at times rob you of your very breath.

As long as I understand that the valley, where bees nest and poison ivy spreads, is where I'll usually be doing my picnicking, I can safeguard my heart from disillusionment. I understand that I won't be spending lots of time sipping sweet nectar on a distant mountaintop.

I really do believe that in this life we will have scrumptious picnic spreads of fried chicken, corn on the cob, and homemade ice cream. But not without ants, mosquitoes, and nasty sunburns.

We do visit mountaintops every once in a while, of course, but the majority of our sojourn is in the valley. After a mountaintop "picnic" with Moses and Elijah, Jesus led his disciples back down into the valley to finish their work amid insults, treachery, and death.

Why? Love. Love motivated Jesus to endure all that was before him in his valley, and it motivated his disciples. His love will keep us secure even in the midst of our thicket-filled experiences.

—Patsy Clairmont

Have Good Trouble

I have told you these things, so that in me you may have peace. In this world you will have trouble. But take heart! I have overcome the world.

—John 16:33 NIV

Recently, I traveled to the Dominican Republic to see the awesome work World Vision is doing there.

As I was leaving on our last morning, Noel, a waiter at the hotel, thanked me for coming, invited me back to the Dominican Republic, and concluded with, "Have good trouble." I did my best to explain the difference between travel and trouble, but the exchange got me thinking about "good trouble."

On our trip, we'd had our fair share of good trouble—luggage that arrived thirty hours after we did, a wheel that came completely off our vehicle as we traveled into the field, and bats in the stairwell at a hotel.

We also saw trouble that was not so good. We saw malnourished babies, overworked mothers, and frightened children who lived in an unsafe and unreliable environment. No one would describe those kinds of trouble as good. However, we saw a hope that was much bigger than their troubles. Through their relationship with World Vision, these mothers had been introduced to another relationship that changed everything for them—a relationship with God. Jesus assured us that while we will have trouble whether we're a woman in the Dominican Republic or a woman in the United States, we can all grab hold of the promise that God will never abandon us in our times of struggle. And through Christ Jesus, we have assurance of final victory.

—Lori Roberson

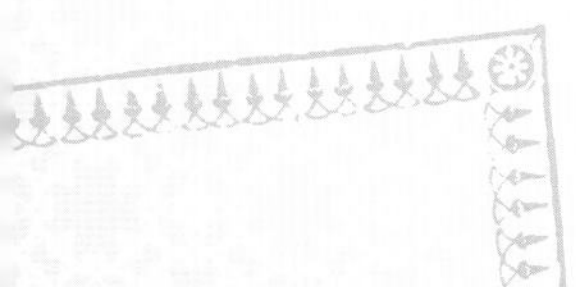

February 16

Facing Loss . . . with Laughter

Weeping may endure for a night,
But joy comes in the morning.
—Psalm 30:5

I have always believed humor and laughter are great ways to mitigate pain. But we must not use humor and laughter to deny the circumstances that cause our pain. When pain results from a loved one's death, we need to face that experience head-on.

After my husband, Ken, died of cancer, I thought I had done that. But I didn't know I also needed to face the overwhelming feelings of disconnectedness and abandonment. They were no laughing matter.

The words of Daniel 11:32 have inspired me for years: "The people who know their God shall be strong, and carry out great exploits." When Ken died, I couldn't be strong until I first stumbled in weakness, expressed it, and with time, stood firm in the God of the universe.

What kind of exploits? I learned to pay the bills, understand the income tax, and cope with a mortgage and those in charge of it.

One of life's hardest realities is letting go and moving on. That process is basically the same for all relationships, whether we're letting go of a spouse, children, parents, or friends. We acknowledge the great pain of disconnect and trace it back to its origin. Then we gather our strength and "carry out great exploits."

Ironically, the process carries the promise of joy in spite of the pain. That promise connects us to Jesus, who said, "You will be sorrowful, but your sorrow will be turned into joy" (John 16:20).

—Marilyn Meberg

Living Life on the Edge

The angel of the LORD appeared to [Gideon], and said to him, "The LORD is with you, you mighty man of valor!"

—JUDGES 6:12

During times of decision making, it sometimes feels as if I've crossed an edge, a point where something is likely to be, but I'm still hovering in its vicinity, still in that free-fall state where I'm wondering what is ahead, where I will land. In the midst of all that wondering, I stay close to God, watching for his guidance, hoping he will catch me.

We can't manipulate God or tell him what to do. We may ask him for some signal communicating a message to us, but that doesn't mean he's going to play the game. Still, we can be watchful and prayerful, hoping he will guide our steps in quiet or dramatic ways so that we constantly walk in his will.

Living on the edge isn't always the most comfortable existence, but it's a place where we tend to do more looking around for help—which, for Christians, means looking for God. When we're teetering over a precipice or plummeting into the unknown, we want to know he's right there with us. That's why the edge can be a *good* place to be.

One of my friends likes to say, "If you're not living life on the edge, you're taking up too much space!" I think he means you're complacent, set in your ways, maybe a little, well, boring! Instead, we need to live life with keen awareness of the opportunities around us, of the other edges that might have the potential to bring us closer to the divine. Watching with a mind-set that expects wonderful possibilities to appear in our lives at any moment gives us a whole new perspective on life.

—Sandi Patty

February 18

Saying Yes to the Unknown

> In the gospel the righteousness of God is revealed—a righteousness that is by faith from first to last, just as it is written: "The righteous will live by faith."
>
> —Romans 1:17 NIV

The greatest adventures of my life have come because I said yes to the unknown.

When I was asked to take a management position at Mobil, I remember being scared to death. I had never held a position where so many major decisions would rest on my shoulders. An enormous budget would be under my stewardship, and I would be responsible for the performance of personnel at my direction.

It was way out of my comfort zone. But something in me told me I could do it. I had the feeling that the doing of it would come from a force outside myself. I simply was going to be the instrument to get the job done. So I took the position. And I did it. And I'm so glad.

If we bite off a bit more than we think we can chew, the Lord brings something into play that wasn't there before we took the bite. It was the philosophy of Henry David Thoreau: "If one advances confidently in the direction of his dreams, and endeavors to live the life which he has imagined, he will meet with a success unexpected in common hours."

The operative word in Thoreau's comment is *meet*. It is in that meeting of our saying yes and the work of the Holy Spirit that—*bam!*—the adventure begins.

God never calls that he doesn't enable. I believe in striking out and watching him work out the details. Once we start something, a momentum begins that propels us toward completion. But it takes really wanting to do it to get started. There's no drive-through breakthrough in life. Nothing of value can be had for nothing.

—Luci Swindoll

The Rhythm of Prayer

> One day Jesus told them [the disciples] a story showing that it was necessary for them to pray consistently and never quit.
>
> —Luke 18:1 msg

Did you know that when some marching bands cross over a bridge they break cadence? The drums and music stop because the sustained beat, noise, and rhythm could cause structural damage to the bridge. Wow! What a visual image of prayer!

Most of us are pretty good in sustaining that rhythm of prayer when we receive one of those APB e-mails about Uncle Lou's cancer surgery or Aunt Jean's heart attack, but do we keep the beat going in the daily grind? What would happen if we did? Would our lives be any different?

Jesus said to always pray and never give up, so it must be that our lives *would* be different! If we fully realized the power of that cadence, we'd keep marching even though we're hot and weary. We'd sustain the rhythm right through the storms and distractions.

I want that kind of prayer life—the kind where I don't wring my hands in despair but keep the beat of prayer going so I can dismantle the enemy's stronghold.

Some of you are growing weary, but I encourage you to maintain cadence! Find another marching band member and commit to pray for one another every day. Band together and sustain the rhythm of prayer even when it means you have to march in all kinds of inclement weather. Keep clashing those cymbals and blowing your horn and don't ever give up. Don't ever, ever, ever break cadence!

—Donna VanLiere

February 20

Fairy Tales and Kingdoms

> He has rescued us from the dominion of darkness and brought us into the kingdom of the Son he loves.
> —Colossians 1:13 niv

Fairy tales have endured for generations. Once upon a time in a faraway land, there was always a kingdom, a prince in search of a princess, and a "happily ever after."

Remember Cinderella? Poor girl had a wicked stepmother and stepsisters who forced her to do all the chores and wear tattered clothes. When the king held a ball so his son could choose a bride, they made sure Cinderella couldn't find her invitation.

She made it to the party anyway, fetchingly transformed—fairy godmothers *do* come in handy—and captured everyone's attention, including the prince. The prince and Cinderella lived happily ever after, and the prince and Sleeping Beauty, the prince and Rapunzel, the prince and Snow White . . .

Little girls for years have heard these fairy tales and imagined what kingdom life must be like. The wonderful truth is that, in Christ, we're part of *the* royal family. We belong to the King of kings. And as his daughters, we are true princesses. We cannot yet behold the magnificent beauty of our kingdom. We cannot see the majestic throne of our King—or the King himself. To those outside of our kingdom, none of it seems real.

But this is no fairy tale. Our spirits bear witness that it's real because the Spirit of our King is alive in us. And we know it's real because we've been given eyes of faith.

One day we will behold its beauty in full. We will stand with awe before that throne and the glorious angels that surround it. We will behold our King.

One day, we will have our "happily ever after."

—Kim Cash Tate

Believing God Knows What He's Doing

O dry bones, hear the word of the Lord! Thus says the Lord God to these bones: "Surely I will cause breath to enter into you, and you shall live."

—Ezekiel 37:4–5

Valleys usually offer a variety of places to spread a cloth and unload a basket of food, but the valley the Old Testament prophet Ezekiel found himself in was full of bones. Even if he had found a shade tree to eat under, one tends to lose one's appetite in the presence of a corpse, much less a whole valley full of disjointed folks.

After Ezekiel took in the view, God asked Ezekiel an odd question: "Can these bones live?"

Huh? Dry bone on top of crispy dry bone? I mean, what're the chances? Why, I've looked at people who were alive and wondered if they would make it, so I know I would have failed the bone-test question.

But Ezekiel didn't guess at God's plan or deny God's power. He answered the question simply: "O, Lord God, You know" (v. 3).

Wow. I wish I could grab hold of the truth in that answer for my life so that, when trials come, I don't immediately assume all is gloom and doom. Instead, I could rest assured that God knows what he is doing, even if it looks like a hopeless, lifeless situation to me.

—Patsy Clairmont

No Crown Without the Cross

> Get behind Me, Satan! For it is written, "You shall worship the LORD your God, and Him only you shall serve."
> —LUKE 4:8

Satan took Jesus to a high place and, in an instant, showed Jesus all the kingdoms of the world. The sight must have been spectacular, and Satan was offering to turn everything over to Christ—on one condition: No Calvary. No agony and suffering. The beauty of it all without the barbaric death that lay just three short years ahead.

On the surface, Satan's offer might seem like a perfect idea: absolute authority rather than death. Yet Satan and Jesus both knew there was more to the matter. Had Jesus accepted this offer, our salvation would have been impossible. In giving up the cross, Jesus would have sinned by worshiping Satan and therefore could not have been the spotless Lamb of God. He would also have failed to fulfill what the prophets said about the Messiah: suffering was to precede glory. By accepting Satan's "gift," there would be no crucifixion, no bloodshed, and no forgiveness of sins.

Jesus declined. He quoted from the book of Deuteronomy, where Moses gave the Law to the people—worship God and God alone (Deuteronomy 5:7). He held true to the promise that God is in control.

I think it's easy to pass over this temptation as we study Jesus' temptation in the desert. We automatically remind ourselves that Jesus was God's Son and the plan had always been for him to suffer for our redemption. We forget that Jesus was also fully man. He knew that in just three short years, he would pay dearly for you and for me.

Yet he stood on that mountaintop and refused to take the easy way out.

—Sheila Walsh

Looking for Edges

Throughout them all you held tight to my lifeline. You never let me tumble over the edge into nothing.

—Isaiah 38:16 MSG

Living life on the edge means we're constantly at the point where something may begin, or not begin, depending on our choices. We're looking around for cliff-edges that hang over good futures, praying that God will guide us in choosing the right edges to step off of. But sometimes we misunderstand, or we go charging ahead without seeking God's guidance. The awful truth is, we make mistakes. Sometimes terrible mistakes.

After we've endured the consequences of poor choices and hard falls, we might move back from that cliff edge and resume the pity party. But I don't think that's where God wants us. I think he wants us out there on the edge, constantly watching for new opportunities to connect with him more intimately, trust him more completely.

Sure, we make mistakes. That's okay. We're out there with a God who allows do-overs. My friend Max Lucado calls God's grace the "supreme force in salvation." It's what allows us to live life on the edge. Even if we make a mistake and step off the wrong cliff-edge, God's everlasting arms are out there. If we call out to him, believing what he has told us and trusting what he has promised us, he'll pick us up from the rugged rocks below and set us back on the cliff-edge again.

It might not be the most pleasant experience we've ever had (and trust me, I've got the "frequent faller" points to prove that I know what I'm talking about here), but God has promised to be with us no matter what and to forgive us when we earnestly ask him to, no matter what.

And he will.

—Sandi Patty

February 24

Agreeing to Disagree

> He who has begun a good work in you will complete it until the day of Jesus Christ.
>
> —Philippians 1:6

Our son Jeff tends to share my Republican leanings, but our daughter Beth has always been what her brother describes as a "bleeding-heart Democrat."

These differences of opinion have made for lively discussions between my two adult children. I stand back in admiration as I listen to Beth express her views, but at the same time, in the core of my being, I want her to think more like I think.

Why? Her views feel like a disconnect to all that we used to be. Is it not safer to agree? Doesn't agreement mean harmony, and doesn't it give me confidence that the mental leash between mother and daughter has not been yanked out of my hands?

I've come to realize that the greatest respect I can show, not only to Beth but to anyone with whom I may be in disagreement, is to agree to disagree. In so doing, I preserve the dignity and right of all persons to be who they are and how they have come to believe.

Scripture tells us it was God who began the "good work" in our kids (and us) and that he'll be the One who continues and finishes it. That will that happen when Jesus returns. Or, if we beat him to the punch, in eternity.

If we, his beloved creation, can swallow that truth, we can relax, drop that mental leash, and let our kids be themselves. Someone smarter than we are holds on to us and our kids forever. That means we never lose connection with him.

—Marilyn Meberg

What Is It About the Bible?

Oh, taste and see that the LORD is good;
blessed is the man who trusts in Him!
—PSALM 34:8

After graduating from college, I lived at home and for two years joined my parents in attending a remarkable Bible class four nights a week and every Sunday. I lived for those classes, took copious notes, and studied my Bible all the time. I was the sponge that drank the ocean.

As I began to have the Bible opened to me in a palatable way, I absolutely fell in love with Jesus Christ. I could not get enough. I went in, dying of thirst, and found the fountain of life.

I began memorizing Scripture and learning about the promises and blessings that were mine by simply putting my faith in Christ. They were there all along, but no one had ever taught them to me. Not only did this time commitment benefit me in terms of a personal, strong doctrinal foundation regarding my faith, but also through those days, weeks, and months it helped my mother and me address the differences that had crippled our relationship for years. The breach between us was healed, and we remained close until she died in 1971.

What is it about the Bible that reaches into the depths of our souls and little by little begins to straighten us out? It digs up our arrogance and pride and enables us to forgive and forget. It creates spaces for understanding that we would not have thought possible, much less tolerated. Nothing of humankind can do that for us. Only God's Spirit has the ability to reach that deep into a life.

The Word of God is powerful enough to change darkness to light and dissatisfaction to joy. Neither Mother nor I had the capacity to change ourselves, but the supernatural work of the Holy Spirit did.

—Luci Swindoll

February 26

Free Food for the Spiritually Starving

> This God of Grace, this God of Love . . . He gave food to those who fear him, he remembered to keep his ancient promise.
>
> —Psalm 111:4–5 MSG

For many of us, the greatest obstacle to understanding God's gift of grace is our tendency to connect God's favor to our behavior. We think that when we do good, God applauds our righteous behavior and that, when we slip and fall, he frowns on us. But God is not a Scout leader or an etiquette coach. His love is lavish.

In our hearts, we know that. But still there is something in us that wants to feel we have contributed in some way to whatever we receive. With the grace of God, we contribute nothing. That's hard for us to swallow. We know we don't bring as much as God does to the table, but we want to feel as if we've done our bit for the team! So, especially when we've slipped in some way, maybe we do an extra shift in the charity group's soup kitchen.

But that practice fails to recognize that God's grace is a gift served out freely to us in his heavenly soup kitchen.

Our son Christian is not a big breakfast eater. He often runs out to shoot hoops with his friends on a summer morning with nothing more than the aftertaste of toothpaste in his system. Then he'll come dragging in and say, "Mom, I'm starving!"

Do you ever find yourself spiritually starving halfway through your day? Fresh grace is available from the moment you open your eyes until you crawl back under the covers at night.

—Sheila Walsh

Why Can't I Cry?

> Those who sow in tears
> Shall reap in joy.
> —Psalm 126:5

Four of my oldest friends and I spent a weekend at a cabin in the mountains. Our only agenda items were to eat and talk for two whole days.

The first day, we took turns sharing what was going on in our lives, where we were in our journeys, the ups and downs, challenges and triumphs. It was a rich, rich time of sharing.

Nobody knew, but I felt like an observer on the outside looking in. This had nothing to do with my friends. They were incredibly embracing of me. It was completely my problem.

I noticed how the other women were able to really be there for each other, body, soul, and spirit. They laughed with abandon, touched generously, and when one expressed sadness, they all shed tears. Except me. It had been years since I had shed a tear. I sat there longing to connect with these friends on an emotional level but not knowing how to even begin.

That night in my bedroom, I asked God with a deep sense of shame and embarrassment, "What's the matter with me? Why can't I feel? Why can't I cry?"

He answered immediately. I knew it was him because his voice was so gentle (when I talk to myself, I sound much more critical).

He whispered to my heart, *Little one, I'm not mad at you for building that wall around your heart. It was my protection for you as a little girl. But it is safe to come out now.*

His words took away my breath, as I realized there was hope that I could be different, that I could change and learn to feel deeply.

What hope I felt to think I might be able to connect at a heart level with a friend!

—Lisa Whelchel

February 28

Far More Than "Typical"

> Now to him who is able to do immeasurably more than all we ask or imagine, according to his power that is at work within us.
>
> —Ephesians 3:20 niv

I'm a practical person by nature. Left to myself, I'll make sensible choices. Careful, planned, I-can-see-where-this-is-going kinds of choices. College. Law school. Clerkship. Law firm. I was living my planned life. I could see the trajectory clear to retirement.

But that was all before I knew the Lord.

I've been an especially slow learner. Rather than believing with big faith when he puts the next step in my path, my mind goes to figuring. And it's gotten good at figuring why something *won't* work.

I was on a roll recently, informing God that something he had placed on my heart wasn't "typically" done. He let me know what he thought of that word, *typically*.

You don't go from slave to prisoner to governor of Egypt, as Joseph did—typically. You don't walk through the Red Sea on dry land—typically. You don't win a battle against a nine-foot giant armed with sword, spear, and javelin when all you have is a sling and some stones—typically. You don't tell the most powerful king on earth (King Nebuchadnezzar of Babylon) that you refuse to bow down to his statue, get thrown into a fiery furnace, and live—typically. You don't get out of a boat and walk on water—typically. You don't get to be born again—typically.

But God! He's the one who made the difference in each circumstance. There's a reason he says, "Behold, I am the Lord, the God of all flesh. Is there anything too hard for Me?" (Jeremiah 32:27). He wants us to know—and be fully persuaded—of his power, might, and sovereignty. God doesn't do anything "typical." He is able to do far more than our minds can conceive.

—Kim Cash Tate

The Subtle Enemy

Now the serpent was more cunning than any beast of the field.

—Genesis 3:1

How could we have missed it? There was Satan, in the garden, seeming so ominous, and yet he could not possess or control Adam or Eve. He could only talk until they agreed. He's doing the same thing today in all of our lives.

Picture this. You are standing at the top of the stairs to the basement of despair and fear, with the enemy at your side. He offers you the first thought, *What if your husband loses his job*?

That first thought came from the old serpent, but now you run with it. *Yes, what if he does lose his job, and we lose the house*? You have now moved to the second step toward the basement of despair and fear. You begin to pick up momentum. *What if we don't have enough food to feed our family*?

The thoughts are coming so fast now that you are no longer in an upright position; you are flying head first down those stairs.

You let the enemy talk till you agreed with him. Now you are in trouble.

You have to fight the battle within the first two steps if you are to win the battle. When you fight the first thought, he can't even drag you down those stairs.

To fight you must disagree. Capture that thought and demolish it with God's Word, such as: "God will supply all of my needs according to His riches in glory" (see Philippians 4:19) or "My God will never leave nor forsake me" (see Hebrews 13:5).

Don't agree with the deceiver. Destroy his words with the only true Word. Yes, you can avoid falling into and having to crawl out of that painful basement!

—Lana Bateman

March 1

Seeking the Right Accessories

He has made everything beautiful in its time.
—Ecclesiastes 3:11

Sometimes we girls think we're ugly because there's no one around to tell us we're beautiful. Or maybe we don't get invited out on the weekends like others do; we go through periods where we feel lonely or left out. It's especially important during those times that we're seeking the right accessories. Here's a list of my top eight *life* accessories:

- Security—trusting that, no matter what, we have a God who loves us
- Identity—in knowing who we are and whose we are
- Value—knowing we are treasured
- Love—knowing God's love for us so we can love others
- Self-control—for making good decisions
- Peace—in believing God is in control
- Joy—in knowing the Source of all joy
- Contentment—in who God made you to be

I've found that wearing these accessories (especially all at once) makes people beautiful inside and out.

Because he wears socks with sandals, my dad, Max Lucado, is not the first person I go to for answers to fashion questions. But when it comes to accessorizing my life, he has taught me a lot! He has made a huge impact on my life by challenging and shaping me in so many ways. Dad reminds me I'm beautiful, inside and out, and he has taught me how to find and have real beauty.

—Jenna Lucado

That's Not Fair!

Here it is again, the Great Reversal: many of the first ending up last, and the last first.
—Matthew 20:16 msg

When we are satiated with God's grace, it is much easier to extend grace to others, but when we are on starvation rations ourselves, we sometimes find it hard to see that same lavish grace extended to those who seem particularly undeserving.

Perhaps no parable illustrates that more clearly than Jesus' story of a vineyard owner who hired his first workers of the day at 6:00 a.m. and agreed on a wage of one dollar. He hired more field hands at 9:00 a.m., noon, 3:00 p.m., and 5:00 p.m. At day's end, he told the foreman to begin with those who had worked only the last hour. When the workers who had sweated in the field all day realized that the tail-end stragglers were receiving one dollar, they assumed their own paycheck would be bumped up accordingly. Not so. They were given the same dollar as the rest.

They furiously complained to the foreman, but he answered, "I haven't been unfair. We agreed on the wage of a dollar, didn't we? So take it and go. . . . Are you going to get stingy because I am generous?" (Matthew 20:13, 15 msg).

The kingdom of God has nothing to do with our scales of justice. From our perspective, it's easy to pick out the good guys and the bad guys; but God says there is no such thing as a good guy. We are all sinners standing in need of the grace of God.

—Sheila Walsh

March 3

Go!

> Go therefore and make disciples of all the nations, baptizing them in the name of the Father and of the Son and of the Holy Spirit.
>
> —Matthew 28:19

The first time I ever left home on my own I was sixteen. I went by train from Houston to Fort Worth to visit cousins. I'll never forget that day. My daddy took a picture of me in my good blue dress Mother had made, my Sunday shoes, and a matching purse. I wore a cute little hat and carried white gloves. *Watch out, world. Here I come!* I was so excited I could hardly breathe—a bit scared because I'd never been anywhere by myself but jazzed at the idea of taking a trip.

The feeling I had that day has never left. Every year since then, I've taken a trip, maybe not a long one, but something that involved packing a bag and spending the night. And more often than not, I've made numerous trips each year.

There has always been something in me that wanted to go! And it's not just my nature; it's compatible with my faith. While inhabiting the earth in bodily form, Jesus had a lot to say about going. He was forever sending someone somewhere on a mission. He commanded his disciples to follow, wherever he happened to be going. And his last word of instruction to us, his followers, before returning to his heavenly Father was "Go!" (Matthew 28:19).

Jesus is interested in our looking beyond ourselves, taking the next step, reaching out, and going.

It's kind of strange that I want to go so much, because I'm truly a homebody. But that doesn't squelch my desire to wander around the world in search of adventure. It's as if that wanderlust were put in me as part of my genetic makeup, and it becomes more of a passion the older I get.

—Luci Swindoll

Though Oxygen Is Flowing

Though I walk through the valley of the shadow of death,
I will fear no evil; for You are with me.
—Psalm 23:4

Have you ever found yourself waiting on God, and he doesn't seem to be answering? I'm sure you have. We all have. And it never seems to get easier. I was in a season when I prayed, read my Bible, and did all I could to listen for God's voice. But all I heard was silence.

All I knew to do was to keep pressing on and doing the next thing. I did my best to move forward and trust moment by moment that God was at work although I couldn't yet see.

Suddenly, the fog lifted. Not only had the pieces of the puzzle begun to fall into place, but I could also see several steps behind me where God had orchestrated even the smallest details to lead me to just the right place. Though I couldn't yet see, God had been moving mountains for weeks to bring all the needed elements together for a positive outcome. In that moment, I was once again overwhelmed and humbled by the love and goodness of a God who loves us, mess makers that we are, so much that he concerns himself with everything—even the smallest detail—that concerns us.

It's so hard to keep moving and to trust what we can't see, especially when it looks like we're headed straight for disaster. But our Father is always there, whether we feel his presence or not.

It's comparable to a safety demonstration on a plane, when the flight attendant refers to the oxygen bags that will drop from the ceiling in the event of a loss of cabin pressure: "Though oxygen is flowing, the bags may not inflate."

Though we can't always see his hand moving, we can trust that God knows and sees every aspect of our lives, and he never stops working on our behalf. While our circumstances change, God's attention and presence never do.

—Lori Roberson

March 5

In the Shadow of His Wings

> Have mercy on me, my God, have mercy on me, for in you I take refuge. I will take refuge in the shadow of your wings until the disaster has passed. I cry out to God Most High, to God, who vindicates me. He sends from heaven and saves me, rebuking those who hotly pursue me—God sends forth his love and his faithfulness.
>
> —Psalm 57:1–3 NIV

The winds of life can blow fierce and strong. Winds of disappointment. Winds of failure. Winds of frustration and sickness and fear and rejection. Whatever the problem, it demands our focus. And the more we focus on it, the more we're carried away by it—to anxiety, incessant worry, loneliness, and sadness.

But there is a place to which we can run for refuge from the fierce winds of life—the shadow of God's wings.

I love this imagery so much that I've colored "shadow of his wings" and "shelter of his wings" everywhere it appears in the Psalms. When the winds blow, I like to picture myself snuggled up under a wide, strong, majestic eagle's wing—protected, out of harm's way. In the shadow of God's wings, I know I'm not alone. I'm tended to, cared for, nurtured, and loved.

In the shadow of God's wings, the wind can rage, but my focus is on the One who is able to rebuke the wind and make it calm (Mark 4:39). That amazes me. He is strong enough to protect and comfort me, while also dealing with the circumstance however he sees fit. He will accomplish all things for me.

Are the winds raging in your life? Crawl up and settle yourself in the shadow of his wings. You'll find refuge there—and so much more.

—Kim Cash Tate

The Seat of Grace

Out of his fullness we have all received grace.
—JOHN 1:16 NIV

My junior high math teacher never seemed to like my friend Peg or me, but he adored the four princesses who sat behind us. They were trendy and cool while Peg and I sported not-cool Toughskins jeans and bad perms.

One afternoon, Peg and I gathered with the other students in the gymnasium for a school assembly. We crossed the floor and climbed up the bleachers for some perfect seats when we heard, "Those aren't available."

We turned to see "Mr. Math" letting us know the seats were taken.

By that time, every other good bleacher seat was filled. We trekked up to the top row—and then saw the four princesses sit in "our" seats down below. Mr. Math was right. The best seats were unavailable . . . to us. Those seats were special and for special girls. We could make do somewhere else.

It's strange how other people color the way we see ourselves. We begin to perceive ourselves as *we think* those around us see us: *You're a good athlete but not as good as your sister. You're thin but just not thin enough. You're a good mom, but have you seen* her *amazing home and kids*?

To love and accept others despite their flaws and failures is a gift of grace in a hypercritical world where people smirk and snicker and whisper catty comments. Grace says, "You're okay with me," without passing any judgment. It sees beyond the frizzy hair and frumpy clothes to the heart of the exhausted single mother, heartbroken widow, or twice-divorced waitress. Grace saves the best seats in the house just for us and stands up to say, "Come on in. It's a privilege to know you."

—Donna VanLiere

March 7

Escaping My Personal Prison

> Thank God for his marvelous love . . . He shattered the heavy jailhouse doors, he snapped the prison bars like matchsticks!
>
> —Psalm 107:10 MSG

By all outward appearances, I was a happy, well-adjusted overachiever. But bulimia had become a way of life for me. I had become the queen of disguise, so much so that I had begun believing my own act.

What I called my "churchianity" was Oscar-worthy. Everyone thought I was so spiritual, so perfect; but I wasn't. Somehow the twelve-inch span from my head to my heart had become the Grand Canyon, and there seemed to be no way to bridge the gap. I felt lost. I had been so busy being who everyone thought I was that I no longer had a sense of being real. And because I knew I was being dishonest, living a lie, I felt worthless.

I believed that if my family and friends knew the real me, they would be ashamed. They would despise me.

The truth was, I despised myself.

Now, don't get me wrong. I wholeheartedly believed Jesus loved me. At least I thought I did.

Jesus became my Savior when I was a little girl, but I don't think I ever allowed him to become my Lord. A lord is the master, someone who has complete power, control, and authority.

Problem was, *I* was the lord of my life.

I reached a turning point when I realized I was trapped in a prison of my own making and that Jesus was the only One who could set me free.

God made me wonderfully uncomfortable, beautifully tortured by the chaos of my condition. I had no idea who I was anymore, but with God's help, I set out in search of the real me.

—Natalie Grant

A Dad's Transforming Love

God, you are our Father. We're the clay and you're our potter: All of us are what you made us.
—Isaiah 64:8 msg

"Dad! Stop!" Those two words summed up a lot of my middle and high school careers. Whether it was trying to put an end to his goofy dance moves or his loud singing in public, I was his nudge in the side or his tug on the shirt to halt all embarrassing activities.

Eventually I grew to love his "embarrassing" quirks and developed a deep gratitude for his influence in my life. I've also read some authoritative reports that show just how important every dad can be.

Look at it this way: Is there a certain store where you buy the majority of your clothes? Maybe you're a GAP girl. Or are you thinking, *I am a thrift store kind of girl*? Maybe hand-me-downs make up your style.

A lot of times there's a primary store we stock our closets from. Dads are kinda like that store. A lot of our style comes from their influence and our relationships with them. I'm not talking just about the way we look on the outside but about how dads help define elements that make up who we are, like how we look at ourselves and everyone around us.

In other words, they affect our *out*look. And our outlook gives us a certain perspective on every aspect of life and every person we meet: it either adds a dull, cloudy gray to our world, or it brightens the colors around us, making everything more beautiful.

It's kind of crazy, but a dad's love can completely transform the way we look. That's because God designed a father's love to be an essential building block in a girl's heart.

—Jenna Lucado

March 9

Depending on God's Word

> Let the word of Christ dwell in you richly in all wisdom, teaching and admonishing one another in psalms and hymns and spiritual songs, singing with grace in your hearts to the Lord.
>
> —Colossians 3:16

Adults don't always say what they mean. That is not true of children. I remember one time when I came home from college for Christmas, I said to my little nephew, "Did you miss me?" He said, "Mimi, I would have missed you for sure, but I forgot all about you." Several years ago, a friend of mine was with her family having a Christmas dinner when her nephew tasted a Jell-o salad she'd made. "Do you like the salad, honey?" she asked. He responded, "Mmmm, not really." Out of the mouths of babes.

It would be manageable if only children were this painfully honest. I remember not long ago being with someone who had just started dating a new beau. She was telling me how much she was enjoying him when she wrinkled her nose and said, "But he has red hair." She said it like she'd just realized he had two heads. As a redhead myself, I'm very used to remarks about redheads, and I just laughed. However when she realized what she had said, she was mortified.

I come from a long line of people who use a lot of words, and not always kindly. Teasing was my father's "love language." My brothers took great delight in taunting me. It's possible that's why I love that God's Word is perfectly clear, no pun intended, no criticism meant, and no teasing or taunting. Just his Word, always true, comforting, caring, and clear.

—Mary Graham

A True Mystery

> When you were younger, you tied your own belt and went where you wanted. But when you are old, you will put out your hands and someone else will tie you and take you where you don't want to go.
>
> —JOHN 21:18 NCV

Menopause is a time of mystery, and it's also an indication that God is a comedian.

The first mystery may be why that hormonal highway of emotions has such incongruous detours. We're floating along on a tidal wave of sorrow because the dryer lint won't come out of the filter in one piece, and the next thing we know, a family member calls hello as he walks by the laundry room, and we angrily reenact an interrogation right out of *Law and Order*: "What's *that* supposed to mean? Where were *you* when your socks had to be sorted?"

And then there are those hairy issues involving hair. This is the part that assures us God is a comedian. At the same time over-the-hill men are consumed with worrying about the departure of hair from their heads, menopausal women are stunned to find the stuff appearing in places on their bodies where it never had the nerve to show up before.

While men are watching infomercials touting follicle stimulants, scalp massagers, and "lifelike" toupees, we're trying to decide whether to have our chin hair bleached, waxed, lasered, or permed.

You just have to wonder sometimes: *What were you thinking, Lord*?

And here's another mystery. Why, just when we finally have time to relax in our Barcaloungers and eat bonbons all day, do we end up with bodies that need—how can this be?—*fewer* calories and *more* exercise!

How *can* this be?

—Barbara Johnson

March 11

The WD-40 Psalm's Lubricating Truths

> Whoever listens to me will live in safety and be at ease, without fear of harm.
> —Proverbs 1:33 niv

If life has dried up your enthusiasm, if your faith feels brittle, or if valley life has left you parched, I encourage you to delve into the life-giving, bone-lubricating truths of Scripture. Write out Psalm 100 and tape it to your morning mirror. I call it the WD-40 psalm.

Read it daily until it sings within your bones. I promise that, when you twirl about in gladness and high-step your way into joy, even your valleys will have picnic potential.

> *Make a joyful shout to the Lord, all you lands!*
> *Serve the Lord with gladness;*
> *Come before His presence with singing.*
> *Know that the Lord, He is God;*
> *It is He who has made us, and not we ourselves;*
> *We are His people and the sheep of His pasture.*
> *Enter into His gates with thanksgiving,*
> *And into His courts with praise.*
> *Be thankful to Him, and bless His name.*
> *For the Lord is good;*
> *His mercy is everlasting,*
> *And His truth endures to all generations.*
> —Psalm 100

—Patsy Clairmont

The Urge to Roam

When the woman saw that the tree was good for food, that it was pleasant to the eyes, and a tree desirable to make one wise, she took of its fruit and ate. She also gave to her husband . . . and he ate.

—Genesis 3:6

I ran away from home when I was four years old. What had possessed me to unexpectedly climb a fence and leave the security of my backyard? I had appealing toys and a good swing. I had not been mistreated and was given a hearty breakfast prior to my "escape."

What possessed Christopher Columbus to head out on repeated journeys into the unknown? (Had I known his name at age four, I could have used him during my roadside conversation with Daddy.)

I did not show wisdom when I expected to be "let go" at the age of four. Sure enough, Daddy quickly caught up with me, ending my short-lived freedom. My parents' concern for my safety and well-being was legitimate, and any sensible parents would do what mine did. What motivated me at an inappropriate age was a Christopher Columbus desire to experience new things, see new things, and feel new things. Understandably, those motivations scare parents. When our kids show immaturity and poor judgment, hurtful consequences can result. So how do we know when to tighten the leash and when to let it drop out of our hands?

We parents need to take refuge in knowing we are incapable of parenting perfectly. It's not in us. We were born from imperfection, and we pass it on.

And whom do we blame? It's that couple who had a short stint with perfection but then chose to chow down on the forbidden fruit.

They so tick me off.

—Marilyn Meberg

March 13

Admitted into the Kingdom

> Help us, O God of our salvation . . . Deliver us, and provide atonement for our sins, for Your name's sake!
> —Psalm 79:9

For those of us living on the edge of the divine, the forgiveness factor operates beneficially on both sides of the equation. When we're the ones being forgiven, we accept that forgiveness, promising to change. When we're the ones forgiving others, we trust God to take care of justice and healing.

On either side of the process, we learn that we cannot make everything right ourselves; only God can.

Fallen-and-forgiven people like me are everywhere among you. In fact, we *are* you—at least we're the imperfect ones among you. We're out there on the cliff-edge, we frequent-faller folks. We're like the shunned woman in Nathaniel Hawthorne's classic novel, *The Scarlet Letter.* She was forced by her community to wear a bright red *A* on her clothing to warn others that there was a sinner in their midst.

Picture me wearing a big red letter *A* on my shirt too. The fact is, we're *all* wearing one of those big red letters, whether or not we recognize it when we look in the mirror. Maybe you see the letter representing *adultery* or *abortion* or *addiction* or *abandonment,* but if you're a believer, you can forget all those words. For Christians, only one scarlet letter is visible: a big red *A* for *atonement.*

God took our old letter and our old life and replaced it with one of his own choosing. Now we know we've been forgiven. Atoned for by Jesus' death on the cross. Admitted into the kingdom of God, where we are promised grace, mercy, adoration, acceptance, and unconditional love. Forever and ever.

—Sandi Patty

A Love That's Hard to Fathom

God did not send His Son into the world to condemn the world, but that the world through Him might be saved.
—John 3:17

Crucifixion was the most humiliating way Christ could have offered to take our sin upon himself. In his time, it was the most extreme form of desecration possible. It said to everyone that this person was under the curse of God. In fact, the Jewish people believed, based on Deuteronomy 21:22–23, that this curse was so strong that to leave the body up for more than a day would infect and symbolically curse their very own land.

We will never be able to fully realize what Christ did for us. Not only was he in physical and spiritual pain on the cross, but he took on a place of public degradation, dying under the curse of his own Father out of his love for you and me.

In Roman law, crucifixion was reserved for the lowest classes and worst criminals. No Roman citizen could be executed this way without a direct edict from Caesar. Not only that, but it is rare to even find evidence of crucifixion because the bodies were usually pulled off the cross and thrown on a trash pile to be devoured by animals. Yet God chose crucifixion for his Son.

Christ's life, and his death, exemplified the extreme measures God took for us.

Jesus didn't have to be born into such poverty. He could have been born into a comfortable middle-class home. He could have died by stoning, as Stephen did in the book of Acts, which was a form of execution more favored by the Jews. Instead, Jesus chose the most humble beginning and the most humiliating end.

Such love is hard to fathom. Such love tells you there was no length too great for the Father to go to out of love for you.

—Sheila Walsh

March 15

Recognizing God's Trustworthiness

> In God is my salvation and my glory; the rock of my strength, and my refuge, is in God.
> —Psalm 62:7

In Psalm 62, David affirms God's worthiness in verse 7 and beseeches everyone to trust him in verse 8. Then David proclaims that, regardless of how much wealth or power people have, no one but God deserves our absolute devotion.

Whether prosperous or poor, human beings aren't worthy of worship. If we put our hope solely in humanity, we're going to need a whole lot of Prozac!

The same holds true, David observes in verses 10 to 12, of trusting in material wealth. And at first glance the tail end of this tune sounds as if David is reversing himself and suggesting that God takes care of us only when we earn a perfect score on our Good Girl report cards. But despite the flavor of our English translations, the original language of the phrase "render to a man according to his work" doesn't actually mean "God gives better stuff to folks who work their fannies off!" In fact, the word *render* comes from the Hebrew root word *šālēm,* which means "being at peace or being fulfilled." So David's point isn't so much about the virtues of a strong work ethic as it is about the worthiness of our heavenly Father. Unlike human leaders, the Lord can be trusted to be absolutely true in his dealings with us. His throne will never be compromised by dishonesty or duplicity. He will never shortchange us to benefit himself. God is and will always be the perfect Ruler.

—Lisa Harper

Seeing Us as God Sees Us

We don't yet see things clearly. We're squinting in a fog, peering through a mist. But it won't be long before the weather clears and the sun shines bright! We'll see it all then, see it all as clearly as God sees us, knowing him directly just as he knows us!

—1 Corinthians 13:12 msg

For most of my life, my vision was horrible, and since the third grade, I have worn glasses or contacts. So I happily anticipated Lasik surgery to correct my vision. Because I couldn't wear contacts for a few weeks in preparation for the surgery, I wore a pair of glasses that was several years old and offered less than my current prescription, but they were my only option.

One day, while wearing my old glasses, I was out running errands and stopped by the library. When I went in, I noticed a man looking at me. I thought to myself, *He's probably checking me out. I've been to the gym, had a pedicure, and look pretty good.*

As I left the book return to go choose new books, I walked by again, and again he was looking at me. It was starting to get a little weird. Finally I approached the checkout desk and passed close by him. It was only then that I realized he was a cardboard Luke Skywalker standing guard over a display of science fiction titles.

With my glasses I could see enough to get around, but my ability to see clearly was flawed. In the same way, we may think we are seeing a good picture of ourselves and God and how we believe he sees us, but it is instead far from clear.

We tend to focus on our weaknesses more than our strengths, our mistakes more than our gifts. But God sees us as wonderful, beautiful, and created for an abundant life of purpose and promise.

—Lori Roberson

March 17

Dad's Unseen Influence

> I am the Good Shepherd. I know my own sheep and my own sheep know me. In the same way, the Father knows me and I know the Father.
>
> —John 10:14 MSG

My family and I used to take the boat out on the lake from sunup to sundown. Dad would pull us on water skis and whip us around on the tube until our arms were as limp as boiled noodles.

One of my favorite parts about going to the lake was getting that long-awaited tan. I loved it when the sun was high and the clouds were nowhere to be found. My white, almost transparent skin would soak in the sun like a sponge soaks up water.

One morning at the lake, the sun was hiding behind a thick blanket of clouds. So rude! Since the sun refused me, I refused the sunscreen. After all, there was no sun to screen, right?

Wow, was I wrong! The next morning I was sleeping like a bear in the winter—until I rolled over. Then I screamed so loudly you would have thought someone had stabbed me with a fork! My skin was as crispy as fried chicken and as red as lipstick. But how could that be? The sun hadn't even been seen the day before!

Well, just because I couldn't see the sun didn't mean it couldn't see me. Just because I didn't feel the UV rays destroying my defenseless skin didn't mean they wouldn't mercilessly burn me.

Just like an unforeseen burn from the sun's rays on a cloudy day, unexpected side effects come from our relationships with our dads. Hopefully your dad has influenced you in a positive way.

I was fortunate to have a healthy relationship with my dad when I was growing up. He was really good about telling me how proud he was of me. Because of that, he gave me one of my must-have accessories: self-confidence.

—Jenna Lucado

Overcoming Difficulties, Step by Step

Yet in all these things we are more than conquerors through Him who loved us.
—Romans 8:37

Fourth-grader Emily wanted to join her class on a field trip to Ohio Caverns, but there was no way her heavy, motorized wheelchair, necessary because of Emily's cerebral palsy, could negotiate the dozens of stairs leading into and out of the cave.

Emily committed the situation to God, and soon his plan was revealed.

He gave Emily's mom the idea of asking the local fire department if they might do a practice cave rescue, carrying Emily, strapped onto a gurney, in and out of the cave. Then, she said, they could prop Emily against a wall of the cave to take in the sights.

The fire chief responded, "Ma'am, we are here to serve!"

Paramedics carried Emily, on the gurney, through the cave. They even carried her in their arms through one narrow passageway so she could see the highlight of the cave, the Stalactite King. Then they strapped her to the gurney again and carried her up the *sixty-six* steps to the cave's exit.

The experience reminded Emily of the paralytic who was lowered through the roof by his friends so he could ask Jesus for help (see Mark 2:1–5).

"I am so thankful for friends who demonstrate that type of selfless love to me on a daily basis so that my life is full and complete, filled with grace because of God's love for me," she said.

Emily learned early how to be more than a conqueror—a lesson every one of us must learn sooner or later, whether we're disabled or able-bodied. She is trusting God. And by his grace, she will overcome.

—Joni Eareckson Tada

March 19

Finding the Real You

> You know me inside and out, you hold me together, you never fail to stand me tall in your presence so I can look you in the eye.
>
> —Psalm 41:12 msg

Is there a secret in your life, something you've held on to for a long time, hoping nobody sees it? Something so painful, so far down in your heart, that you dare not even speak of it? If so, there's something you should know: you're not alone. I know you might not believe it now, but maybe soon you will. In the meantime, can you muster up enough courage to personalize those words and simply say, "I'm not alone"?

My poor self-esteem reared its ugly head as an eating disorder. What consequences are *you* struggling with as a result of a poor self-image? Do you have secrets that make you feel worthless? In your effort to exert control, are you inflicting damage on yourself physically or emotionally? If so, you're probably overdue for a moment of divine intervention.

Please open your heart and your mind to God's presence and pray this prayer: "God, wake up my mind to the truth of who I am, who you created me to be, and to the truth of who you are. Gather the feelings and emotions in my head and give me the courage to be honest about myself. And most of all, give me faith to believe what you have to teach me as I study your Word. I want a divine awakening, Lord. I need to know you're here with me. Amen."

Be receptive to God's love for you, his gift of peace—watch for it, expect it—even in the unlikeliest places.

He surrounded me with his comforting love and acceptance as I lay curled around the toilet on the floor of a bathroom, devastated by bulimia. Where will *you* be when you finally give in to his extraordinary, healing grace?

—Natalie Grant

It Is Finished!

> Christ redeemed us from that self-defeating, cursed life by absorbing it completely into himself. Do you remember the Scripture that says, "Cursed is everyone who hangs on a tree"? That is what happened when Jesus was nailed to the cross: He became a curse, and at the same time dissolved the curse.
>
> —Galatians 3:13 msg

At the moment Christ let out his final cry on the cross, the veil in the temple was ripped from top to bottom (Matthew 27:51).

No longer was there a need for a temple, for Jesus is the temple. No longer was there a need for a veil to hide the presence of God in the holy of holies, for Jesus is the place where you and I come face-to-face with God our Father.

Jesus took our shame on himself so you and I can come into our Father's presence, as a child would run into the arms of a papa who loves her. What more, dear sisters, needs to be said? It is finished! We are free!

As I reflect on what the death and sacrifice of Christ say to you and to me, I am overwhelmed. To be loved like this demands something in return.

If God looked at our fragile, broken lives and determined that no price would be too high to salvage them, then I don't want to miss one moment of my destiny. I am tired of us looking at our reflections in the old mirror of what seems true to us. Instead, let's see ourselves in God's mirror.

—Sheila Walsh

March 21

When God Is Up to Something

> If you want to be perfect, go, sell what you have and give to the poor, and you will have treasure in heaven; and come, follow Me.
>
> —MATTHEW 19:21

For years, I thought God was all I needed. I thought if I looked to people to meet my needs, that would be idolatry. But God showed me that in order to grow deeper in my relationship with him, I needed friends to whom I could acknowledge my need and on whom I could allow myself to depend.

I wanted to take time to understand and experience intimacy with God, myself, and others. I longed to be able to extend my daily Bible time to include unhurried moments to simply be with him and to think and listen. And I longed to share leisurely lunches with a close friend.

But there didn't seem to be time in my calendar for either of these desires. I had a manuscript due to one publisher within the next six months and another book left on my three-book contract with another publisher. I couldn't see time on my calendar to develop intimacy for at least another year, and I didn't want to wait that long.

As it turned out, God was way ahead of me. When one publishing company was bought out by another publisher, I was able to be amicably released from writing the first book. Then, within weeks, my other publisher asked if I could change the focus of the last book in the three-book contract. I didn't feel equipped to write the book they requested, so I offered to step down so someone else could write it.

It was a win-win situation for everyone.

Don't you just love it when God is up to something?

—Lisa Whelchel

Hard-to-Believe Truths

So are we Jews better than others? No! We have already said that Jews and those who are not Jews are all guilty of sin.

—Romans 3:9 NCV

If you're like me, you've thought, *Sure, I understand that we're all sinners in a broad sense, Lord, but there are some of us who mess up a lot less than others. You can't tell me that doesn't count for something.*

It is so tempting to categorize sin, to see others as less deserving of God's grace than we are. But living a grace-filled life requires us to lay down our internal scales of justice, not only as we see ourselves but also as we see and judge others.

It's hard to extend to others what you have not allowed yourself to be blessed by, but the truth remains:

- As you are, right at this moment, God loves you.
- He knows all that is true about you, and he loves you.
- Even when you can't forgive yourself, he forgives you.
- There is nothing you can do to make him love you more.
- There is nothing you can do to make him love you less.

This is the grace of God.

Take a few moments to absorb these truths. Are they hard to believe? Look at your past and bring it to the foot of the cross, where it may be easier for you to receive the grace of God. That's where you will surely understand the truth of Martin Luther's statement that we must completely despair of ourselves "to become fit to obtain the grace of Christ."

—Sheila Walsh

March 23

Things of Value Are Not Free

> Tune your ears to the world of Wisdom; set your heart on a life of Understanding. . . . Believe me, before you know it Fear-of-God will be yours; you'll have come upon the Knowledge of God.
>
> —Proverbs 2:1, 5 msg

One of the greatest lessons I tucked under my belt during the years I worked for an oil corporation was this: things of value cannot be had for nothing. My time working there was the testing ground for that truth. I learned that, more often than not, deferring the rewards of today gives us the future we dream of tomorrow. We have to spend in order to get, and time, energy, and money are our only mediums of exchange. Count on it, anticipate it, and accept it.

When we realize there's no shortcut to having what we want, life gets a bit easier. We're not nearly as frustrated because we settle into the patterns that pay off in our souls and bodies. We quit thinking that life somehow owes us a living. We work. We pray. We study. We're attentive to details. We put first things first. We risk. We believe God means what he says. Unless we live out of these truths, there really is no tomorrow. Everything becomes one endless, tiresome "today," and there's no growth or change. In short, wisdom never comes.

I remember asking God for wisdom. It was as though he asked me one day when I was praying, "What do you want most, Luci?" I thought about some of the choices I'd made that led to dead ends. After turning all this over in my mind, I answered, "Wisdom, Lord."

Well, when we ask for wisdom, all kinds of things begin to happen. Things we hadn't planned on. God comes in like a flood, altering our world—changing the things we once valued, restructuring relationships, taking away this desire and adding that one, putting our priorities in a new alignment. God grows us up!

—Luci Swindoll

A Little Lifeline of Encouragement

You, LORD, hear the desire of the afflicted; you encourage them, and you listen to their cry.

—PSALM 10:17 NIV

When I graduated from high school, my one and only dream was to work at Disney with the Kids of the Kingdom group. When I turned eighteen, the minimum age to audition, I hurried to Anaheim and performed the song and little dance that the show's staff taught the fifty to seventy-five auditioners. I wasn't the best dancer, but I had grown up singing. I knew I could do *that*!

When my turn came, I watched the judges' faces while I sang and felt a surge of confidence when I saw them smile. When I finished enthusiastically singing "Don't Rain on My Parade," the room erupted in applause. I left the audition feeling sure I was a shoo-in for the group.

A few weeks later, when I learned I *hadn't* been accepted, my parents watched me mourn the death of my dream and tried everything they could think of to encourage and comfort me. But I wouldn't even come out of my room.

Finally Dad slipped a little note under my door. I still have it today. It said, "Today, I watched my little girl transform from a caterpillar into a butterfly." He went on to say other loving things, including how proud he was to see me handling a great disappointment with such maturity.

Was he kidding? Crying hysterically and locking myself in my bedroom didn't seem very mature to me! But now that I have children of my own, I remember that event through a parent's eyes, and I see that Dad was offering me a little lifeline of encouragement to help me get back on my feet and get on with my life.

—Sandi Patty

March 25

Losing the Leash

> Train up a child in the way he should go,
> And when he is old he will not depart from it.
> —Proverbs 22:6

Many years ago, soon after my son Jeff's eighteenth birthday, he and a friend wanted to drive into Los Angeles to attend a rock concert. I considered the forty-five-minute drive on the crazy Los Angeles freeways. I pictured a haze of marijuana smoke in the arena, where I suspected most attendees would be drunk.

"Mercy! Are you out of your mind?" I muttered for hours.

I still clenched my imaginary parental leash tightly as my husband, Ken, pulled me aside and became Jeff's lawyer.

He pointed out that during the two years Jeff had had his driver's license, he had continually proven his competence. He also reminded me that Jeff had a "dependability gene" we'd seen since early in his life.

"But what if his better instincts and training desert him and he's caught up in all I've tried to protect him from?" I wailed.

"Marilyn, you've done your part. Now it's up to him. Sit back, let go, and cheerfully tell him to have a good time," Ken said.

Around 1:45 a.m. the night of the concert, I was lying in bed, staring at the ceiling while trying to remember Scripture verses, when I heard the key in the front door. Jeff stealthily walked into the bedroom, leaned his six-foot-five-inch frame against the doorjamb, and whispered a sweet, "Good-night."

"I love you too, baby," I answered. "I have complete confidence in you."

I heard him smile in the dark. We were still connected.

It was time to lose the leash.

—Marilyn Meberg

Wearing a Headlight of God's Word

You are all children of the light and children of the day.
We do not belong to the night or to the darkness.
—1 THESSALONIANS 5:5 NIV

My husband gave our six-year-old grandson an unusual birthday present. He thought a youngster would have great fun navigating the dark by donning a headlamp such as miners wear. This six-year-old was pleased with the prospect of lighting up otherwise scary places.

He's not the only one. Regardless of our age, nothing is more welcome in darkness than light. Even a lit match in a dark place brings a sigh of relief. A speck of light gives us a place to head for; it offers hope.

God sent his Son, Jesus, into the world to be the Light Bearer so that he might expose and illuminate the darkness of our own hearts as well as the evil that hovers in our land.

Jesus came to redeem us in the midst of darkness and chaos so that we might become "children of the day." As children of the light, we partner with Christ to bring illumination to those around us so that we might offer them the hope he has given us.

His Word becomes our headlamp, showing us the next step to take and reminding us that we aren't alone, even in the valley of the shadow of death.

Take a moment to imagine what a difference one small candle makes in a dark room. In fact, sit in a dark room for several reflective moments and then carefully light a candle and see the impact it makes. It is a strong reminder of what we can be while living in this dark world.

—Patsy Clairmont

March 27

You Are You for a Reason

> Tell it to God—he's the one behind all this, he's the one who dragged me into this mess. Look at me—I shout "Murder!" and I'm ignored; I call for help and no one bothers to stop. God threw a barricade across my path—I'm stymied; he turned out all the lights—I'm stuck in the dark. He destroyed my reputation, robbed me of all self-respect. He tore me apart piece by piece—I'm ruined!
> —Job 19:6–10 msg

No one gets to choose where she is born or who her parents are. One child is born into great wealth and favor, and another child opens his eyes into a world of poverty and AIDS in a small village in Africa. One child is welcomed into loving arms, while another is unwanted and unloved.

In your own life, perhaps you longed to be the girl at the table next to you. Or the woman down the street or across the country. The one who appears to have everything she could ever want or need—and more. But instead you feel trapped in a life not of your choosing.

Is any of it an accident? I know for sure that, in God's original plan, life was never meant to be this way. The brokenness we suffer was not God's choice but ours. When Adam and Eve, made in the image of God, reached outside the life he had lavished on them, we all fell. Now the whole planet limps and weeps along. But in the midst of all of that, I believe you are you for a reason. You are not an accident; you are a woman with an eternal destiny.

It takes some of us a long time to understand that. Often it means letting go of what we think should have been and bowing our hearts to the sovereignty of God. He can take the least likely of lives and love large through them.

—Sheila Walsh

Recognizing Our Inestimable Worth

Judge not, that you be not judged.
—Matthew 7:1

One of the most debilitating spirit-breakers I know is the tendency to judge the worth of others as well as ourselves on the basis of performance. With this mind-set we assume that if what is done is good, so is the person. If what is done is not good, neither is the person.

It is a common error to assume we are worthy persons only as long as we perform well. With that mind-set, we believe that what we do is more valuable than who we are.

Jesus says in John 13:34 that we are to love one another, even as he loved us. Just as Jesus first considered the worth of the person, so must we. Though someone's performance may displease us, our role is not to judge, alienate, or condemn. The cleansing of sin and the modification of behavior are God's job. The recognition of the inestimable worth of each of God's children is ours.

There is a vast difference between acceptance and approval. We are not mandated to approve of wrong behavior but to accept others as worthy of God's love and provision. Acceptance and support can help wounded spirits heal.

The greatest example of seeing the worth of the person apart from performance was set by Jesus. He consistently cut through the externals of performance to the interior of the heart, and each time he affirmed the worth of that individual by the way he treated him or her.

—Marilyn Meberg

March 29

Singing My Heart Out

> Hear, O kings! Give ear, O princes! I, even I, will sing to the LORD; I will sing praise to the LORD God of Israel.
> —JUDGES 5:3

An unusual opportunity for great adventure was placed in my path at a time when my daily routine was lived stereotypically as I worked eight to five each day. Answering a tiny newspaper ad in the *Dallas Morning News* about chorus auditions, I was accepted for the 1959 season with the Dallas Civic Opera Company.

For fifteen years, from 1959 to 1973, I sang my heart out. It didn't come without sacrifice and tons of expended energy, but it gave me one of the greatest experiences of my life. I know now it would have been unattainable at any other point in my life, and if I'd waited, I would have missed it.

The experience introduced me to fascinating people from all over the world, and it enlarged my boundaries in a way nothing else could. Even though everything was brand-new to me, I entered in with abandonment and joy. With every new person I met, every new performance, I was renewed. It was wonderful!

The year I stopped singing in the Dallas chorus I painted a small plaque that lists all thirty-four operas in which I sang. My favorite, *Lucia di Lammermoor* by Donizetti, is the first on the list. The plaque hangs in my library at the end of a bookcase. There are lots of memories in that room. I turn the corner out of my studio and—*bam!*—I'm transported back thirty-eight years.

I thank God I had such a unique, life-changing experience that so broadened my world and my understanding of it. And here's what's amazing—during those busy years I hardly ever left town!

—Luci Swindoll

Embracing the Untouchables

> You shall love the LORD your God with all your heart, with all your soul, and with all your mind. . . . You shall love your neighbor as yourself. On these two commandments hang all the Law and the Prophets.
>
> —MATTHEW 22:37–40

Jesus' words in Matthew 22:37–40 clarify the difference between legalism and the law. The Pharisees were legalists, trying to impress God by following the letter of the law. But Jesus' surprising answer was that God was looking at their hearts, not their rule books. Legalism reminds me of the caste system that existed in India for many years and still exists in many areas, although it is technically illegal.

The system divided Hindus into four main categories: priests, warriors or ruling class, merchants, and unskilled laborers. Below them were the untouchables—people deemed so low they could not even be included in the system.

This might seem extreme to you at first, but I believe such a system exists in many parts of the church. After those at the top—the pastors or bishops—are the wealthy members who contribute to the church's financial health. Next is the majority of the people—those who work hard to keep the doors open. Then there are those who are dependent on the church for help and support. And below them all are the untouchables—those struggling with unacceptable issues, such as addiction.

But instead of using God's criteria of love and grace, we use our own human understanding of worth to satisfy our innate need to find where everyone fits into the big picture. I wonder how many wonderful opportunities to encounter Christ in others we have missed because of our blurred spiritual vision.

—Sheila Walsh

March 31

Working My Way to Wholeness

> Your Father knows the things you have need of before you ask Him.
> —Matthew 6:8

During a difficult time in my life, I was crying constantly without knowing why. Desperately searching for a way to deal with my jumbled-up feelings, I became addicted to exercise. I exercised like a maniac and, as a result, lost twenty-five pounds in six months.

I thought, *I've always struggled with my weight. I've exercised before and still couldn't drop a pound. What's different this time?*

As clear as a bell, I heard the Lord impress upon my heart: *you're not going to need that protection anymore.*

Instantly, I knew what he was referring to, even though I had never told anyone my secret: there was sexual abuse in my past. Now I knew I had to deal with it. I wanted to be strong and brave and independent, but the truth was I needed help. I needed a friend to share my burdens, even if I had to pay someone to listen to me.

I found a place where I could go for outpatient intensive therapy. For six straight days, I had back-to-back counseling sessions from 7:00 a.m. until 9:00 p.m. No two sessions were the same. Some of them were with individual doctors, but many of them were in a group setting.

At times during those six days, I felt like I was visiting the eye doctor, seeing things like I'd never seen them before. It was strange. There were so many things in my life that I had only seen from my perspective, usually the perspective of a child, and that is the view I had had of them for the rest of my life.

There, in that mental-health facility with the help of my counselors and group-session friends, my eyes were opened to newer, truer ways of looking at my life.

—Lisa Whelchel

Blessings Are Supplied in Untold Ways

Command those who are rich in this present age not to be haughty, nor to trust in uncertain riches but in the living God, who gives us richly all things to enjoy.
—1 Timothy 6:17

The author Randy Alcorn, who wrote a book titled *Heaven*, researched his topic very carefully. One of my favorite things that he concluded from his research was that animals will be in heaven since they are a part of God's creation, they were saved in Noah's flood, they were at the birth of Christ, and they are mentioned in the book of Revelation.

As a child, I didn't have pets, but for most of my adult life, I've lived with a small house dog. At first, I wanted nothing to do with a pet, mainly because I have issues about the house being hospital clean. But I accidentally fell in love with a dog, her puppies, and a few puppies since. As a result, I'm very happy to imagine sweet puppies in heaven.

My dog at the moment is Bailey, an adorable little cockapoo born shortly before 9/11. As a tiny puppy, he was exposed to *God Bless America* playing on the TV several times a day, and he began to sit up and howl with whoever happened to be singing. He now sings when we ask him—usually for birthday parties and celebrations. This little furry creature has become a great blessing to many. Last week on his way home from the groomer, he stopped in a home for the elderly and sang at one of their parties. They asked for his card for future events.

God gives such delightful gifts to us and for no apparent reason except to make us smile. And, perhaps, to remind us to be thankful. God certainly does richly supply us with all things to enjoy.

—Mary Graham

April 2

A Glimpse of the Pearly Gates

He will swallow up death in victory; and the Lord God will wipe away tears from off all faces.
—Isaiah 25:8 KJV

I'd like to blame my tendency toward confused communication lately on the fact that I was diagnosed with a malignant brain tumor in 2001. But the fact is, I've always been just a little bit absentminded, so I'm not sure the brain tumor has anything to do with it. (When the doctor told me what the problem was, I thought, *Wouldn't you know? All these years I've wished my brain would grow, and instead I get a growth!*)

People treat you differently when they find out you have cancer, especially people who are acquaintances rather than close friends. They look at you differently, and a lot of the time, I don't like the unspoken words in their eyes: *Poor you. You've got cancer. You're going to die.*

It's made me want to wear a T-shirt that says:

Yes, I have cancer.

Yes, I'm going to die.

And so are you.

My situation has sent me crying to God, complaining about the way he was bringing my life to a close. But then . . . unexpectedly . . . I kept on living!

I've spent my life looking forward to heaven, and just when I thought I had caught a glimpse of the pearly gates, what do you know? God wasn't ready for me yet. Either that or, as the old saying goes, the more you complain, the longer he lets you live. So I've vowed to stop complaining (or at least try to stop).

Instead, I hope to follow that old maxim that says, "Live each day as though it's your last . . . and someday you'll be right!"

—Barbara Johnson

Coming out of Hiding

He made the entire human race and made the earth hospitable, . . . so we could seek after God, and not just grope around in the dark but actually *find* him. He doesn't play hide-and-seek with us.

—Acts 17:26–29 MSG

I grew up attending churches that didn't seem to know any other invitation hymn except "Just As I Am." To be honest, by the time I was eight years old, I didn't like that hymn one bit. I knew I couldn't sing that hymn honestly because I wasn't coming to God "just as I am," and I didn't plan on coming clean with him any time soon.

The older I got, the better I became at hiding the real me. In fact, I became a world-class fake. On the outside I was a good Christian girl who "had it all together." I was an impressive youth leader who said all the right things. I had lots of friends and wore all the right clothes. Everyone else bought into my disguise, but I couldn't fool God. It was silly even to try. He already knew my heart completely.

What did it take to set me free? It took the courage to take off my mask, to come out of hiding.

How amazing it was when I finally realized I can be real with God. I don't have to worry about criticism or fear rejection when I come to him.

Psalm 51, David's confession to God after being confronted about his sin with Bathsheba, is beautiful in its truth: "Generous in love—God, give grace! Huge in mercy—wipe out my bad record. Scrub away my guilt, soak out my sins in your laundry. I know how bad I've been; my sins are staring me down. . . . What you're after is truth from the inside out" (vv. 1–3, 6 MSG).

Truth from the inside out. Just as I am. Once and for real.

That's what I want for myself.

—Natalie Grant

April 4

Choosing Life with Open Hands

> Regard prisoners as if you were in prison with them. Look on victims of abuse as if what happened to them had happened to you.
> —Hebrews 13:3 MSG

Many years ago, after our son's arrest for murder was front-page news, we received many comforting cards in our mailbox. We collected them in a large basket. One day depression was pulling me into the grip of despair. I picked up the basket to go through the notes. I felt a sense of shock and sadness when I realized how many *sympathy* cards we had received—the kind people send when someone has died. I screamed at the top of my lungs, "My son is *alive*! He is not dead. He is *alive!*"

The heart-wrenching truth was that someone else's son was dead at the hands of my son.

My husband and I faced the most important decision in this hellish journey: Would we die too—emotionally, spiritually, and even physically—or would we choose life? We could not change what had happened, but we could decide how we would live our lives in the middle of razor wire, sympathy cards, and deep disappointment.

Choosing life, instead of a slow death, has been the beginning of rediscovering hope. Jesus himself said, "I came so they can have real and eternal life, more and better life than they ever dreamed of" (John 10:10 MSG).

Life instead of death. Hope instead of despair. Even joy in the midst of terrible sorrow. A new kind of living—harder, but better in some ways, than before. Maddening because we hate the process but richer because of the pain.

Life. Pure and simple. It's a choice, a new kind of normal.

—Carol Kent

No One Is *That* Perfect

The one who loves me will be loved by my Father, and I too will love them and show myself to them.
—John 14:21 NIV

I never realized how much I depended on my dad's encouragement until I left for college. I started feeling more insecure about myself, and it took me awhile to realize that I was stressed because I wasn't living with my biggest fan anymore. The girls in the dorm weren't going to say, "Jenna, I am so proud of you!" the way my dad did.

That's when I realized how much my relationship with Dad really defined a lot of who I was. Since then I've learned that three big areas of life are significantly influenced by a daughter's relationship with her dad:

First, having an interactive, healthy relationship with her dad improves the way a girl looks at herself. Second, a dad shapes the way a girl looks at others and has relationships with them. For instance, a dad models what a marriage relationship looks like. Third, the way a girl looks at God is greatly influenced by her dad.

But even if we have the best dad in the world and he gives pounds of encouragement and gallons of love, we will still struggle with fears and insecurities. We may measure our worth by our popularity or want to be liked by a certain guy. We may find ourselves wanting to be a little thinner, a little smarter, a little more athletic, or . . . fill in the blank.

Whether your dad is wonderful, terrible, or somewhere in between, remember that no earthly dad is perfect enough to flawlessly complete our look, help us be totally confident, have healthy relationships, or always see God in the right way.

Take it from one who knows.

—Jenna Lucado

April 6

Love So Great

> About the ninth hour Jesus cried out with a loud voice, saying, "Eli, Eli, lama sabachthani?" that is, "My God, My God, why have You forsaken Me?"
> —Matthew 27:46

As that awful day passed while Jesus hung on the cross, I can only imagine the heaviness in the air as God passed judgment on his people. To us it would be frightening enough, but to Jesus, the separation from his Father must have felt as though a knife had pierced his heart.

It is impossible for us to know the full sense of how the Father and Son were divided at that moment, because we are not told. All we know is that Jesus knew his Father was not there as he tasted the very essence of hell—separation from God. And yet in that moment was triumph, too, as Jesus once and for all took every sin, every ounce of shame and condemnation we will ever deserve, and embraced it. It was ordained that he would take our place under judgment, and with love he accepted that role.

Such is his love: he believed we were worth dying for.

I will never be able to wrap my mind around that truth, for it is beyond human understanding. But I have staked my life on it. Jesus believes I was worth it all. Jesus believes that you were worth every blow he took, every thorn that ripped into the delicate tissue in his head, and every strike of the hammer against the nails that pierced his wrists.

You are loved and valued more than you could ever hope or ask for. The greatest love story that Hollywood ever thought up could not hold a candle to the flame that burns in God's heart for you, dear sister!

—Sheila Walsh

An Appreciation for Fog

Mark the blameless man, and observe the upright;
for the future of that man is peace.
—Psalm 37:37

Fog hung in the New Mexico night sky like ancient draperies as our plane began its descent through the thick folds of fabric to the runway below. But then the pilot pulled the plane's nose sharply up and headed back toward the shrouded stars. After circling, he announced over the intercom that he was going to "try" to land again.

Now, call me finicky, but "try" sounded way too unconfident. I wanted more assurance—like certifiable proof of pilot training, character references from someone other than his mother, and the results of his last sobriety test.

He said the fog had created a heavy barrier, preventing him from seeing the runway, even feet away from touchdown. He laughed as he reported our predicament.

Somehow, I didn't catch the humor.

On the next attempt we made it, but then the airport immediately closed the runway until dawn, when the sun helped burn off the soupy weather.

To think, all that drama over something as elemental as air!

Most of us dislike fog; we want it cleared away so we can see where we're going. But I believe sometimes fog that hides the future protects us from fretting over difficulties to come—difficulties we're not ready to face. Events in our future will surely pierce our hearts like sharp sticks that can't be dislodged. For now, I'm comforted to know that, in God's sovereign hand and perfect timing, my worst dilemmas will be redeemed for good.

—Patsy Clairmont

April 8

Outside the Empty Tomb

> After rising from the dead, Jesus appeared early on Sunday morning to Mary Magdalene, whom he had delivered from seven demons. She went to his former companions, now weeping and carrying on, and told them.
> —Mark 16:9–10 MSG

Can you imagine what that moment was like for Mary Magdalene as she knelt at the entrance to the empty tomb, weeping?

Jesus had saved her life, and then she had watched as he was beaten and executed. Now this was all she had left, the bitter blessing of anointing his body with myrrh and aloe, but even that had been taken away from her.

In agony of soul, she reached out to a stranger for help . . . and found herself at the wounded feet of Christ, who spoke her name.

There is something so deeply personal and intimate about hearing someone say your name. Only a few moments before, Peter had been there, and John had been there, but Jesus chose to show himself first to Mary. She was chosen to be the first evangelist!

I don't know how you view your life or the events that have brought you to where you are today. I don't know how inadequate you may feel or what physical ailments you may have. But I do know that there is nothing about your life that is an accident.

When we look only at external circumstances, we are in danger of missing the whole point of the miracle and gift of the life we have been given.

After the death and resurrection of Christ, Pilate was still in power, Herod still ruled, and the Roman soldiers still rode their horses through the streets of Jerusalem—but everything had changed. When you know that the God who holds the universe in place knows all that is true about you and loves you enough to die for you, how could life ever be meaningless again?

—Sheila Walsh

Believing We Are *Priceless*

We find ourselves standing where we always hoped we might stand—out in the wide open spaces of God's grace and glory, standing tall and shouting our praise.

—Romans 5:2 MSG

During counseling sessions before my Lap-Band surgery a few years ago, I got a glimpse of the future, when it might be possible for me to finally believe that I'm pretty, even through ordinary eyes.

That kind of thinking doesn't happen because you get some kind of "extreme makeover, personal edition." It doesn't happen because you lose weight. Actually, you can adopt that mind-set even if your appearance doesn't change at all. Liking what you see in the mirror comes when you realize that *you have value* as a living, breathing human being.

The weight-loss counseling was secular, but I've had enough Christian-based therapy to understand that Christians have an extraordinarily powerful reason to believe we have value. Our whole faith is grounded in the fact that God himself came to earth and endured unimaginable agony on our behalf. He did it not just on our behalf collectively but on behalf of each of us individually. Even if I'd been the only person on earth, Jesus would still have done it. He would have come to earth and gone through the crucifixion just for *me*. Overweight, emotionally scarred Sandi. And for *you*.

And remember. Jesus didn't go through that ordeal so that we could merely survive. He said he did it so we could "have life, and that [we] might have it more abundantly" (John 10:10 KJV). Or, as the *The Message* version puts it, so that we could have "more and better life than [we] ever dreamed of."

If we can just believe that, we can understand that we are *priceless*.

—Sandi Patty

April 10

The Most Commonly Asked Question

> If you seek God, your God, you'll be able to find him if you're serious, looking for him with your whole heart and soul.
> —Deuteronomy 4:29 msg

One of the things I find most irritating about my frequent memory failures is forgetting where I put things. You've heard the adage that the journey of a thousand miles begins with a single step. Well, for me, any journey always begins with one last trip to the bathroom and a frantic search for my car keys.

The most amazing thing we women lose—at all stages and all ages of our lives—is our purse (often with our car keys in it). We've all done it: set it on top of the car while we're loading groceries, put it down on a changing-room chair while we're trying on clothes in the mall, left it in the taxicab, forgotten it on an airplane, walked out of a restaurant while it remains under the table, overlooked it as we hurried out of the doctor's office when we were late picking up our kids from school.

Yes, we forget our purses, lose our handbags, misplace our wallets, and leave our pocketbooks behind. But how can that be? We might as well leave our brains behind (which, for some of us, also happens) as leave these little (or not so little) envelopers of essentials. Our whole *lives* are contained in those things! Driver's license, credit cards, keys, address books, membership cards, family photos, cameras, cell phones, calculators, garage-door openers, dental floss, cosmetics, mirror, hairbrush . . . oh, and occasionally, money.

With so much of our lives stuffed in there, it seems impossible that we could ever walk off and forget it. But we do.

Yes, in many homes, the three little words that are heard most often are not, "I love you" but "Where's my purse?"

—Barbara Johnson

April 11

No Borders

The earth is the LORD's, and everything in it,
the world, and all who live in it.
—PSALM 24:1 NIV

I took my first trip to Europe in 1966, accepting an invitation from some opera friends who lived there. To take that first trip, I saved twenty-five dollars a month for five years, and when I landed on foreign soil, there wasn't a day when my feet touched the ground. I walked on air, elated over everything—the countries, cities, people, art, music, food, languages, flights, and accommodations. I had discovered a new world and knew then I'd never get my fill. That twenty-one-day trip opened a whole university of wonder—a zoom lens into endless possibilities. It whetted an appetite that has never been satiated.

Shortly after I got home from that first trip to Europe, I bought a world globe. Nothing fancy, just a round ball on a stand that I could twirl and watch the countries go by. Every place I saw or touched, I wanted to experience for myself. I wanted to go there.

When the earth is in front of us, in a round ball, with all the countries and oceans delineated, it makes everything seem accessible, within reach. No borders or boundaries or impasses. I love that.

Problems that exist in actuality between nations and continents can't be seen on a world globe or map, and everything is peaceful. Anything is possible. Every act of kindness or desire for betterment seems doable.

This kind of outlook gives us the capacity to dream big, dare to try new things, and believe we can overcome detours and obstacles that get in our way or hold us back. If the world isn't such an ominous, scary place, then we are more inclined to reach out to others and give our hearts to them.

—Luci Swindoll

April 12

Never Going Back

> As far as the east is from the west, so far has He removed our transgressions from us.
> —Psalm 103:12

When Satan torments you about some past confessed sin, remember that what Jesus did on the cross was complete and total. By dying on the cross he totally removed our sins so that we no longer have to deal with them. Our sin has been cut off—gone as far as the east is from the west—and God chooses to remember it no more (Psalm 103:12). That is good news!

If you find it hard to let the impact of that good news sink right to the depth of your heart and soul, try this: one thing I have found helpful from time to time when I have felt burdened by a past failure or persistent flaw is to write it down on a piece of paper, examine it, bring it before the Lord, and then burn it.

Let me give you an example. I used to have a problem with saying that I had done things I hadn't done or listened to CDs I hadn't listened to or seen movies that I hadn't seen because I wanted to "go with the flow." I would hear myself do it and think, *This is ridiculous. Why did I just say that I saw that movie when I didn't*? It was only when I recognized and owned this as sin that I could deal with it. So I wrote out on a piece of paper:

Father,

Sometimes I say things that aren't true because I want people to like me. I know that this is wrong and ask you to forgive me.

Then I lit the piece of paper and threw it in the fireplace. As it burned, I thanked my Father for his grace that covers my sin. As I watched the burning paper turn to ashes, I knew that, with God's help, I would never have to go back there again.

—Sheila Walsh

Finding What We Really Need

Take My yoke upon you and learn from Me, for I am gentle and lowly in heart, and you will find rest for your souls.

—Matthew 11:29

In the early days of Women of Faith events, Joni Eareckson Tada was a guest speaker in a few cities. Joni is a heroic woman of faith in every sense of the word. Injured in a diving accident as a teenager, she has used her weakness to demonstrate God's power in her life.

Joni first spoke for us in 1997 in Sacramento. At that point, Women of Faith was not setting up the arenas on our own. It had never happened before and has never since, but in Sacramento in 1997, the arena was oversold by about a thousand seats.

The mistake was discovered about twenty-four hours before the event, and the team came up with amazing solutions, one of which was to rent smaller plastic chairs so that the floor could accommodate more people.

We explained all of this Friday as people arrived, but in the end, there was drama. Some women were uncomfortable and felt cheated, and some even felt angry. I mentioned this as a prayer request to Joni just before she spoke. When she rolled on the stage in her wheelchair, she began with these words, spoken so kindly: "I understand some of you are not sitting in the chair you want to be sitting in tonight. Neither am I. And I know so many who would love to be sitting where you are tonight—even if only for tonight."

There was a hush over the room. And from that moment, we had one of the best, most memorable events in our history. Everyone was challenged and inspired. Sometimes what we ask for is not what we want. We ask for comfort, but we want our spirits to be moved, our hearts lifted, and we want to be changed. We can miss all of that if we're not careful.

—Mary Graham

April 14

Practicing the Art of Confession

> The sacrifices of God are a broken spirit; a broken and a contrite heart—these, O God, You will not despise.
> —Psalm 51:17

God desires us to come before him with humility. The type of gifts we give God aren't as significant as the texture of our hearts. For instance, rather than your reluctantly committing to be a small-group leader during a season when it doesn't work with your schedule, God would be more pleased if you honestly declined and then earnestly prayed for the small-group ministry. Rather than grumbling about giving extra money to the church mission fund, how about inviting some missionaries over for dinner?

Our offerings to God aren't about earning his forgiveness or approval but about gratefully acknowledging his holy and perfect grace.

The tail end of Psalm 51 (vv. 18, 19) makes it clear that repentance can impact an entire community. And I find it interesting that some scholars think these concluding verses were actually added long after David penned the first part. They think the group petition that comes next was inserted as a sort of exclamation point after the Israelites returned to Jerusalem from captivity in Babylon to find the ramparts of their hometown ransacked. Thus, this explicit request to have the walls rebuilt: "Do good in Your good pleasure to Zion; build the walls of Jerusalem" (Psalm 51:18 NCV).

Whether it's poetical appendage or it originated with David, this portion makes the point that, even when it comes to a gathering of believers, we must still admit our mistakes if we hope to enjoy God's favor.

—Lisa Harper

Helped by Heartache

The Lord is near to those who have a broken heart.
—Psalm 34:18

My friend and coworker Sheila Walsh gave me the children's book *The Miraculous Journey of Edward Tulane.* Inside the cover an epigraph reads, "The heart breaks and breaks and lives by breaking."

As I pondered that line, I realized that if our hearts didn't break, they would burst from pain and we would die. I never thought about heartbreaks helping us to survive this fractured world we live in, and yet they do.

When my dear friend Carol buried her adult son, Jeff, I wondered if her splintered heart would ever heal. I've watched her walk through twelve years since her loss, and I realize that while today Carol's life isn't paralyzed by Jeff's death, she still walks with a heart-limp because there is nowhere she can go to escape the reality of her loss.

Yet what I've witnessed, as my shy friend steps through the fog of despair and wrenching loss, is a growing boldness, a wider faith, a deeper compassion, a fearlessness toward death, and a heightened commitment toward her family.

It took time for Carol's dance to return because it's hard to move your feet on a dance floor covered with loss, depression, and anger; but now she actually glides with greater grace than before. Her movements have an added lilt and precision. And others watch . . . and marvel . . . and wonder . . . and hope—hope that their own dance will return as well.

—Patsy Clairmont

April 16

We Are God's Chosen

> I have chosen you and have not turned against you.
> —ISAIAH 41:9 NCV

We have all had our hearts broken by someone who did not choose us or by someone who rejected us. Some of us have even said under our breath, "We could have had a great life together, but . . . oh, well."

God never says, "Oh, well." He is relentless in his love pursuit of us while at the same time honoring our right to say, "No, I'm not interested." It breaks the heart of God when we don't let him fulfill his desires for us.

Meaning for life comes when we realize God made us because he wanted to. God made the first move; we choose whether to make the next one. It is a sobering freedom to abandon the love God has for us. In so doing we abandon the very reason we were born, and our lives then are reduced to a meaningless existence.

Abandon means "to choose against; to desert." How blessed we are that, in the cocooning security of God's choice to love us, we also have his promise to *never* abandon us. He will never choose against us. No human being in our lives can make such a declaration of steadfast love.

My prayer is that you choose to accept the very reason for which you were born and that you rest in your place of one whom God will never abandon, never throw away.

—Marilyn Meberg

Finding Level Ground Beneath the Cross

For the law was given through Moses, but grace and truth came through Jesus Christ.
—John 1:17

We live in a very fast-paced world, and all too often we find ourselves at the end of another day without having connected with anyone in a meaningful way. Is that because sometimes we're unwilling to reveal our real selves to others?

Most often, I imagine, we don't tell others about our needs because we don't want to be thought less of. We don't want others to see that we've made mistakes or failed in our Christian walk.

A common thread throughout human history is our inability to live up to God's standards. But another thread can be traced: our desire to squeeze people into a mold of our making—to embrace a dead religion rather than a living truth. Both realities would leave us miserable . . . if it weren't for Christ.

In *The Message,* Eugene Peterson translated John 1:16–17 in this jubilant way: "We all live off his generous bounty, gift after gift after gift. We got the basics from Moses, and then this exuberant giving and receiving, this endless knowing and understanding—all this came through Jesus, the Messiah."

The ground at the foot of the cross is even. There are no podiums for those who feel most worthy. There are no pits for those who feel they don't belong. The only way to break free from this dead, stale religion is with the glorious gift of fresh-baked grace every morning for the rest of our lives!

—Sheila Walsh

April 18

God Put the World on Our Hearts

> The ways of right-living people glow with light; the longer they live, the brighter they shine.
> —Proverbs 4:18 msg

A dear friend of mine, Joanne, fought cancer valiantly for seventeen years but finally lost. Two days before she died, I called Joanne to visit a bit, not realizing death was so near. When I told the person who answered who I was, she said, "Oh, yes . . . Joanne wants to talk with you."

In a weak, barely audible voice, my friend said, "Luci, you are a gift to the whole world. Thank you for being in my life"—then handed the phone back to her caregiver.

I cried when I heard Joanne's voice, knowing she probably wouldn't last long in that weakened condition. And I'll never forget her words or that enormous compliment. But it was a great deal more to me than an expression of kindness. It was God's injunction through the soft, sweet voice of Joanne. He was saying, "I have given you life, Luci. It's a gift. Now I want you to live that live by embracing the whole world."

God has put the world in my heart. He's put it on all our hearts. His desire is that we would go into it—in whatever way we can. He has a gift for the entire world, and it is in us, his people.

When we realize our lives are to be given away, everything about our outlook changes and grows. God takes our youth and gives us his truth in exchange. We see and do things differently as a result. We think beyond our own borders. The world becomes accessible through the power of God's Spirit and love. We capture each moment, embrace the journey, and go forward.

—Luci Swindoll

Spending Time at Our Wits' End

They reel to and fro, and stagger like a drunken man, and are at their wits' end. Then they cry out to the LORD in their trouble, And He brings them out of their distresses.
—PSALM 107:27–28

To be human is to spend some time at our "wits' end," perhaps reeling to and fro. Most of us have expended time and energy trying to find solutions to our various wits'-end dilemmas.

Sometimes we use problem-solving skills that seem sensible to us, and in so doing we may see our circumstances change for the better. When that happens, we sigh with relief that yet another crisis has been averted.

But what if we *can't* figure these things out on our own? What if, at our wits' end, we feel lost in pain, confusion, desperation, and fear? Those are the kinds of emotions that drive us to "cry out to the LORD" in our trouble. To be at our wits' end is, according to *Webster's*, "to have [our] back against the wall."

The good news is, when our backs are against the wall—he is there. God is always at our wits' end. How do we know? Because God is wherever we are. Wherever we may wander, in foolishness or fear, God does not leave us.

That astounding truth is accompanied by yet another astounding truth found in our scriptural theme passage, Psalm 107:27–28: when we cry out to the Lord, he brings us out of our distresses. Why does God do that? The answer is repeatedly stated throughout the entire chapter of Psalm 118.

He does it because "his love endures forever" (NIV). In spite of our mindless wandering that may produce wits'-end dilemmas, "his love endures forever."

—Marilyn Meberg

April 20

Celebrating My Second Birthday

> My child, pay attention to my words . . . They are the key to life for those who find them; they bring health to the whole body.
>
> —Proverbs 4:20, 22 NCV

During counseling before my Lap-Band surgery a few years ago, I kept coming back to that point of realizing *weight loss is an inside job*. It's ultimately more about *thinking* than *eating*.

That's why I'd failed at the dozens of other weight-loss diets and programs I'd tried. I just hadn't been convinced that I was worth the effort to endure whatever it cost me in time, money, or sacrifice. The old shame and the old way of thinking would come sneaking back in, and once again I would fail.

A year after the surgery, I complimented a woman about how good she looked. She said thank you and then leaned in closer and said something like, "You should have seen me a couple of years ago. I've lost nearly two hundred pounds."

"Wow!" I answered. "That's amazing. How did you do it?"

"Well, I didn't do it on my own. I don't know how you feel about this, Sandi, but I had gastric bypass surgery."

I grabbed her hands. "Yes, you *did* do it on your own. I had Lap-Band, and I know *we* still have to do the hard work. It's still hard, isn't it? We still have to watch what we eat and exercise and stick with all those lifestyle changes, but now . . ." I stopped and hugged her. "Can you believe we've done this?"

She told me she now celebrates two birthdays: the day she was born and the day of her surgery. "Because that's when I got my second chance to live a healthy, productive life."

I so get that!

—Sandi Patty

My Best Friend Forever

But there is a friend who sticks closer than a brother.
—Proverbs 18:24

It may sound corny, but truly, my best friend has always been Jesus. I somehow understood this from as early as I can remember. I wasn't raised in a church-going home. But as a small child, barely able to read, I was given a large picture book of Bible stories; whenever I was afraid or lonely or sad, I would look at the pictures and read the stories. I turned to him even then for comfort. He became my refuge before I ever knew him as Savior.

Later, my father was invited to a church revival service. Our whole family went. From the moment I walked through those church doors, I started to cry. I sat in the pew weeping the whole night. I didn't know why, and I was so embarrassed, but I couldn't stop crying.

I understand now that the presence of the Lord was in that place. Jesus walked straight through the wall that was already in place around my heart and touched my pain with his healing love.

At the age of ten, I asked Jesus, "Come into my heart, forgive my sins, and be my Lord." But even before that official invitation, Jesus had been snuggling up like a cat offering gentle companionship to the most frightened places of my soul.

Throughout my years in Hollywood, Jesus was more real and present to me than any other person in my life. If I were to picture my isolated heart like a deserted island, then it has just been Jesus and me in there for years.

Now, when you spend that much time with someone, you become really close, and my friendship with Jesus has been constantly growing in depth and breadth from the beginning. Maybe even from before the beginning.

—Lisa Whelchel

April 22

Heeding God's Voice

> I wait for the LORD, my whole being waits,
> and in his word I put my hope.
> —PSALM 130:5 NIV

During a turbulent season of my life, suffering the consequences of the poor choices I'd made and looking for a way out of the mess I'd landed in, I had a strong and enlightening dream.

In it I'm clinging to a scrawny little tree that's growing out of the very edge of a cliff. All around me a storm is raging, and the powerful wind is blowing me away from the cliff and out over the abyss. Far below I can see the sharp rocks that will undoubtedly end my life. I can feel myself growing weaker by the second.

Suddenly, above the howling roar of the wind, I hear a voice, and instantly I recognize it as God's.

Let go, God says.

In the dream, I close my eyes. I can't bear to look at the murderous rocks any longer.

Let go, God says again.

My life is almost over. The only thing I have left is a choice. I can choose to let the wind blow me over the edge, or I can *choose* to let go. I can *choose* to follow God's voice *now.*

That's what I choose. I let go, and down I fall.

But, unknown to me, the wind has changed. It's blowing the other way, no doubt in obedience to the voice who stilled it one stormy night on the Sea of Galilee two thousand years ago (see Matthew 8:23–27).

In my dream, the wind has changed direction, and when I choose to heed God's voice and let go of the tree limb . . . I fall onto solid ground.

—Sandi Patty

Brer Rabbit's Redeeming Lesson

Then God saw everything that He had made,
and indeed it was very good.
—Genesis 1:31

I think God put animals here on earth because they please him and because he knew they would make our valley life easier. It's not that they don't require upkeep; let's face it, they can be a handful and a wallet reducer. But they give so much more than they require—affection, protection, comfort, and enjoyment.

I have many friends who are either cat or dog owners. They all would testify to how much valley joy they have experienced because of their animals.

Being a dog lover, I would pirouette backwards to have a dog. But since I spend so much time on the road, I'm relegated to enjoying other people's pets and stories about animals in books on my shelves. One of my favorite "pets" in book form is Brer Rabbit. He is that sassy, smart, and seasoned rabbit who loves living in a briar patch—a fact that saves his life, leading him to exclaim: "I was born and raised in a briar patch. Oh, my Lord, he's sure been good to me!"

I love Brer Rabbit's story because it reminds me of the redeeming value of having been born and raised in brambles. Life is full of briars that can puncture us, or we can adapt, patch up life, and find refuge in the midst of piercing pain. And here's why: 'Cause our Lord, he's sure been good to us.

—Patsy Clairmont

April 24

A Hair Solution

> People throw lots to make a decision, but the answer comes from the Lord.
>
> —Proverbs 16:33 NCV

Each spring for the first three years I lived in Texas, I planted a gorgeous garden of flowers—petunias, snapdragons, and pansies, to name a few—and each spring the rabbits ate them.

Then, one day at the beauty shop, I was complaining about my rabbit problem when a woman getting a root touch-up said, "I can tell you exactly how to get rid of your rabbits—human hair."

She explained her method, and a short while later I hurried home with a plastic bag full of hair clippings my stylist had swept into the trash can that day. I eagerly started hairing up my flower beds but soon lost my enthusiasm for the project. My back hurt, my fingers lost "nobility," and the hair—brown, black, blonde, gray, and multicolored—gave me the creeps.

I was nearly finished when a friend showed up, curious to know what I was doing. After I told her, she stared wordlessly at me for at least a full minute. "Marilyn," she whispered conspiratorially, "do you realize you are spreading the DNA of perfect strangers all over your property? I'm sure that's not even moral!"

I accused her of watching too many episodes of *CSI*.

Soon I had proof the solution works: no more rabbits! My friend now has a rabbit problem in her flower beds, too, but she refuses my hair solution, despite its proven success in my snapdragons. When I offer her clippings, she says she cannot accept my offer to share hair because it would compromise her moral standards!

—Marilyn Meberg

Identifying the Real Problem

As the Father loved Me, I also have loved you;
abide in My love.
—John 15:9

Max Lucado has always been a faithful, involved, loving dad. I know how to love myself because he loves me. As I watched him love other people, I learned to love others. I watched him love God, which taught me how to love God.

But having a good dad doesn't mean there haven't been times when I climbed some mountains of self-doubt, experienced spiritual confusion, and settled for superficial friendships.

My dad's love was not strong enough to keep me from kneeling in front of the toilet and trying to make myself throw up. He couldn't prevent me from thinking I was fat.

I remember, in particular, one Easter when I consumed a potluck of calories and then, afterward, felt guilty, and angry with myself, wondering, *Why did I do that*?

Summer was around the corner. I had been on a strict diet to look good in my swimsuit. I thought throwing up would serve as punishment and also relieve the guilt I felt.

But what was the real problem?

First, I believed the world's lie that we aren't beautiful unless we wear a size 0. Second, I cared more about my appearance than my heart. I was willing to harm myself physically, emotionally, and spiritually just to be thin. Third, I didn't feel good enough or pretty enough. My dad called me "beautiful" all the time, but I still turned to magazine covers for my definition of beauty. I made a big mistake by trying to find all my security in my dad's love and in other people's approval. It's just not possible. Ever. When I did that, I was constantly insecure and unsatisfied with myself.

—Jenna Lucado

April 26

Finding What Was Lost

> Imagine a woman who has ten coins and loses one. . . . When she finds it you can be sure she'll call her friends and neighbors: "Celebrate with me! I found my lost coin!"
> —Luke 15:8–9 MSG

In 2005, my husband, Don, gave me a beautiful diamond ring for our anniversary. A few months later, I took the ring off to take a shower before leaving on a weekend trip. I put it somewhere in the bathroom where I would be sure to remember it and where it also would be safe from falling down the drain.

And then, when I looked for it again a few minutes later, it was gone! It had vanished. Simply evaporated into thin air.

I frantically tore the bathroom apart, looking everywhere—and folks, it's not that big a bathroom! But I could not remember where I'd put it, and despite my best efforts, I could not find that ring.

Several months went by, maybe a year and a half. Then one day I walked into our bathroom, and the ring was lying on the counter by the sink. A cleaning crew had apparently found it.

I screamed. And shrieked. And cried. I ran out of the bathroom, up and down the hall, down the stairs, in and out of the kitchen, screaming and crying, so happy I simply couldn't contain myself.

My family probably thought maybe Publisher's Clearinghouse had miraculously shown up in our bathroom to announce that I'd won a million dollars a day for life.

To lose something I valued so much had been crushing. Embarrassing. Frustrating. I had spent hours looking for it, shed tears regretting its disappearance. And then to find it again . . . the joy was simply indescribable. It made Jesus' parable about the woman's lost coin very real to me.

—Sandi Patty

Why Can't We Get It?

The LORD is with me; I will not be afraid. What can mere mortals do to me?
—PSALM 118:6 NIV

Throughout the Bible we're told that God is always with us. It's an awesome promise but one that is difficult for many of us to incorporate into our daily living. For some reason, its truth is beyond our grasp. We may believe God's love endures forever in some sort of mystical, far-from-us way, but if the whole truth were known, it does not seem real for our nitty-gritty reality.

Why can't we get it—that when we call out in our distresses, he will bring us out of our troubles?

I think the problem lies in the contrast between what we believe and what we think. In our hearts we *believe* that God's love endures forever, but in our heads we sometimes *think* in a way that creates roadblocks to faith. Our faulty thinking might lead us to have questions like these:

- If he loves me so much, why do I hurt so much?
- Am I being punished? I thought I was forgiven.
- Who's in charge of my life? Can I trust that answer?
- Why is faith so hard? What if I don't have enough?

Faulty thinking leads to shaky faith, and shaky faith can put your back against the wall. Through prayer, Bible study, and, sometimes, the help of godly teachers, you can find your way to a faith that is practical and within your grasp. You can eliminate faulty thinking, get past the roadblock, and find your way to a faith that endures.

The God who is always there cares even more about your quest for faith than you do. His intent is to meet you where you are in your faith need and to lovingly show you what it means when he tells you he will bring you out of your distresses.

—Marilyn Meberg

April 28

Exhilarating Vulnerability

He restores my soul.
—Psalm 23:3

I cashed in some of my airline reward miles and flew to Los Angeles to visit a group of friends from my years in California. We hadn't all been seated around the table together since I moved to Texas.

It was just like old times . . . only it wasn't because I was not the same, and my friends sensed that immediately. For one thing, we hadn't been talking more than fifteen minutes before tears began to roll down my cheeks.

Second, my friends were used to me asking questions. I loved to ask them questions that let me really get to know and love them. I always loved getting to really *know* these friends, not just know *about* them.

But I realize now that this is probably why my friends could never put their finger on why they didn't feel close to me. I always was interested in them, but my interest and listening were also defense mechanisms to avoid opening up my own heart.

So my friends were surprised when I suddenly became vulnerable with them, sharing my own hurts and fears and uncertainties.

This was an all-new situation, and an amazing thing happened when I began to let others inside my heart for the first time. They threw open the gates of their own hearts and invited me into the deepest recesses, where their own questions and secrets were stored.

I was the one who was then surprised: so this is what it feels like to be interdependent! Why had I been scared of this for so long? It was exhilarating.

—Lisa Whelchel

The Impossible Commandments

The law of the Spirit of life in Christ Jesus has made me free from the law of sin and death.

—Romans 8:2

The laws God gave to his people in the Old Testament reveal much more than rules; they reveal his heart. God prefaced the Ten Commandments by restating his relationship with his children: "I am the Lord your God, who brought you out of the land of Egypt" (Exodus 20:2).

It doesn't seem like the commandments should be that difficult to follow: honor God and keep him first. Take a day off. Honor your parents. Don't kill anyone. Don't sleep with anyone else's husband. Don't shoplift. Tell the truth. And if your friend has a new purse, be happy for her!

God didn't demand twenty hours of community service every day or six hours of hymn singing before bedtime. On first examination, abiding by the Ten Commandments should come naturally. Instead they bring into sharp focus our complete inability to obey God in our own strength.

In this day of self-help gurus and feel-good books, it's easy to avoid the truth that we are *all* sinners. We were born into this sin as children of Adam and Eve . . . and our culture does not want to hear about it. Look on the best-seller list and you'll find book after book telling us we are the light of the world, we are like gods, and all we have to do is embrace that.

That is a demonic lie. Our freedom doesn't come from becoming God but by embracing what God has done for us through his Son, Jesus Christ.

—Sheila Walsh

April 30

Capture the Moment

> Keep my message in plain view at all times. Concentrate! Learn it by heart! Those who discover these words live, really live; body and soul, they're bursting with health.
> —Proverbs 4:21–22 MSG

I'm crazy about postcards. During my first trip to Europe in 1966, I wrote sixty-one cards. Postcards are one of the simplest ways to capture the moment. They're colorful, easy to acquire, quick to write, and inexpensive. In a few minutes' time you tell somebody on the other side of the world that you love her and are thinking of her.

I write cards all the time, even from home. I wrote one last night to one of my Texas pals.

I've written postcards to myself too. When I saw the Taj Mahal in India, I asked the friends with whom I was traveling to add to the card I had written to myself. They did; we all signed it. I mailed it, and bingo!—it arrived after I got home. I was a happy girl with a treasured memory right in the palm of my hand.

Moments come and go so fast, but they make up the whole of life. Little bitty moments here and there. Life is short and irrevocable. No matter what we do to lengthen the moment, we can't. No matter how eager we are to shorten uncomfortable events, that can't be done either.

If we don't learn to live fully in the present, much of life passes us by, lost forever in the cobwebs of time, often unremembered. Time can't be retrieved except in our memory banks. That's why we must be all there at any given moment, even during times that are frightening or difficult. Everything has a purpose, and if we don't want to miss that purpose and the adventure along the way, then we must be conscious, alert, curious, and openhearted. When we capture the moment we're in, we're fully alive.

—Luci Swindoll

Longing for the Trust That Mary Had

The angel said to her, "Rejoice, highly favored one, the Lord is with you; blessed are you among women!"
—Luke 1:28

It must have been such a startling moment for Mary when an angel appeared right in front of her and told her she would become pregnant and bear God's child.

"But how?" Mary answered. "I've never slept with a man."

The angel explained: "The Holy Spirit will come upon you, the power of the Highest hover over you. . . . Nothing, you see, is impossible with God."

"Let it be with me just as you say," Mary answered. (See the whole conversation in Luke 1:34–38.)

My heart longs to trust God the way Mary did—ready to serve, no matter what the gossip, the criticism, and the misunderstanding from others. I long to pray with an honest heart, "Be it unto me according to thy word" (Luke 1:38 KJV).

I read her poignant words and think, *How could she do it? How could she be so trusting? So surrendered? Was it her youth? Her shock? The result of a lifelong, intimate dependence on God?*

And then I find myself asking, *Do I even want to say that to God when the consequences could be so painful? Do I want to get to a place where I give him that much power? Do I really understand that he already has that power and that my resistance only hurts myself?*

I think I understand what trust is, and I demand it of others, but what is it *really*?

Among the dictionary definitions for the word *trust* is another word: *hope*. It was an epiphany for me to discover that, even in the dictionary, the words *hope* and *trust* are used together.

—Carol Kent

May 2

We Don't Need Bags of Candy

> The LORD is my shepherd; I shall not want.
> —PSALM 23:1

Darlene lived across the street from me until I was five. She was just a bit older than I and an only child. I was the youngest of eight children. All anyone in my family did was boss me around.

That is precisely why I loved Darlene. She was my best friend, and I loved her with my whole heart. When I was four, Darlene started to school. The elementary school was about half a block away. She was very afraid to go to school by herself. So I volunteered to walk her to school in the morning and go back in the afternoon and walk her home. Her mother gave me a nickel twice a day, one when I picked up Darlene and the other when I saw her safely home. I could have been rich except for one thing. There was this little store between our houses and the school.

On the way to and from the school, I bought five cents' worth of penny candy, which was a whole bag. I had enough candy that year to protect myself from my brothers' incessant teasing. I, who never had any power over them, now had all the power with nothing more than a little brown paper bag of sweets.

How often as a child of God I feel helpless, unarmed, and weak. I find myself looking for ammunition, appeasements, or armor to protect myself from the words or ways of others. Sometimes when I pray, I want to provide something that enables me to negotiate better terms with God. Then I remember I no longer need a little brown bag of anything to come to my defense. The Defender of my soul lives in me, to love me, provide for me, and protect me from anything that is not his perfect will for me.

—Mary Graham

Awaken to Wonder

Remember His marvelous works which He has done,
His wonders, and the judgments of His mouth.
—1 Chronicles 16:12

Wonder means "that which arouses awe, astonishment, surprise, or admiration." Quite honestly I can walk out to my backyard and experience all of that. My heart is filled with awe when I examine the tatted lace of the Queen Anne that grows like royal trim at the edge of a wooded area. I was equally astonished yesterday when, after a summer storm, a rainbow arched across the heavens. One day I was amazed to see prehistoric birds land in my yard. Okay, okay, so they weren't that old, but the sandhill cranes sure looked like it. I've never trusted birds taller than I am.

Wonder is all around us: in a night sky, a summer storm, a waterfall, or a tadpole's wiggle. It's definitely present in a baby's birth, the notes of a songbird's hymn, and the gossamer beauty of a butterfly's wings. Wonder fills us when a child utters his first word, when a baby bird takes its first flight, and when our heart flutters with first love. And nothing compares to the wonder a mother feels when her baby moves inside her womb for the first time.

When have you gone in search of wonder? Where? What did you find? Name three wonders in God's creation that thrill your heart just to think of them.

Are you standing in a "wide place," or are you hemmed in by hardship? Look around. Open your eyes. God's handiwork is waiting to inspire you and fill you with wonder.

—Patsy Clairmont

May 4

Finding Meaning in Misery

> I will give you the treasures of darkness
> And hidden riches of secret places.
> —Isaiah 45:3

We tend to think Christians should not experience calamities because we believe God will steer bad things away from us. Of course, we allow for little calamities like root canals, fender dings, or bad weather during vacation. But when the big stuff hits—earthquakes, floods, fires, tornadoes, hurricanes—we think God is indifferent to our suffering. It doesn't help when these events are categorized as acts of God.

I believe we can find solutions to many calamities by paying attention to how we think about calamities and what we believe about them. Maintaining faith, confidence, and trust in God's sovereign intent may not make the problem disappear, but it can change how we respond to it—and whether we feel defeated by it.

When we find ourselves thinking and believing God doesn't care, doesn't intervene on our behalf, or simply leaves us alone to work things out, some mental repair work is in order. Depending on how we think and believe, we can decide whether we want to pull ourselves out from beneath the rubble or curl up and simply lie there hoping to die.

When I'm in the eye of a storm, I remember God's sovereign intent to bring good out of bad, his promise to give me "treasures of darkness and hidden riches of secret places." And I trust him to provide soul wealth, which gives the calamity personal meaning.

—Marilyn Meberg

The Danger of Distraction

[Martha] had a sister called Mary, who also sat at Jesus' feet and heard His word. But Martha was distracted.

—LUKE 10:39–40

Luke 10:38–42 tells about a visit Jesus and his disciples made to the home of a woman named Martha and her sister, Mary. During that visit Mary "sat at the Lord's feet listening to what he said" (v. 39 NIV). Martha, in contrast, scurried around the house "distracted by all the preparations that had to be made" (v. 40 NIV).

The picture I get is that the guests had dropped in unexpectedly and Martha was frantically trying to serve the group some quick refreshments while also picking up the clutter, getting the beds ready, and then assembling enough food to feed a bunch of hungry men.

Whew! Just thinking about it wears me out. Apparently Martha was having to do all the work single-handedly because her silly sister wasn't lifting a finger to help. Mary was sitting in there with the company, looking doe-eyed at their friend Jesus, and hanging on his every word as if her life depended on it. No wonder Martha was cranky!

Finally she marched into the living room and snapped at Jesus, "Lord, don't you care that my sister has left me to do the work by myself?" she fumed. "Tell her to help me!"

Jesus' reply resonates down the centuries to identify the essential priority all of us should have today: "Mary has chosen what is better, and it will not be taken away from her" (v. 42 NIV).

Jesus' words are profound, yet he shared them with kindness and gentleness. He doesn't shout with dramatic arrogance. No, we have to look for the crucial lesson in his simple reply; we have to stop and listen carefully and absorb what he's saying. We can only hope that's what the distracted Martha did too.

—Sandi Patty

May 6

God's Gift to Keep Our Faith Strong

> Faith is the substance of things hoped for,
> the evidence of things not seen.
> —Hebrews 11:1

As a child, I developed a sudden fear of my own death after my beloved pet turtle, Leroy, died. Hearing my concerns, my mother gently coached me in how to receive Jesus into my heart. I immediately prayed a five-year-old's version of the sinner's prayer—something like, "Dear Jesus, I believe you are God's only Son and that you died on the cross and arose from the dead, and I hope you will forgive me for my sins and take me to heaven when I die so I can live with you forever. Amen."

Mother assured me that should my untimely death occur, I would instantly be in heaven. What a tremendous relief for my young, anxious heart!

Looking back, I realize I didn't have a clue at that age what real faith is. The faith I did have was in my mother, who explained salvation to me. It made sense that God loved me (I saw no reason then why he shouldn't), and I liked the idea of Jesus living within me forever.

God graciously provided me with a gift to help develop my faith and keep it strong. I call this type of gift a *faith object.*

As a child, my faith object was my mother. I trusted her; she was reliable, and she was also tangible. I could see her and hear her voice. She said there is a God who loves me, and his Son, Jesus, forgives sin, and with his forgiveness, I would live in eternity.

As adults, we have a different faith object, and we have only one. It's the Bible. It's tangible, I can see it, I always have access to it, and I have faith in what it says.

—Marilyn Meberg

We Just Keep Showing Up

Their message goes out through all the world; their words go everywhere on earth. The sky is like a home for the sun.

—Psalm 19:4 NCV

In 1995, I was invited to speak at several conferences the following year. The conference organization (which has become Women of Faith) was founded by author and entrepreneur Stephen Arterburn as a source of encouragement to women across America.

Steve wanted women to have fun, get away from their routines for a weekend, and sing and worship the Lord with other women. With this vision as a springboard, he invited Patsy Clairmont, Barbara Johnson, Marilyn Meberg, and me to be part of the tour. "Make 'em laugh!" was more or less our instruction when we began.

We were all busy with our own ministries, but because we knew and loved each other, we all said yes to doing eight "Joyful Journey" conferences around the nation. The following year, 1997, Steve invited Thelma Wells and Sheila Walsh to join us. We loved them right off the bat. They fit right in with our wackiness!

God was doing something—we could feel it. Every time we spoke at another venue, we experienced fresh excitement. Thousands of women were discovering what it meant to be a "woman of faith," to trust God with their desires, their families, their problems, their lives. Talk about adventure! Since then we've spoken to four million women.

I, for one, didn't even dream that God would swing open this door—a wonderful, exciting way to come together with fabulous women I love and admire for a common purpose that has eternal value. We tell our stories, worship together, and pray for each other and the women in our audience. We travel around the United States and the world, reaching the people God has put in our paths. It's all in his hands. We just keep showing up.

—Luci Swindoll

Finding Comfort in the God of All Hope

> The darkness shall not hide from You, but the night shines as the day; the darkness and the light are both alike to You.
> —Psalm 139:12

During a trip back to my hometown in Scotland, I happened to go by the old psychiatric hospital where my father died many years earlier. That hospital had been the place of nightmares to me as a child, and those images from my past seemed to replay inside my head. They were the same painful images I had always tried to bury beneath a mountain of "stuff," whether it was food or new clothes or seeing three movies in one day.

Anything to keep the wounds anesthetized. As a teenager and continuing into my early thirties, whenever I felt the familiar sadness creep over me, I stuffed myself with food until I could hardly walk.

Here's what I've learned since then: Dwelling on the past does nothing, but learning from it and then letting it go does. By the grace of God we can accept what is true about our past, and in Christ our very wounds and scars can be redeemed. Pain reminds us to bring our wounds to the wounded healer so he can make us better. In turn, we can comfort others as we have been comforted and look to a future free from hurt.

As I revisited the place where my father died, God brought me full circle. I was no longer a five-year-old girl haunted by a nightmare but a fifty-one-year-old woman comforted by the God of all hope who holds our past, our present, and our future in his hands.

—Sheila Walsh

Moms Making Up Christ's Body

So we, being many, are one body in Christ, and individually members of one another.

—Romans 12:5

When my kids were in junior high, I put together a little group I called my MomTime friends. These girlfriends were decidedly younger than I was and had small children, so I considered the group a wonderful mentoring opportunity.

My mental-health counselor agreed and encouraged me to practice being more transparent, vulnerable, and open to receiving, rather than reverting to old patterns of asking others to share their hearts while never opening mine.

This felt extremely uncomfortable. I told myself I had really good, godly reasons for my defense mechanisms. *Who wants a weak leader*? I reasoned. *If I'm vulnerable about some of my doubts and hurts, they might think I don't believe the biblical promises I share with them.*

Worse, it never crossed my mind that I could receive from these young women as much as they could ever get from me. Oh my, the treasure chest I almost missed opening! From this group I see God's wisdom in calling us the "body of Christ." He could have called us his heart or his hands or his mouth. But, no, he knows we need every part of the body to be healthy. This wholeness and interdependence with a variety of friends are also what guarantee healthier relationships.

These friends have taught me that we can minister just by being who we are. We don't have to *do* ministry to be used by the Lord in someone's life.

—Lisa Whelchel

Drop Your Purse and Dance

> God's thunder sets the oak trees dancing a wild dance, whirling; the pelting rain strips their branches. We fall to our knees—we call out, "Glory!"
>
> —Psalm 29:9 MSG

When things are going well, it's easy to sing and dance. But sometimes what we most need is a break amid hardship and heartbreak: when our dreams have been crushed, when our heart is aching, when we are soul weary. That's when a lighthearted touch, a composition of joy, or an unexpected twirl can diminish the tide of sorrow so we can catch our breath.

Last year our family went through some crushing blows. I could hardly breathe I was in so much emotional pain. I was confident of God's redemptive presence in the midst of our hurt, but we still had to walk through the shadowed valley.

Little things helped. Even listening in to our grandsons' playful conversation was resuscitating, and though I had no desire to kick up my heels, I found it consoling to be encircled in an embrace.

One evening my husband, Les, and I arrived home after running errands to hear music throughout the neighborhood coming from a nearby party. The song playing was Patsy Cline's "I Fall to Pieces," which I found sadly appropriate for our situation. Without a word, Les took my purse and set it on the driveway, slipped one arm around my back, and with the other took my hand in his. He waltzed me around and around under the stars. And I was deeply comforted.

When was the last time *you* danced? Are you too tired, too mired down by life's busyness or sorrows to take a twirl? Give yourself a break and sing anyway—until your heart dances with joy.

—Patsy Clairmont

Get Your Priorities Straight

[Martha] said, "Lord, do You not care that my sister has left me to serve alone? Therefore tell her to help me." And Jesus . . . said to her, "Martha, Martha, you are worried and troubled about many things. But one thing is needed."

—Luke 10:40–42

In every Bible version I can find, the story of Mary and Martha in Luke 10 reports Jesus answering Martha's complaint with the patient tone of a wise and loving teacher.

She was fuming at him that her sister, Mary, was sitting there, listening to him instead of helping her with preparations for their houseguests.

"Martha, dear Martha," Jesus says to her in *The Message* version. We imagine him smiling and shaking his head a little as he looks into her eyes with wisdom and love. Some translations have him saying, "My dear Martha," or "Martha, Martha."

The Lord's answer to Martha clearly identifies what our number one priority is supposed to be. His words give us the perspective we need in order to understand what's really important: *Jesus is the most valuable "possession" we can ever have—because he gives us the hope we need to survive the loss of everything else.*

Making Jesus our first priority makes it easier to categorize the rest of our lives. When we filter everything through our focus on him, we see our blessings as gifts and our hardships as challenges that draw us closer to his sustaining love and strength.

And the best thing is, once we've found Jesus, we can never lose him. We find him by confessing our sins to him, asking him to forgive us, and then believing what he says is true. Doing so sweeps us over the edge of the divine into the Savior's arms, where he promises to hold us for all eternity.

—Sandi Patty

With Christ, Change Is Possible

The Lord is near to those who have a broken heart,
and saves such as have a contrite spirit.
—Psalm 34:18

During a difficult time in my life, I wrote myself a letter that also served as a prayer from the deepest part of me. It said, in part, "Down deep inside I am lonely." I cried out to God in that letter and exposed all my anger, fears, regrets, inadequacies, and despair. Then I wrote, "What can I do about it?" As the Holy Spirit brought things to mind, I made a list of ten ideas I thought might make a difference. Then I went back to bed and, for the first time in weeks, slept soundly.

I retired two years later, in 1987, and worked for a while at Insight for Living, the international radio Bible ministry of my brother Chuck. But in 1992 I had so many speaking dates on my calendar I decided to once again retire and trust the Lord to meet my financial needs on his own terms.

It hadn't occurred to me that he would keep bringing me all kinds of unexpected opportunities year after year, including an invitation to join the team of speakers who went on to become part of Women of Faith.

We never know how things will turn out, do we? Feeling stuck or overwhelmed makes us despondent and causes us to stay put a lot longer than we need to. For me, writing that predawn letter so many years ago taught me things I'll never forget. Once I saw my effrontery and self-centeredness on paper, I knew change was necessary—and, with Christ, possible.

I had no idea all that he had in mind for my future. But since then, God has shown me that wherever I am in life can be my very best place.

—Luci Swindoll

Work Hard

The LORD repay your work, and a full reward be given you by the LORD God of Israel, under whose wings you have come for refuge.

—RUTH 2:12

My mom came from a family of do-it-yourselfers. She and her three sisters all looked forward to a day of productivity, but I wouldn't say they were workaholics, because they also knew how to sit a good chair.

They didn't hesitate to roll up their sleeves and glow from their efforts and later collapse into porch chairs with glasses of sweet tea. Soon they would move to the kitchen where they would make the best chicken and cornbread dinners you ever ate.

My mom was a strong model of a hard worker, but she was a reluctant teacher. She would rather do it herself than hassle with a child who couldn't produce up to her high standards. It didn't take me long to learn that, because I couldn't please her, I should let her do what needed to be done. Out of her desire to have things perfect and to keep peace, she let me slip out of the learning loop, and I grew up allowing others to carry my workload.

It's demeaning to wake up as a young adult and realize you're lazy. I discovered how hard it is to learn an industrious lifestyle once you are grown—not impossible, just hard. By God's grace and much effort, I've turned into a hard worker. In fact, now I have to watch that I don't tip in the other direction because I want to make up for lost time. In place of my slothful lifestyle is a strong sense of dignity and satisfaction. As I inched toward change, I often drew on Mom's demonstrated work ethic. She ended up being not only my model but also, indirectly, my teacher.

Never underestimate the impact of your family's offerings. You've learned more than you know. Trust me.

—Patsy Clairmont

May 14

Never Alone

> He heals the brokenhearted
> And binds up their wounds.
> —Psalm 147:3

As Christians, we are not asked to pretend our wounds don't exist but to let go and stop holding on to them so tightly. The truth is that whatever happened in a particular moment of our lives, that's where we were at that moment. We acted on the understanding we had then. In God's sovereignty he brought us from where we were, to where we are right at this moment. We were never alone, never abandoned.

Perhaps your father sexually abused you. Perhaps your husband is an alcoholic and came home drunk again last night. Perhaps you're dealing with some serious issues with a child or other family member. You would be justified in asking, "How can you say that should have happened?"

My answer would simply be that being set free from the past means accepting what is true, not what we wish were true. If you had a father who was sick enough to hurt you, that's who he is. You may wish he were a different person. But he was not. And you can't change that reality.

Rather than sink under the devastation of what happened, we add a new truth about what should have happened. We say, "God, you should have been there!"

God answers, *My beloved child, I was there. I held you although you could not see my arms. I caught each tear that fell. You were never alone.*

—Sheila Walsh

A Regret About Pets

God made the wild animals according to their kinds, the livestock according to their kinds, and all the creatures that move along the ground. . . . And God saw that it was good.

—Genesis 1:25 niv

Every one of my closest friends has a pet—a dog or cat or horse or goldfish or something that is dependent upon someone for its care—in some cases more than one. But somehow that kind of responsibility has never appealed to me. I regret that. I've become fascinated with wild animals in Africa, so I've wondered how that can be. I can't quite figure it out.

When I was growing up, both of my brothers had dogs, and my dearest girlhood friend had a cat. (Actually, the cat had her, which is the case with all "cat people," I'm told.) I had neither and, I'm sad to say, never wanted an animal.

It makes me chastise myself in a way; I view myself as somewhat coldhearted. I don't think I wanted the responsibility, but had I had the responsibility, I think I would have become a softer person, more generous in my spirit toward all creatures because that is the way all my animal-loving friends are. This may be a silly thing to confess, but as I think back, I do believe I would do this differently.

The only roommate I ever had raised Chihuahuas. The most adorable was Bonnie, and she was darling. As Bonnie grew older and frailer, she stopped eating and lay in her little bed from morning till night. One evening, I came home from work and found her dead on the floor. I cried and cried and was depressed for weeks.

Maybe that's why I never had an animal of my own. Perhaps I don't trust my emotions. Perhaps I fear that loving an animal would make me too vulnerable.

I just wish I had done that differently a long time ago.

—Luci Swindoll

May 16

Love, Loyalty, and Redemption

> Blessed are you of the LORD, my daughter! For you have shown more kindness at the end than at the beginning. . . . All the people of my town know that you are a virtuous woman.
>
> —RUTH 3:10–11

The book of Ruth presents a heartwarming story of love, loyalty, and redemption. Through her mother-in-law, Naomi, Ruth learned about God's love and became a believer.

Understanding the part of Ruth's story told in Ruth 4:1–12 requires a little knowledge about the practice of redemption during those times. Close relatives had the responsibility and opportunity to purchase the land of a family member sold due to poverty. This had been the case regarding the land that had belonged to Naomi's husband, Elimelech, before he died.

Another family member had first choice to redeem the land—that is, to buy it back from the one who purchased it when it was sold due to poverty. That other family member backed out when he was told that he also got Ruth as a wife in the deal. This left the option to Boaz, who quickly exercised the option and redeemed the land, taking Ruth as his wife in the process.

In the end, Ruth was redeemed and used by God to bring to the world the ancestors of David and Jesus. Ruth rose above her situation and embraced life God's way.

Like Ruth, you are valuable to God and the world. Through you, God wants to do things you never imagined possible. The choice is yours—RSVP to a pity party of one or decline the invitation through God's strength.

—Patsy Clairmont

Leaving the Ranks of Simpletons

A prudent person sees trouble coming and ducks; a simpleton walks in blindly and is clobbered.

—Proverbs 22:3 msg

One of the leading causes of marital conflict is money issues, and one of the greatest ways to prevent this problem is communication. My husband, Ken, certainly tried to communicate with me about our finances, but every time the subject came up, I slipped into a coma.

Three months after his death, I began to receive crabby letters from something called a mortgage company. I didn't like their attitude.

Finally I called Luci Swindoll and read her the crabby letter I had received that day. She responded with hilarity and disbelief. She said, "Marilyn, do you know the meaning of the word *mortgage*?"

I admitted I'd heard the word, but it had no personal appeal.

She said, "Honey . . . you are going to lose your house if you don't pay your mortgage."

The phrase "lose your house" got my attention. Luci drove me to visit the crabby people, who were apparently softened by the term "distraught widow." They became especially courteous when I assured them I would never miss another payment. I paid what I owed and then went to lunch with Luci.

I narrowly missed a major calamity simply because I wasn't prudent; I didn't know what I should have known. Soon afterward, thanks to wise, compassionate friends and the help of trusted financial advisers, I retired as president of Simpletons Anonymous.

Ken would be proud of me!

—Marilyn Meberg

May 18

Deserving of Pursuit

> Get up, my dear friend, fair and beautiful lover—come to me!
> —Song of Solomon 2:10 msg

I love listening to my parents tell how they fell in love. They had graduated from the same college in a small West Texas town, and each had randomly moved to Miami, Florida. Dad was a minister, and Mom taught at the school affiliated with the church where he worked.

It's funny to hear their different perspectives. Dad says he fell in love the first night he laid eyes on Mom. But Mom says, "It took me a little while. I just thought he was funny at first, and I wanted to be his friend. Eventually, the friendship evolved into love."

Dad never gave up. Having immediately fallen in love, he pursued my mom until she walked down the aisle at the same small Miami church where their relationship had begun.

Hearing their history and watching my dad love my mom taught me the importance of the guy chasing the girl. I didn't want to be a girl who called a boy before he called me. I wanted a guy who had confidence, and a truly confident guy will approach the girl before she approaches him. After all, which is harder: for a guy to look you in the eyes and ask you out on a date or for him to shoot you a text saying, "Wanna hang out?"

Looking someone in the eyes is a lot harder than looking at a cell phone keypad. Each of us deserves a man who isn't going to take the easy way out. So I wasn't a girl who initiated the flirting, because my dad had taught me what my role was.

I know that I deserve to be pursued, and so do you!

—Jenna Lucado

The Sweetest of Gifts

Are not two sparrows sold for a copper coin? And not one of them falls to the ground apart from your Father's will. . . . Do not fear therefore; you are of more value than many sparrows.

—Matthew 10:29, 31

My friend Ney Bailey makes me feel valuable. The first time we had lunch together, she asked questions and then follow-up questions, and I found myself talking about something I never would have imagined sharing out loud with someone. But I loved talking about me . . . and that was so unlike me.

I told her about my disappointment over a recent broken friendship, when I'd been told that I was "too heavy" with emotional burdens for the friendship to continue.

When Ney asked me how I was feeling about that hurt now, I answered, "Now, I'm thinking, maybe I was too heavy, like a pot of gold is heavy. Now I'm thinking she missed out."

Ney grinned. "I'm so glad to hear you say that," she said. "That tells me that, even in the midst of rejection, you know you are valuable. You are worth what was given for you. God gave Jesus for you."

This is the gift Ney possesses. In her presence, you feel a reflection of how God must feel about you.

After that lunch we started talking by e-mail. I would send her an e-mail before I went to bed, telling her about my day. When I woke up in the morning, I would rush to my computer (even before the coffeepot) to read her reply. She would take each paragraph and respond to it.

Is it just me, or is this the sweetest of gifts: for someone to put so much value on your life and what you have to say that they will take the time to receive your words and offerings and then respond to each one of them personally and uniquely?

—Lisa Whelchel

May 20

A Hard Life Filled with Rejoicing

> He will yet fill your mouth with laughing, and your lips with rejoicing.
> —Job 8:21

Job was "blameless and upright," and he "feared God and shunned evil" (Job 1:1), yet he lost everything that was dear and valuable to him—even his health. Before his miserable ordeal ended, the only thing left was his questioning but enduring faith that God was still in control.

Ironically, within Job's story I find an unshakable promise of joy. It comes in a set of platitudes spoken by Job's friend Bildad: "He will yet fill your mouth with laughing, and your lips with rejoicing" (Job 8:21).

In the midst of my own misery, God did exactly that for me. After one of our sons was killed in Vietnam and another in Canada by a drunk driver, and after a third son disappeared into a homosexual lifestyle, I felt miserable and numb, unable to cope.

One day I got in my car and headed for a high viaduct, planning to step on the accelerator and send the car hurtling through the guardrail to the jagged ground far below. I wanted to kill myself and end my misery. But at the last minute, I worried that I wouldn't be killed in the crash but instead would be only maimed and, as a result, locked up in a home for the bewildered.

Suddenly I knew I didn't want to kill myself. Instead I prayed the prayer of relinquishment: "Whatever, Lord. Whatever happens, I know you'll see me through it."

Praying those words seemed to replace the heaviness in my heart with a bubble of joy that has inspired me to seek out the cheer hiding in each day I've lived since then—even in the dark, gloomy crevices that appear when my life threatens to fall apart again.

—Barbara Johnson

Embracing What Is and What Can Be

> The thief does not come except to steal, and to kill, and to destroy. I have come that they may have life, and that they may have it more abundantly.
>
> —JOHN 10:10

Sometimes we have to make peace with what happened in our past so that we're able to let go of that hurt and move on. Instead, so many of us put ourselves in situations to be hurt over and over by the same person because we know things *should* be different. We cling to our dreams of what we wish the past could have been, and by doing so we set ourselves up to be hurt again and again.

If this is you, I encourage you to let go of that past—your "what should have been"—and embrace your "what is" and your "what can be." Truth is powerful. At times it is heartbreaking, but ultimately it will deliver you.

Even as we deal with the painful habits of our past, it is important to remember that we have an enemy whose sole focus is to destroy what God loves. And that is you! The devil is a thief who would love to rob you of your identity in Christ. Don't let him. Jesus came to give you life—real life.

Because of Christ, we don't have to live in the past; we can be present today and tomorrow to live a life that is better than one we could have dreamed for ourselves. We can make peace with the truth of the past, and we can learn from the past. But Christ calls us to be free to live today and tomorrow with purpose and passion.

—Sheila Walsh

May 22

Open Your Blinds, and *Voilà!*

> I'm staying alert and in top condition. I'm not going to get caught napping, telling everyone else all about it and then missing out myself.
>
> —1 CORINTHIANS 9:27 MSG

It really doesn't matter where one goes to find adventure in nature. It lies all around us, in our own backyards and under rocks and trees. Maybe I can see it easily because I really want to. It's that simple. I'm always on the lookout. I carry my camera, journal, and watercolors wherever I go.

One year I was in Portland, Oregon, and outside my hotel window was majestic Mount Hood. I saw it with early morning light, midday light, and when the evening shadows were long across it. Every minute of the day, it was beautiful. I took out my watercolors and painted it in my journal—just to snatch that moment for a later recollection.

When I lived in the desert, I quite often saw roadrunners. They are fascinating to watch. Once I saw one in the backyard with a small frog in its mouth. It hustled up my grapefruit tree and sat on one of the branches eating the frog and tormenting two mockingbirds. I took a snapshot. Why not? I don't have to be in some far-off place to see the beauty of this world. I just open my blinds, and *voilà*! It's there.

Whether adventure takes us to our own backyard or to a distant continent, the spirit of adventure is all about participating fully in the moment we've been given as a gift. We often plan one thing and, on the way, experience another that's even more interesting, meaningful, or unusual. We have a part to play, a song to sing. Each experience life serves up is an opportunity to savor a moment we will never taste again.

I, for one, don't want to miss a morsel.

—Luci Swindoll

Considering Life's Conundrums

Solomon answered all her questions; there was nothing so difficult for Solomon that he could not explain it to her.

—2 Chronicles 9:2

How do we put together the pieces of life's puzzles that keep us confounded? If I'm a conundrum even to myself (and I assure you, I am), how can I understand someone else's jigsaw existence? We humans are so intricate, so layered.

The Bible cuts through intricacies, layers, and even generational influences and helps us to understand some basics about our human condition. For instance, we're told that those who hate being corrected are stupid (Proverbs 12:1). The lesson is clear: listen up, or be a loser.

And we're told that a woman who causes her husband shame is rottenness to his bones. (Hmm, would that include Eve? Or was theirs an equal-opportunity sin?)

Proverbs 14:23 tells us that idle chatter leads to poverty. Is that referring to poverty of our spirits, or is it financial? Perhaps it's both. Yes, yes, I'm sure it is.

The human condition begins to make sense as we glean the head-on truth of the Word, which is not to say that, even if we were scholars, people wouldn't perplex us or certain Bible verses wouldn't stump us. But when we receive what we *can* understand, it opens our understanding a little more, like one puzzle piece fitting snugly into another. When it comes to studying the Bible, we read it and reap.

—Patsy Clairmont

May 24

Remembering God's Rescuing Hand

> When your children ask . . . , "What do these stones meant to you?" Then you shall answer them that the waters of the Jordan were cut off before the ark of the covenant of the LORD; when it crossed over the Jordan.
> —JOSHUA 4:6–7

The counseling I've received during the last few years has shown me how important it is to me to keep a journal of my thoughts and activities.

Journaling lets me look back on the journey I've taken and remember how God has guided me, corrected me, rescued me—how he's always been there for me.

Sometimes as I scan back over the words I've written in my journal, I feel like the Israelites must have felt, standing in the promised land and looking back at the altar of stones they'd built on the banks of the Jordan River.

God told them to take stones out of the Jordan and use them to build the altar so that in the future, when their children asked why the stones were there, the Israelites would be reminded to tell them the story of how God had been faithful to bring them to the land he had promised them. God had stopped the waters of the Jordan that day so they could cross, just as he had rolled back the waters of the Red Sea when they were fleeing from Pharaoh.

God directed the Israelites to remember the story and tell it to their children "that all the peoples of the earth may know the hand of the LORD" (Joshua 4:24).

That's what journaling does for us. Later, when we review what we wrote, we remember our story—and see God's hand at work in our lives. And we trust him to work in us and help us again.

—Sandi Patty

Accepting the Gift of Forgiveness

I have blotted out, like a thick cloud, your transgressions, and like a cloud, your sins. Return to Me, for I have redeemed you.
—Isaiah 44:22

When Jesus died for the sins of the world, *all* sin was taken to the cross. My responsibility is to accept God's gift of forgiveness by confessing my sin to him and receiving his cleansing. That forgiveness sets me free from what would have condemned me.

There are those who believe that if we have a sin of any kind, even in our thinking, we would be condemned by it if sudden death occurred. In other words, we would need to be continually "confessed up," or that unconfessed sin would doom us to eternal punishment. If I am thinking uncharitable thoughts about the driver in front of me and am suddenly killed by a collision with an eighteen-wheeler, do I go to hell because of those uncharitable thoughts?

Instead, consider Scripture's invitation to us to live in God's amazing grace: "The Spirit of life in Christ, like a strong wind, has magnificently cleared the air, freeing you from a fated lifetime of brutal tyranny at the hands of sin and death" (Romans 8:2 MSG).

"Brutal tyranny" is living in constant dread of an eighteen-wheeler suddenly descending upon me during a moment of sinful thinking. Instead, let us wrap ourselves in God's specific and definitive promises, including, "His huge outstretched arms protect you—under them you're perfectly safe" (Psalm 91:4 MSG).

Scripture assures us that God's caring heart is fully engaged with ours and that he will never, ever leave us alone.

—Marilyn Meberg

May 26

Remembering the Dance

> David danced before the LORD with all his might.
> —2 SAMUEL 6:14

Years ago I met a woman who had been discarded by a philandering husband. The wife went into an emotional tailspin as her husband was given the home where they had raised their five children so the other woman could move in. She left with only a suitcase and a crushed spirit.

Their adult children were dizzy with confusion, but their main heartache was their mom. They worried that in her defenseless state she would become so despondent she would take her own life. The daughters checked on her daily.

One day their mom was washing dishes when a love song came on the radio, filling the air with romance as she filled the sink with her tears. She cried out, "I don't even have someone to dance with."

That's when she saw him: tall, somewhat stoic, but definitely available. She grasped his slim waist, and they danced around and around as she laughed with surprised delight. As she twirled, she spotted her daughters in the doorway staring. They thought their mom finally had cracked when they found her dancing with a broom.

She stopped and wiped away a few old tears. "No, I haven't lost my mind or my hope. Memorize what you've seen because there may come a time in your life when you go through great loss, and I want you to remember to keep dancing."

Try it sometime yourself when your world has been turned upside down. Crank up the radio, hold the Lord in your heart, and dance again.

—Patsy Clairmont

Finding Purpose in Broken Pieces

For God so loved the world, that he gave his only begotten Son, that whosoever believeth in him should not perish, but have everlasting life.

—John 3:16 KJV

Herb Kliewer was forty-nine years old when he broke his neck in a fall and was left totally paralyzed. He ended up in a nursing home where all he could do was lie in bed staring blankly into the air.

There is nothing left of me but worthless broken pieces, he thought. *What good am I now*?

Suddenly, "It was almost like Jesus was right there by my bed," Herb said. "I felt him telling me, 'Broken pieces are all I need.'"

That moment changed Herb's life. Yes, his body was still broken, but he knew without a doubt that God was right there with him. Hopelessness faded in the bright light of that assurance.

Soon God allowed the feeling to come back to Herb's hands and then to his arms. No longer was his entire body paralyzed.

Herb learned to hold a pen again and began copying Bible verses that were especially meaningful to him. His favorite is John 3:16, which reminds us that God loved us so much that he gave his Son to die for us. For Herb, in the nursing home. For you and me exactly where we are and who we happen to be.

Herb has taught me a wonderful lesson in perseverance. He's shown me that one's purpose doesn't depend on understanding God's plan or why God allows awful—or even good—things to happen.

God's purpose is more often focused on the moment, on how we respond to a tough circumstance right now, this instant, every day.

—Joni Eareckson Tada

May 28

A Lesson in Faith

My strength is made perfect in weakness.
—2 Corinthians 12:9

If I could choose, I'd make every day easy. I'd make the weather perfect, the plans ideal, the people in my life exactly who I chose. Or would I?

Sometimes the greatest pleasures in life are not the ones we choose or can envision for ourselves. Sometimes they start as great disappointments wrapped in huge fear. Such was my experience on February 19, 1969. My niece, Ruth Ann Hill, was born in Anchorage, Alaska, where her dad and her mom, my sister Jan, were living at the time.

Growing up and especially throughout my high school and college years, Jan was my best ally. Having come from a lineup of eight children, I find I've been close to different siblings at different times for different reasons. In college my best friend was Jan, ten years older than I. It was hard enough when her husband was transferred so far away, but when they were expecting their first child, it seemed even harder to be so far from them.

Ruth Ann was only a few minutes old when the doctor informed her parents that she was born with Down syndrome. When Jan phoned my family, I felt overwhelmed—not just that the news was very different than had been anticipated but that the distance between us felt even greater than before. However, whatever my reaction was that day forty-three years ago, there's been no greater blessing in my life than sweet Ruth Ann. And I'd dare to say, no one has ever loved me more.

Sometimes when things don't turn out as we planned, even though the different plan might not seem perfect, it's quite possible God has great blessing in store.

—Mary Graham

The Joy of E-mail Journaling

Encourage one another daily.
—Hebrews 3:13 NIV

I'm blessed to have a daily e-mail relationship with one of my friends, writing her every day about what's going on in my life and enjoying reading her daily replies. While she was out of the country recently, I continued to write her an e-mail every night, even though I didn't send them.

I had always wanted to keep a daily journal, but I stink at it, so this was as close as I would ever come to doing so. I had started countless daily journals in too many Januarys and never made it past February. How fun it was finally to discover the joys of writing to a friend every night, describing all the goings on of my day, and the ins and outs of my heart.

I was journaling!

I also was growing in a way I hadn't anticipated. By expressing my thoughts and exposing my heart to another human being, I was learning about myself through the reflection in another's eyes. My daily writings became like a diary and a mirror all in one.

Sharing my life with another person in writing was so much more fun than actually keeping a journal just because I knew it was a spiritual discipline that was good for me. It seemed kind of like the yummy, pink, liquid antibiotic I used to give my kids when they had an ear infection. The medicine was so delicious the kids didn't even know they were taking something good for them.

Keeping in touch with others through e-mail is especially beneficial during busy seasons of life, when our work schedules are particularly heavy, or when keeping up with small children all leaves little time for phone calls. I encourage you to develop a daily e-mail "journal" with one of your friends.

—Lisa Whelchel

May 30

You Can't Help but Love Him

She opens her mouth with wisdom, and on her tongue is the law of kindness.

—Proverbs 31:26

When I was a teen, I met another teenage girl whom I enjoyed hanging out with, except she had an annoying habit: she obeyed her mother. She even sought her mother's counsel.

One day I asked her, "Do you always listen to your mom?"

"I didn't used to," she answered, "but then I ended up pregnant and had to give up my baby because I was so young. During that time, I thought a lot about things my mom had said to me about my choices and the kids I ran around with, and I realized everything she had said was true. So to answer your question, yes, I do listen to my mom. I'd be foolish not to because she's lived longer than I have and knows what she's talking about."

At that stage of my life, I had no plans to listen to anyone, so I found this girl's answer tedious. Down the road of my rebellion, I paid a big price to be stripped of that pride. I learned that God offered me truth, and I'd be foolish if I didn't receive it. He's been around a lot longer than I have, and he knows what he's talking about.

The more I study God's Word and spend time in prayer, the fuller my reservoir of truth is. Then, when I'm caught between a rock and a hard place, I can draw from that well. I don't have to flail about like one without hope. No doubt about it, the more I learn about him, the more I love him. You can't help but love the One who loves you and makes such provision for you.

—Patsy Clairmont

The Most Wonderful Fairy Tale of All

The Son of Man has come to seek and to save that which was lost.

—Luke 19:10

As a little girl, I watched fairy tales through cynical glasses, never quite believing the knight-in-shining-armor myth. I told myself I didn't want to be rescued. I wanted to be the one doing the rescuing.

I know now that life had taught me not to look for a rescuer. No one was coming, so I'd better take care of myself.

Now, at fifty-two, I believe in the most wonderful fairy tale of all—which is actually a true story. I believe that I am loved and pursued by the greatest Prince who ever lived. I believe he sees me as I am and loves me completely. I believe now that, as my friend Max Lucado says, I have never lived an unloved moment in my life.

No, this is not some kind of female midlife crisis. I don't believe that, because I love Jesus, I will be spared pain and sorrow. I don't believe all my prayers will be answered as I would like them to be, but I do believe that God is in control and is watching over me.

Do I still have moments of doubt? Sure. But the voice in those moments is far less convincing than it used to be. With Christ as my guide, I have been able to face the truth about my past and not just accept it but embrace it.

You can do the same. Every painful step on our various journeys has led us to where we are today, and I for one celebrate that.

—Sheila Walsh

June 1

Enjoying God's Gifts of Wealth and Work

> When God gives someone wealth and possessions, and the ability to enjoy them, to accept their lot and be happy in their toil—this is a gift of God.
>
> —Ecclesiastes 5:19 NIV

The Bible has a lot to say about what we ought to believe about money. Ecclesiastes 5:10 says, "Whoever loves money never has enough; whoever loves wealth is never satisfied with their income. This too is meaningless" (NIV).

Underscoring this Old Testament teaching about money is the New Testament commentary in 1 Timothy 6:10: "The love of money is a root of all kinds of evil, for which some have strayed from the faith in their greediness, and pierced themselves through with many sorrows."

Scripture does not teach that having money is evil; it's the craving, wanting, and seeking after it that can cause soul cave-ins. Balanced thinking about money is the goal. We are encouraged to enjoy our work and accept our lot in life as gifts from God.

My belief about money is to agree with God and know that it is he who gives me financial gifts. If I crave more than he gives me, I'm flirting with evil.

He is the supplier of all my needs. That does not mean I lie in my hammock waiting for my daily supply. I partner with God and work where he directs me to work. Then, perhaps before dark, I can flop into my hammock and thank God for the "wealth" I'm receiving from him each day.

—Marilyn Meberg

A Burning-Bush Kind of Sign

> The angel of God appeared to him in flames of fire blazing out of the middle of a bush. He looked. The bush was blazing away but it didn't burn up.
>
> —Exodus 3:1–2 MSG

Before we were married, my husband Don mentioned that he'd often wished he could someday adopt a child and name him Sam, after his adoptive dad.

One day, when we had been married about six months, one of my friends, Shari, asked if we knew anyone who might consider adopting a baby that her lawyer husband was involved with as a legal representative. She was *not* asking us if *we* would consider adopting the baby. After all, she knew perfectly well that between us, Don and I already had *seven* children.

But we did consider it. A day or two later, we asked to see the newborn. Shari and her husband took us to the hospital for the visit; as we sat in the car in the parking lot, Shari insisted that we ask God for some kind of convincing sign—a burning-bush kind of sign, she called it—that would tell us his will for us about adopting the child.

Later, when they came pushing the little plastic bassinet into our waiting room, Shari was crying, unable to speak. All she could do was wave toward the baby.

I knew the infant had endured some difficulties during delivery, and I worried that serious problems had developed. But it turned out Shari was crying tears of joy. As they came closer, I could see what her awkward gestures were about. It was the little sign taped to the bassinet.

A name tag. The nurses had given the baby a temporary name when he was born.

They'd named him Sam.

—Sandi Patty

June 3

Laughing at the Detours

> I will instruct you and teach you in the way you should go; I will guide you with My eye.
>
> —Psalm 32:8

Several years ago, Marilyn Meberg and I got stranded due to bad weather when we were coming home from a speaking engagement on Mackinac Island, off the coast of the Michigan mainland. In order to catch our plane on time, we had to take a horse and buggy, boat, taxi, and bus. Literally!

At every juncture, one more thing went wrong. We could have had a miserable day. But we were together, and there was absolutely nothing we could do to improve our lot in life, for that day anyway. So we decided to make the most of the adventure; as a result, we had the time of our lives. We've looked back on that day as the most spontaneous fun we've ever enjoyed in our long friendship.

Throughout that unpredictable day, we played a ridiculous game. "Marilyn, they say we'll miss the boat because of the fog, but I don't think we will. I'll buy your breakfast if we do," I said.

She replied, "You little optimist. Of course we'll miss the boat. If we don't, breakfast is on me." She bought breakfast.

We bet lunch on whether or not the taxi would be waiting in the designated spot. She bought lunch too.

And so the day went. We were in a pickle, but our experience was delightful. We laughed ourselves silly. When we got home, I was very full and Marilyn very poor. She'd picked up the tab for all three meals and every snack.

It's all in the attitude. Once we learn to capture these unexpected moments of surprise and potential disappointment, an even greater spirit of adventure is born in our hearts.

—Luci Swindoll

June 4

A Two-Way Lift

The helpless commits himself to You;
You are the helper of the fatherless.
—Psalm 10:14

Recently I was riding from an airport to a hotel when, to make conversation, I asked my driver, "So what fills your days with joy?"

"Oh, that would be the Man Upstairs who puts breath in my body each day," he responded.

"Great answer," I said.

Suddenly the driver honked his horn in short, passionate blasts. It startled me and the drivers of vehicles around us too; they quickly moved to far lanes. The man continued to honk and to point toward a car on the far outside lane. I glanced nervously in that direction to see two older women driving and chatting, seemingly unaware of this young man's attempts to gain their attention.

He must have honked his horn fifteen times before the woman driving looked over and saw him. A big smile crossed her face, and she waved.

Then he said proudly, "That's my aunt. My mother died when I was a child, and she stepped in the gaping hole of my loss."

After a quiet moment, he whispered, "Yup, that's my heart driving that car."

What a tender statement of gratitude, birthed out of a tragic loss. Thank God for such women who are willing to step in to accompany those unable to go on alone.

That man could have been bitter and withered in soul, but because of God's provision, the light of hope shone on his face. I'm sure some still nights he wears a mottled veil of grief, but in the daylight hours he's pressing on. What a lift he gave my life that day—and every day since!

—Patsy Clairmont

June 5

God Believes in You

> Create in me a clean heart, O God,
> And renew a steadfast spirit within me.
> —Psalm 51:10

My first encounter with Patsy Clairmont was through tears as I sat backstage after speaking for the first time at a Women of Faith conference. I felt like I had failed miserably. I so wanted to do a good job. The emotional baggage I was dragging around back then equated love and acceptance with being good and performing well. That day I hadn't measured up to the standard I had set for myself, and I was distraught.

This was about more than doing my job, and, I confess, this wasn't about performing for an audience of One either. I knew God loved me, but I wanted these women to like me. I thought that meant I needed to earn their approval by impressing them with my speaking skills. It was all I could do not to run out of that arena. I didn't feel like I deserved to be there, and I felt in way over my head.

I was choking back tears when Patsy pulled up a chair beside me and spoke with such insight and understanding:

"I know how you feel because I have been there myself a million times," she said. "The standard we set for ourselves is perfection, and that is never attainable, and then we beat ourselves up when we fall short. You don't have to be perfect. Just be you. God called you to this position, and he knew who you were and what you had to offer that no one else could when he chose you."

She looked me in the eye as she concluded, "He believes you can do this. Can you rest in his faith in you?"

—Lisa Whelchel

Created for More

This I say, therefore, and testify in the Lord, that you should no longer walk as the rest of the Gentiles walk, in the futility of their mind.

—Ephesians 4:17

Sometimes I feel like the world is made up of two kinds of people: people pleasers (those who go to great lengths to be loved and yet never feel they deserve it) and people who are never pleased with anything (who can't seem to see beyond their own wants and needs).

Pleasers learn from a very early age—in part through parenting or lack thereof—to bury their own feelings, to accept responsibility for anything that goes wrong, or to think they should be able to fix any troublesome situation that arises for their loved ones.

On the other hand, people who are never pleased with anything tend to be just the opposite: their feelings are the most important in any situation, they are never to blame for anything that goes wrong, and they would never bother trying to fix what is not their fault.

Those who live in what the apostle Paul called "the futility of their mind" spend more time trying to know what others want from them than they do in pursuing knowledge of God. When we spend all our energy trying to earn another person's affections, trying to do all we can do and being all we can be for another human, our lives are sucked up in an endless vacuum.

We were created for more than a desperate search for approval and acceptance, for more than a life of fear. God told his children in Isaiah 43:1, "Now this is what the Lord says. He created you, people of Jacob; he formed you, people of Israel. He says, 'Don't be afraid, because I have saved you. I have called you by name, and you are mine'" (ncv).

—Natalie Grant

June 7

The Craving for *More*

> I gave you . . . your master's wives into your keeping. . . . And if that had been too little, I also would have given you much more! Why have you despised the commandment of the LORD, to do evil in His sight?
> —2 SAMUEL 12:8–9

When I was a public school teacher, a fellow teacher ten years older than I began to confide in me about her various marital indiscretions. Because we frequently shared playground duty, I couldn't always escape her.

I finally asked her why she was such a party girl. She answered, "I just need more than my husband can give me."

That woman was out of control, and she wasn't wanting more love. Her actions stemmed from sexual addiction fueled by lust—wanting more.

In spite of knowing better, many people buy into Satan's favorite lie: *There's more.* The lie says, *There's more excitement, greater intimacy, and deeper love out there; you can have more.*

The crafty enemy of our soul knows full well that his lie is hard to resist. It worked on Eve; it works on us.

Satan's sole intent is to watch the moral and physical destruction of God's people. A method that has worked for him from the beginning of time is to dangle a baited hook in front of each of us.

What's the bait? *More.*

Whenever our eagerness for more causes us to swallow the bait, we're hooked. Our enemy jeers and cheers, chalking up another victory. Then he rebaits.

But remember: God promises to bring good from all things. One of the ways he brings good from something as disastrous as infidelity occurs when we come to the realization that he, the God of all creation, is the ultimate *more.*

—Marilyn Meberg

Who Are We Really?

Therefore, whether you eat or drink, or whatever you do, do all to the glory of God.
—1 CORINTHIANS 10:31

Luci Swindoll and I had barely settled into our seats on the flight when a woman walking by stopped dead in her tracks and said very loudly, "I know I know you. Oh, yeah! You're the comedian, and you're the emcee." (Luci is a longtime speaker at Women of Faith events; I am president of Thomas Nelson Live Events and emcee at many events.) Then the woman walked on by. Luci and I smiled. *Labels*. What people see and even assume about us is so interesting. Perception is not always reality, and I really wish I could remember that *all* the time.

Nicole Johnson, dramatist for Women of Faith events, has written a sketch called "The Label Maker." It's a funny yet poignant piece about how quickly we judge others and call them a "name" in order to put them in some category in our minds. Her sketch is brilliant and carefully challenges us to keep our hearts open toward others, as opposed to filing others into a category that helps us keep everything and everyone straight.

Meanwhile, God loves everyone, from those who seem to us the most lovable to those we consider tyrants. He loves us personally and unconditionally. That amazing reality flows from who God is, not from the object of his love. Out of his heart of perfect love, God loves. And he gives us the capacity to love as he loves us: wholeheartedly, completely, perfectly.

There is some truth to the fact that Luci is funny and I emcee events. But it's not who we are. It's not who God made us, and it's not what we were created to be. Who we are is complex and cannot be labeled. The reality is we were all created to love and be loved.

—Mary Graham

June 9

Finding a Father

> I will be a Father to you, and you shall be My sons and daughters, says the Lord Almighty.
>
> —2 Corinthians 6:18

After my husband Don's adoptive parents had both died, he felt a yearning to know the rest of his story, to find his birth parents. Unfortunately, by the time he learned who his birth mother was, she too had died. But her relatives carefully, and a bit hesitantly, gave him what clues they had to guide him in his continued search for his father.

Finally, after much seeking and a roller-coaster ride of hopes and disappointments, the day came that the phone rang and Don heard his birth father's voice for the first time. What a moment that was!

Since then Don's dad—we call him Pop—has become a wildly beloved and completely cherished member of our family, even living with us for several months at a time.

Don has gotten acquainted with his siblings, and wonderful things have happened. It's been amazing. Maybe the most poignant moment came when Don went to visit his dad in West Virginia for the first time.

That night, after Don had gone to bed, he heard a knock on his bedroom door. It was Pop, carrying a glass of milk and a plate of cookies. He'd come to tuck Don in and tell him a bedtime story. He'd never gotten to do it when Don was a boy growing up, he said, and he wanted to make up for all those boyhood bedtimes he'd missed. What a cherished moment that was, not just for Don and Pop but for all of us who felt blessed by hearing them tell the story later.

—Sandi Patty

Laugh a Lot

Go, eat your bread with joy, and drink your wine with a merry heart; for God has already accepted your works.
—ECCLESIASTES 9:7

Many times as a kid I would hear my mother's laughter from another room. Even though I had no idea what was so funny, I would laugh too. It just seemed that, when Mom laughed, the day was brighter and my heart was lighter.

Laughter is not only positive but also powerful. Along with being a magnet that draws others in, it also serves as medication for our interior lives. That cancer wards incorporate laugh clinics into hospitals ought to tell us a great deal. And shared laughter makes even enemies friends, if only for a moment. Our world could use a good dose of friendly. "The joy of the LORD is your strength" (Nehemiah 8:10).

Now, I realize this verse is talking about a much deeper level of spiritual experience than just laughter, but I do believe laughter is a part of that joy. But I've bumped into some folks who I thought laughed far too much. Their constant giggles felt like a nervous reaction instead of a spilling over of pleasantness. Tittering breeds an uneasiness in others because it doesn't feel authentic. It's like fear and insecurity are dressed up in a funny voice.

So we're back to the "balance" word. Honestly, I don't think we can discuss emotions without having to hit the balance button again and again. I promise you that in this topsy-turvy, inside-out world, we won't be able to maintain balance, but it should always be our goal. And along the journey, let's take time to chortle every day. It will smooth out some of the bumps in the road and help others up steep inclines.

—Patsy Clairmont

June 11

No Time for a Break

> Make straight paths for your feet, so that what is lame may not be dislocated, but rather be healed.
> —Hebrews 12:13–14

Life is full of serendipitous and surprising detours—not all of them easily accepted at the moment. We've all experienced life taking sudden turns. When these things happen, we have the choice either to embrace our experience with a sense of trust or to spend our energies fighting the inevitable. We can respond to challenges and opportunities with "Why not?" or we can react to reality with "Why me?" It's truly up to us how we'll encounter what is around the next bend.

Some time ago, I broke my leg. The orthopedic surgeon put seven screws into the fibula in my left leg, attaching it to the larger bone next to it.

Since the break was so serious, I could envision my whole life stopping for a time. It was a classic opportunity for me to determine how I would deal with formidable obstacles. I could feel defeated, put my schedule on hold, stop traveling, and mope around—all of which were tempting. Or I could turn that time of healing into an adventure. The choice was mine and mine alone.

I decided to go for the latter. I determined to do whatever it took to keep my spirits up. I took God at his Word that he would be with me and take care of me, that he'd go before me and straighten the crooked places, that he'd be my Comforter, Friend, and Great Physician.

Something about that choice had a rush in it for me. An edge. An excitement. Each day, I couldn't wait to see what would happen! I was glad I had chosen to live as fully as I could under the circumstances.

—Luci Swindoll

Embracing the Truth About Our Past

Scorn has broken my heart and left me helpless . . . But as for me, afflicted and in pain; may your salvation, God, protect me.

—Psalm 69:20, 29 NIV

I have a theory about our earthly form. I have absolutely no Scripture to back it up, but here it is, and you can do with it what you will: How we view ourselves determines how far we believe we can progress on this spiritual journey. If we see ourselves as "less than" every other woman, we will hold back and not fully live the life that Christ died to give us. If we understand that on the outside we express the brokenness of a fallen world, but internally we are being redeemed every single day, it could change everything.

I think each of us is in disguise. No matter what we look like, God sees that we still look like daughters of Eve. I don't think it matters whether you are a size 2 or a size 2X, whether you are blonde or gray, tall or short. I think our bodies are just earthly manifestations of the fact that our planet is fallen. I also think they teach us a lot about who we are and what we value.

When you see a woman who is morbidly obese or almost transparently thin, do you judge her? Do you find yourself looking critically at another's hairstyle or clothing or any other physical aspect? Do you do the same with yourself?

Perhaps instead, these less-than-perfect manifestations should arouse our compassion and care.

Our brokenness shows in different ways. But what shows on the outside is of little importance compared to God's quest for our hearts. God doesn't want us to spend our lives looking in the rearview mirror or superglued to what appears to be true now, but rather by faith looking to the view ahead.

—Sheila Walsh

June 13

The Thoughtfulness of Friends

> As God's chosen people, holy and dearly loved, clothe yourselves with compassion, kindness, humility, gentleness and patience.
>
> —Colossians 3:12 niv

One of the first things I noticed when I became part of the Women of Faith team was how sincerely supportive and intimately invested these women are with each other. One weekend, minutes before I was to leave the hotel for the arena for the conference's Friday-night session, I discovered I hadn't packed the shirt I was planning to wear. I quickly threw on Saturday's outfit and rushed out the door.

During the conference, I mentioned to speaker Sheila Walsh that I might have to wear the same outfit the next day.

She said, "I brought some extra clothes; come to my room tonight and see if anything appeals to you."

That evening Sheila loaned me the most gorgeous shirt and purple suede jacket. The next day, I got so many compliments. I felt beautiful.

Sunday morning she told me to keep the shirt and jacket. I immediately had two reactions: first, I can't accept this gorgeous jacket; second, I really want it! I graciously refused.

She gave me the most tender reply: "Honestly, Lisa, it would make me very happy for you to do this. It really was God's idea. I woke up with his words in my heart: 'Give this to my little girl from me.'"

I was deeply touched by both my friend and my Father. I'm discovering that friends are good for just about all that ails you.

—Lisa Whelchel

Whatever, Lord!

Though He slay me, yet will I trust Him.
—Job 13:15

Two important principles have helped me survive the trials of life with joy in my heart: first, remember that we are pilgrims here, not settlers. Whatever we're enduring in this life is temporary.

As Christians we have mansions waiting for us in heaven; that means our final exit here will be our grandest entrance there! If you keep your focus on that heavenly promise, then you'll know that, no matter what life throws at you, you and God can handle it.

Second, instead of whining, "Why me?" learn to say, "Whatever, Lord!" God is in control. Nothing comes into our lives without passing through his filter.

He has a plan to bring us through our earthly existence to join him in a glorious eternity. So vow to have the same faith Job had and say, in the midst of your troubles, "Though he slay me, yet will I trust him."

—Barbara Johnson

June 15

Seeing What's Today

> The LORD blessed the latter days of Job more than his beginning.
> —JOB 42:12

Consider Job. People have been for centuries. Job lost everything that mattered to him except his wife. And as if that weren't enough, he was covered in oozing sores. His wife thought he should curse God and die. That was her only recorded contribution. Sad, but understandable coming from a woman who had just buried all her children. She had given up, thrown in the proverbial towel. We hear it in her grief-torn, anger-laded words.

Job hung on even when friends arrived and said all the wrong things. Just when Job needed them the most, their counsel only added to his indignities. But then Job began to see past his pain, past the people, and past the opinions, to flickers of light in the dark night of his soul. He heard God speak, and the Lord's every word glowed with a future.

Job entered the lantern-lined path of hope. His life-picture shifted, and his end years flourished.

A life of faith involves seeing past what's happening today and believing in God's redemptive care in our tomorrows. How do we respond like Job? Let's see . . . Job didn't run around frantic (my tendency); he sat down and listened (not so much my tendency); he didn't give up even in the face of despair (hmmm); he knew God's voice (I like that); and he leaned into God's sovereignty (my life goal).

From Job's example we can see five luminous lanterns of hope that we can use during our night-seasons to know God hasn't forgotten us. We can: be still, listen, believe, discern, and accept.

—Patsy Clairmont

Choosing a Landing Spot

You pulled me from the brink of death, my feet
from the cliff-edge of doom.
—Psalm 56:12 msg

Sometimes when I think of the choices I've made throughout my life and the consequences that have come as a result of them, I think of the nursery rhyme describing ol' Humpty Dumpty sitting on the wall.

He's up there teetering this way and that. Finally he falls, and look what happens.

Disaster!

But what if he'd managed to fall on the other side of the wall? Maybe there would have been wise and helpful people waiting there—not all the king's horses and all the king's men but folks who actually knew how to help him put his life back together again.

Consider that maybe Mr. Dumpty had a choice as he teetered atop that wall. Sometimes we teeter on edges, looking on either side of a wall. Neither landing site looks comfortable; there are rocks and sharp points to be endured. But sometimes, if you look a little farther in this imaginary scene, you can make a better choice by checking out the first responders waiting to pick up the pieces.

On one side, maybe you can see a hearse surrounded by a coroner's crew, or maybe a trash truck is waiting to haul you off to the landfill. "Off to the dump with you, Mr. Dumpty!"

On the other side, you see a team of rescuers. Look! That's an ambulance waiting, with its motor running. And what's that painted on the top of the ambulance? Why, of course! It's a big red *cross*.

—Sandi Patty

June 17

Calling Home

> Whether you turn to the right or to the left, your ears will hear a voice behind you, saying, "This is the way; walk in it."
> —Isaiah 30:21 NIV

My mother's thoughts generally stayed close to home while my daddy thought far away. When I was in college, Mother's letters told of neighborhood happenings; Daddy's quoted Scripture and poetry. Mother mailed a new blouse or skirt, and Daddy sent books and my allowance. Both had their place. She kept my feet on the ground, and he helped me dream.

"You can be anything you want to be," Daddy would say to me. "You can go anywhere you want to go, achieve anything you like. You just have to line your desires up with the Lord's and go. You have to take a few risks and head out."

Once when I was really little and spending the night at a friend's house, I got very homesick at bedtime. I called Mother and Daddy and asked them to come pick me up. I was embarrassed and told Daddy how sorry I was that I wasn't able to stay. I felt like a baby and asked him if he was mad at me because I called.

"Honey," he said, "of course I'm not mad at you. You can always call when you're afraid. I will always come get you if you need me to. But remember this—you are never alone wherever you are in life. God is with you. God will take care of you. Never be afraid to talk to God when you get homesick."

As we drove home that night, Daddy tucked into my heart a seed-thought that has, over time and travels, grown into a giant tree, enabling me to go far and wide, high and low, across the world, virtually unafraid and excited about what lies down the road or over the horizon.

And when I'm homesick, I talk to God about it.

—Luci Swindoll

God's Eyes Are upon Us

[Hagar] answered God by name, praying to the God who spoke to her, "You're the God who sees me!"
—Genesis 16:13 MSG

Hagar was Abraham and Sarah's slave, a woman with no home of her own and no rights. Even her name meant "fugitive."

You can read her story threaded through Genesis 16–21. She bore Abraham's son, Ishmael, and eventually fled with the child into the desert with only bread and one skin full of water. They wandered until they ran out of food and water and were very close to death. Hagar laid Ishmael under a bush to die and then sat down a short distance away and wept what had to be the bitterest tears a mother could shed, thinking about the impending death of her only child.

Genesis tells us that God sent an angel who told Hagar to take the boy by the hand, for God's promises were not derailed by human circumstances. As she stood, a well appeared. Hagar and Ishmael were saved.

One of the things I love most about Hagar's story is the mercy God extended to her. The past was the past, but God gave her a future. To everyone else, Hagar was a nobody, but not to God.

If you are a woman who feels forgotten, I pray that Hagar's story will help you see that God never forgets you. Hagar fled to the desert, in a sense removing herself from the only help or hope that seemed available to a slave girl. Life moved on for Abraham and Sarah. No search party was sent out to find the young woman.

She was left by this world to die—but she was not forgotten by heaven. The God who sees never took his eyes off Hagar.

And he never takes his eyes off you.

—Sheila Walsh

June 19

Holding Nothing Back

> You changed wild lament into whirling dance.
> —Psalm 30:11 msg

I certainly was not prepared for what happened to me in Ghana, West Africa, a few years ago. I was on a mission trip with World Vision, the relief organization that does so much for people in developing countries. Women of Faith was invited to participate in one of their projects, and I had the happy privilege of being included in the traveling troupe.

One afternoon we were all invited to a *durbar,* a large assembly where numerous African groups and tribes come together dressed in the full regalia of their culture. There must have been three thousand people there—men, women, and children. The festivities lasted three hours in the searing heat of the summer sun.

At one point the chairperson whispered in my ear, "The Ghanaian queen mother would like to dance with you." I knew I didn't want to offend the queen by refusing to dance, although the idea sounded strange.

So, self-consciousness aside, I walked out into that dusty field, bowed to the queen mother, and together we danced to the beat of those wild, wonderful African drums. It didn't take me long to get into the spirit of the affair.

The crowd was wildly enthusiastic. Either we were fabulous, or they knew how to respond to the queen mother's performance. I held nothing back, and neither did she. Here we were: one white, one black; one young, one old (I was the young one); one American, one African; one single, one married; one in jeans, the other in finery; two women, dancing together for all the world to see and enjoy.

I'll tell you, if that wasn't a memory to cherish, I don't know what was.

—Luci Swindoll

Got to Have Soul

Now when he had finished speaking to Saul, the soul of Jonathan was knit to the soul of David, and Jonathan loved him as his own soul.

—1 Samuel 18:1

The general busyness of life and our daily homeschool schedule don't leave much time for leisurely lunches with girlfriends. But when I get the chance, I'm reminded how much I need them.

Recently, a girlfriend and I met at one of my favorite restaurants. Well, we started out chatty—what our kids were doing for spring break, upcoming trips and events, ministry involvement. But two hours in, when the plates had cleared, we began peeling back the layers.

For me, that's the best part of conversation. Chatty banter has its place, but it only touches what's happening on the surface, and then usually in the best light. In the end, we've parted with our struggles intact and unshared.

I love when conversation reaches the soul, when we share what we're *really* dealing with and how we *really* feel. I love when we're deep enough to just listen and, once we've heard the struggles, to grab hands and pray.

Isn't that what true friendship should be about? If we're living on the surface, how can we help one another? How can we "bear one another's burdens" (Galatians 6:2) if we don't know what the burdens are? How can we encourage and pray for one another if we appear to have it all together? How can we truly connect if not from the soul?

And often it's only a matter of taking the time.

Pick up the phone. Go out to lunch. Friendship is a precious gift, and unless we invest in it, the deepest parts are left untapped. I don't want my friendships to bob along on the surface. They've got to have some soul.

—Kim Cash Tate

June 21

Establishing *No*

> Your eyes saw my substance, being yet unformed. And in Your book they all were written, the days fashioned for me, when as yet there were none of them.
>
> —Psalm 139:16

Geographical boundaries can be confusing if there is no fence. "Did I plant pansies on your side when I thought I was on my side?" A fence serves as a boundary, defining where you end and I begin.

We also need boundaries to protect ourselves and create emotional endurance in the face of challenging personal situations. Otherwise, those who have no respect for boundaries—all too often they are family members—are prone to swoop down and take flowers no matter which side they are on.

The key to emotional endurance is knowing where I begin and you end. When that boundary is threatened, the word *no* is needed.

In Eden, God set a boundary for Adam and Eve, telling them every beautiful and delicious fruit was up for grabs—except the fruit of one tree. That tree was a "no" tree. Don't touch it; don't eat it. A simple boundary.

Scripture teaches that our worth and value are not to be touched. They are not up for grabs. God placed a "no" upon the souls of his beloved creation that says, "Don't you dare defile my cherished treasure, the work of my hands, the temple in which I live, the life for whom I died."

We begin in the mind of God, and we will conclude in the arms of God. In the meantime, a "no" protects us from any behavior that says we are not God's beloved. Therefore, there are times we must say no, even to those closest to us.

—Marilyn Meberg

Finding Safe People

Above all things have fervent love for one another, for "love will cover a multitude of sins."

—1 Peter 4:8

One of the most critical lessons in friendship is learning to identify safe people. I, unfortunately, learned this the hard way. The moment my heart began to open up, I wanted to let everyone in. Because I had so little real life experience with friendships, I didn't know you had to be careful who had access to the deepest recesses.

I was incredibly naïve. If a man comes up to you wearing a trench coat lined with gold watches on the inside, trying to sell them to you at a deal, you can't be shocked if you ask him to come over to your house for dinner and then discover, after he's left, that the jewelry in your bathroom drawer is missing.

After some very painful disappointments, I have learned a few things about how to identify safe people. Now I know to pay attention to warning signs to discern people with unsafe areas.

For instance, I listen closely to conversations with my friends. If my friends are loose-lipped, judgmental, petty, negative, or condescending while talking about someone else, then odds are they probably talk about me the same way when I'm not around.

By the same token, if someone looks for the best in people, gives them the benefit of the doubt, or doesn't join in when others gossip or gang up on a person who is not present, then I can know that person is probably safe holding my reputation even when I'm not there to protect it myself.

—Lisa Whelchel

June 23

A Forgiven Past and a Blessed Future

> By faith the harlot Rahab did not perish with those who did not believe, when she had received the spies with peace.
> —Hebrews 11:31

Rahab is described in the Bible as a harlot, but she came to recognize the God of Israel as God indeed.

Rahab gave birth to Boaz, whose wife, Ruth, gave birth to Obed, who was Jesse's father, who in turn was the father of King David. As a result, Rahab is included in the lineage of Christ quoted by Matthew in his gospel (1:5). God forgave Rahab's past and blessed her future.

How much time have you spent looking in the rearview mirror of your life? You may have had an unhappy childhood and have never been able to let go of wishing things had been different. Whether it was an irrational mother or an indifferent father, you still feel the wounds deeply. Are you trapped in the "it *should* have been different" place? If so, I have great empathy for you.

We all long to know we are loved and valued. The fact remains, however, that no one is completely whole; therefore, no one can love perfectly. But spending too much time looking in the rearview mirror can lead to a wreck.

Perhaps it is time for you to let go of what you wish *were* true and accept what *is* true. No matter how difficult life has been, God in his wisdom placed each of us in our unique place and time.

—Sheila Walsh

Welcoming Adventure with a Grateful Heart

Call to Me, and I will answer you, and show you great and mighty things, which you do not know.

—Jeremiah 33:3

When we trust God outside of our comfort zones, anything can happen, anywhere. And sometimes what happens is utterly delightful. Would that we could always have curiosity and verve about life, saying "Yes!" to its strange and unusual possibilities. God gave us life and vitality and a sense of wonder and an enormous capacity to flourish emotionally, personally, and spiritually. Why do we often hold back? Why do we wait? What are we afraid of? Why not live fully and completely—regardless of the circumstances we encounter? Why not do life differently?

The most interesting people I know drink in life and savor every drop—the sweet and the sour. The good and the bad. The planned and the unplanned. And isn't that what God intends? When Jesus modeled humanity for you and me to see, he was out there—everywhere! He took risks. He embraced life and responded to everyone and everything, the tender and the tumultuous. His capacity for life was without measure. And we are designed like him. Fully human and fully alive. I don't want to miss anything he has in store for me, even if the path he takes me on winds through some pretty rough terrain. Right in the midst of what seems to me to be a detour from the map, I'm often gifted with something precious and unforgettable.

Capturing the moment is a choice, a way of life. It requires us to wake up, live life, and be present—here, there, and everywhere. Sometimes that's scary; sometimes it's exhilarating. Always it's an adventure I keep learning to welcome with a full and grateful heart.

—Luci Swindoll

June 25

A Shrug . . . and a Tug

> Keep vigilant watch over your heart . . . Avoid careless banter, white lies, and gossip.
>
> —Proverbs 4:23 msg

Dads affect how we look at our friendships and how we interact with our friends. I have a very vivid memory of my dad teaching me how to treat friends: I was riding in my mom's station wagon when I was in middle school. There were two rows of seats in the back, and I sat next to my friend in the middle, while my sister and her friend sat behind us.

I leaned over and told my friend that I thought my sister's friend was fat. Right as I said it, the car went quiet. I froze, and my heart immediately sank. *Did she hear me? Should I say something*?

I decided to shrug it off. But the more I tried to shrug, the more I felt a tug. I had to relieve my conscience.

Later that day, I told my dad what I had said. He gently explained that it is good to never go to bed with problems unresolved. The faster you apologize or correct the situation, the better you will feel. He encouraged me to call her and clear my conscience. The ironic part of the story is that I ended up confessing what I had said, but she had never even heard me! I ended up ratting myself out!

Even so, it felt good to be honest and open. Dad taught me to be a good friend to others, even when it's not easy.

—Jenna Lucado

The Gift of Living Water

We know that this is indeed the Christ, the Savior of the world.
—John 4:42

When Jesus approached Jacob's well in Samaria, a Samaritan woman was taken aback when he asked her for a drink. The Jews and the Samaritans didn't interact. "You . . . ask a drink from me?" she inquired (see John 4:9).

Jesus replied, "If you knew the gift of God, and who it is who says to you, 'Give Me a drink,' you would have asked Him, and He would have given you living water" (John 4:10).

He then ladled this invitation to her lips: "Whoever drinks of the water that I shall give him will never thirst. But the water that I shall give him will become in him a fountain of water springing up into everlasting life" (John 4:14).

The woman knew she wanted this water, but first Jesus exposed her past so she would understand that he was offering the only well that could replenish her withered soul. The woman went into the city and told the men that a stranger had told her "all things that I ever did." Then she posed the question each of us must one day consider: "Could this be the Christ?" (John 4:29).

The men went to see for themselves. She who had drunk in Jesus' words had whetted their shriveled hearts.

One statement in Scripture about this woman particularly captures my interest. After speaking with Jesus, the woman "left her waterpot" (John 4:28). You don't leave your waterpot behind in such a dry land unless your thirst has been quenched.

Are you thirsty? I invite you to join me in the Valley of Water at the well of his Word. I've found the more I sit at his well and drink, the more natural it is for me to go there first instead of sprinting for my old waterpot of stagnant answers.

—Patsy Clairmont

June 27

Healthy Connectedness Through Healthy Separateness

> Jesus was taken into the wild by the Spirit for the Test. The Devil was ready to give it. Jesus prepared for the Test by fasting forty days and forty nights.
>
> —Matthew 4:1–2 msg

The subject of personal boundaries and our right to establish them is sometimes confusing to those of us who believe we are to give to others without being concerned about ourselves. The truth is, it is impossible to have healthy connectedness with others without knowing healthy separateness.

Establishing boundaries begins when we learn our own value, competence, and strength. Those qualities come when we depend on the individual gifts God has placed within us. And not only has he placed within us gifts, he also places within us his Spirit. We would all benefit from the example of Jesus, who separated himself from everyone to fast and pray for forty days. In doing so, Jesus connected more deeply with the Holy Spirit within him, which prepared him for his earthy ministry.

God does not see us as merely a clump made up of individuals. God loves and cares for us as individuals. Each of us is called by name. The decision to receive Christ is an individual choice. To honor our bodies as his temples is an individual choice. To set aside time for private prayer and worship is an individual choice.

To maintain our separate individuality, boundaries are necessary. They help us ensure that our commitment to the needs of others is balanced and prudent. When our boundaries sag, we tend to overcommit; as a result, we become fatigued and overwhelmed.

Saying yes can be Spirit-induced, but so can saying no.

—Marilyn Meberg

The Gift of Grace

For it is by grace you have been saved, through faith—
and this is not from yourselves, it is the gift of God.
—Ephesians 2:8 NIV

When I was a kid, my friends and I would spend all day in the yard, and when we got hot enough we'd run to the back patio, open the water spigot, get down on our hands and knees, and open our mouths up for a drink of water that splashed all over our faces.

Like me, you probably hoped for a life that would exceed your dreams, but as those dreams collapsed along the way, you've simply settled into your routine in a culture of ungrace. That's not a word, but it should be. Ungrace pulsates in our offices, communities, homes, and the media, and it tells us that, regardless of what has happened, we must *do* more! We must be better, look better, and make ourselves better. But to love someone regardless of their quirks and mistakes is a breath of hope in a world that turns more upside down than right side up. That is the gift of grace.

At some point, life blindsides us with something: abuse, foreclosure, disease, unplanned pregnancy, divorce, death, job loss, or financial collapse that takes our breath and buckles our knees. But isn't there more? The beauty of grace says yes. There's still love after the affair, still joy after the diagnosis, and still hope after the bankruptcy. With what strength you have left, turn your face up toward that spigot of grace and let it splash all over you.

Grace is always with us; it is real, and it is an indescribable gift that has the power to change your life. It does come with one condition, though—like any gift you have to hold out your hand and accept it.

—Donna VanLiere

June 29

The Good in Challenges

> God always answers, one way or another, even when people don't recognize his presence.
>
> —Job 33:14 MSG

I'm learning to recognize situations when my God-given intuition is being overruled by my tendency to sink into impulsive second-guessing, a habit that originated not with God but during an episode of childhood abuse at the hands of a babysitter.

Every time I overcome that challenge, I move closer to the edge that separates my past life from the life God wants me to have today, one that's blessed by health and happiness.

Such blessings have taught me there's value in challenges. For one thing, they can bring us closer to God. When we face some overwhelming problem or when we're urgently trying to overcome some despised thing, we cry out to him, begging him to help us. And in response, as the friend of Job told his problem-prone pal, God *will* answer.

The apostle Paul instructed us to "be cheerful no matter what; pray all the time; thank God *no matter what happens*" (1 Thessalonians 5:16 MSG, italics added). We should be thankful for the problems we encounter, because God may be using them to snap us out of whatever distractions we've drifted into. As Job's friend also said, God may use our difficulties to "get [our] attention through pain" (Job 33:19 MSG).

When God finally *gets* our attention, we're wise to keep it focused on him—because that's how we'll get through the next challenge, which is probably waiting right around the corner.

And through it all, we have to remember that, no matter what kind of tangled-up mess we've landed in, God is going to use it for our ultimate good.

—Sandi Patty

Buckets and Thimbles

I know, my God, that you test the heart and are pleased with integrity.
—1 CHRONICLES 29:17 NIV

I learned a lot about making close friends by spending a few semesters in the school of hard knocks. After some heartbreaking betrayals and disappointments, I realized there were warning signs I could have paid attention to in some of my first attempts at finding a close friend with whom I could trust my heart.

Giving me some much-needed guidance, my Bible study teacher, George, drew a picture of a bank account on a dry-erase board and explained to me that my emotional account was overdrawn. He asked me to list all the people in my life who were withdrawing energy, emotions, thoughts, and time from that account—all the places where I was spending myself. Then he asked me where the deposits were coming from to refill my reserves.

George's visual helped me see that, in most of the relationships in my life, I was giving out but not receiving enough to avoid emotional bankruptcy. It was critical that I get in relationship with some people who weren't only interested in receiving but who were also able to give and replenish me.

My friend Ney Bailey calls this the bucket-thimble model. Some people have the capacity to contain a bucketful, some a cupful, and others a thimbleful. If I'm a bucket-person and I'm in a relationship with someone capable of containing only a thimbleful, then when I share, I'm prone to overwhelming them.

And even if that thimble-person gives all she's able to give, she just isn't capable of giving me all I need. I need to take an honest look and not expect more from her than she is able to give. To have the friends I need, I have to find another bucket-person, a few cup-people, or a handful of thimble-folks.

—Lisa Whelchel

July 1

Sipping the Refreshing Water of God's Truth

> Gideon said to them, "I will not rule over you, nor shall my son rule over you; the LORD shall rule over you."
> —JUDGES 8:23

One definition of a *valley* is "the extensive land area . . . irrigated by a river system" (American Heritage Dictionary). The valley has a water supply that keeps it fruitful. Likewise, if we are to be lush and productive, we need a river to run through us. Partaking of a Bible study, whether we do it on our own or with others, will start the irrigation.

Lately I've been spending a lot of time in the book of Judges in the Old Testament, drinking in the refreshing water of truth that God calls us, just as he called Gideon, to be more than we ever dreamed. Imagine that.

Gideon was full of fear, yet God called him a mighty man of valor. God didn't extricate Gideon from his woes but instead watered Gideon's life right in the midst of enemies and chaos. Gideon would grow into his valor.

It doesn't matter how insecure we feel, how feeble our résumé may appear, or how many times we've botched up our lives; God has a higher plan for us, and it begins with his wellspring within us. (I recommend sipping from Gideon's story in Judges 6–8.)

—Patsy Clairmont

Taking Pleasure in God's Creation

The heavens declare the glory of God; and the firmament shows His handiwork.
—Psalm 19:1

Pleasure is one of God's gifts. The Bible confirms this in verses such as James 1:17: "Every good gift and every perfect gift is from above, and comes down from the Father of lights."

Even so, from the Puritans to the Amish, Christians have historically felt a certain distrust of pleasure, sometimes citing such seemingly crabby verses as 2 Timothy 3:4, which warns us not to love pleasure more than God, and 1 Timothy 5:6, which says the one "who lives in pleasure is dead while she lives."

If these words are taken out of context, we might not believe pleasure is one of God's gifts. How could it be? If sounds as if pleasure and trouble go together.

As in all things, we want to maintain a balanced and thoughtful understanding of what the Bible teaches about pleasure. Scripture is not telling us to avoid pleasure; it does, however, encourage us to experience pleasure with disciplined common sense. For many people, the challenge is to keep pleasure in a state of balance.

God intends his good and perfect creation to be appreciated by us and to give us pleasure. I love that, after each of God's creative acts recorded in Genesis, he stood back and "saw that it was good" (1:10). He encourages us to see just how good! Seeing the grandeur of his creation gives me enormous pleasure. I join the psalmist in believing it is a sweet way to worship: "In Your presence is fullness of joy; at Your right hand are pleasures forevermore" (Psalm 16:11).

—Marilyn Meberg

July 3

Backstage Pandemonium

> The steps of a good man are ordered by the Lord,
> and He delights in his way.
> —Psalm 37:23

Several years ago, my band and I were part of a show that included cowboys performing rope tricks on horseback. My pianist, Steve, missed the regular rehearsals, but he did arrive for what we call the tech rehearsal. We didn't have time to brief him about the other performers. He just sat down at the piano, and things immediately started.

As the handlers were leading the horses into the backstage area, one of the animals slipped and fell. By that time, we were performing one of our songs. The director came running onstage yelling, "Horse down!"

Steve wasn't sure what he was supposed to do. "Excuse me?" he asked.

"Horse down!" the director yelled again.

"I'm having trouble understanding you," Steve said. "It almost sounded like you said, 'Horse down.'"

"That's what I said," the director barked: "Horse down!"

Poor Steve hadn't even known there were horses in the show. For a few moments chaos reigned, while Steve sat quietly at the piano.

The handlers finally put resin on the horses' hooves to give them some traction, and rehearsal resumed without further calamities. But we're still laughing about the story many years later.

—Sandi Patty

Your Sin Has Been Paid For

For by grace you have been saved through faith, and that not of yourselves; it is the gift of God, not of works, lest anyone should boast.

—Ephesians 2:8–9

Scripture gives us a frighteningly clear picture of how, if we are given what we deserve based on our deeds, we're all in trouble.

Until Jesus, the world lived in condemnation. The only way out of that condemnation was to live purely and perfectly. We were to conscientiously follow the Ten Commandments and participate in the animal sacrifices for sin when we messed up.

With Jesus came a new order of things. We are no longer held accountable for the perfection we could never achieve or for the good works we could never accomplish, because Jesus rescued us from the sinful limitations of our humanity. Ephesians 2:8 describes the new way for us: God saved you by his special favor when you believed. And you can't take credit for this; it is a gift from God. Salvation is not a reward for the good things we have done, so none of us can boast about it. We are God's masterpiece. He has created us anew in Christ so that we can do the good things he planned for us long ago.

Old Testament thinking was, "You get what you deserve if you sin." The disciples and Job's comforters were thinking in the old way. Jesus came to show his creation that a new way is possible because he died for sin. You may have sinned a whopper, but you don't ever have to crawl up on the cross. With that incredible truth comes this additional amazing truth: You are not paying for your sin right now as you read these words. Your sin has already been paid for. It's a done deal.

—Marilyn Meberg

July 5

Focusing on the Light

As long as I am in the world, I am the light of the world.
—JOHN 9:5

I vividly remember standing in the National Gallery in London in 1995, eager to see a special exhibit featuring just one painting: Joseph Mallord William Turner's *The Fighting Temeraire*. Some scholars consider this painting a thoroughly perfect picture.

The *Temeraire* was a man-of-war that had fought heroically at the Battle of Trafalgar. But in Turner's painting it is being towed by a steam tug to be broken up. The famous ship and tiny black tugboat are on the left side in the painting, and a great light is on the right, off in the distance.

What captivated me was the light, not the ship or the tugboat or the fact that all the ship's fighting days were over.

If the painting could speak, I think it would have said to me, "There is still magic in the world, Luci. It's in the light . . . in the distance. Don't fret over what's been lost. Concentrate on the light."

When I remember Turner's work, I think of Jesus as the light of the world. Keeping my eyes on him, I can do anything. I can walk in light even on my darkest days.

Living in the light is one of the most difficult tasks we have. It means getting out of the way so there is no shadow blocking the source. Light is illumination—whether emotional, financial, mental, physical, or spiritual. To capture the light available to us is one more aspect of divining the spirit of adventure. The more light we live in, the more we grow and change.

When we simply do what God asks, no matter how hard it seems, and when we keep our focus on the Light of the world, an amazing brightness comes, all within the embrace of his love.

—Luci Swindoll

The Key to Deliverance from Bitterness

Forgive us our debts, as we forgive our debtors.
—Matthew 6:12

The bloody hostility that erupted in Northern Ireland in the mid-1960s was, in essence, a resurgence of the hatred that had existed for several hundred years between Protestants and Catholics.

At the beginning of the 1970s, British armed forces moved in, essentially as a peace-keeping force, but the violence only escalated. One of my most poignant memories as a child growing up in Scotland was watching the news one night while young children threw rocks at soldiers. A reporter asked one of them why she was throwing rocks at the soldiers.

"Because I hate them," she said.

The reporter asked why.

"Because my mammy told me I do."

Hate and bitterness are contagious. Think of the countless countries that still deal with civil unrest, whether for religious or other reasons. Look at the racial tension and hatred that are still alive here in America. The trouble with that kind of deep-seated bitterness is that no amount of revenge is ever enough. For every blow struck by one side, the other retaliates with a fresh one, and the cycle continues. There is never enough blood spilled to wash away the bitterness.

And as devastating as unforgiveness is on a national or tribal level, it is lethal to the individual. When we are unable, or refuse, to forgive, we become hostages to the pain of the past. God has given us the key to deliverance from this captivity. Like a golden thread, it is woven through the Bible, from Genesis to Revelation: *forgiveness.*

—Sheila Walsh

July 7

Looking for Friends, Avoiding Perfection

> He who walks with integrity walks securely,
> But he who perverts his ways will become known.
> —Proverbs 10:9

I was on a quest to make new friends, and Karla and I really "clicked" when we met during one of my speaking engagements. We had read the same books and loved to have philosophical discussions that had no beginning or end and were full of questions with very few answers. Besides that, Karla was just a whole lot of fun.

Plus, she appeared to be a perfect Christian. Looking back, I realize that should have been my first alert that she wasn't a "safe person" for me and could not be the close friend I needed.

I've since learned to pay attention to what somebody does, not just what she says. I know that sounds elementary, but this has been a hard thing for me to accept. I tend to want to believe someone's words to me, even when the actions don't align. Now I look for people who can be real and honest about their shortcomings and struggles, and I've learned again that there is no such thing as a perfect person.

If you think you are meeting one, run!

Perfect people cannot connect with you at a real level because they cannot connect to themselves at a real level. That's why they must wear the mask of perfection.

If it is so important to them to give the illusion of perfection, then they will expect perfection from you too. That is not possible, and you will always feel "less than" around them.

Thankfully, I eventually learned to "listen" to actions as well as words and weigh them together more carefully as I sought out imperfect friends I could trust with my heart.

—Lisa Whelchel

We Matter to God

Now, my God, I pray, let Your eyes be open and let Your ears be attentive to the prayer made in this place.
—2 Chronicles 6:40

I passed a friend driving in the opposite direction on the road today. The moment I recognized her car, I began honking and waving (it was a slow speed zone); however, she drove on by completely oblivious to my friendly gyrations. Of course, she wasn't being intentionally aloof, but I still felt a tiny twinge of disappointment that she didn't notice me and that I didn't register as the smallest of blips on her radar.

Unfortunately, many people feel the same way about God. All too often humans assume they're invisible—or at least insignificant—when it comes to our Creator and Redeemer. Not that they necessarily imagine God to be callous or cruel; they just figure he's so preoccupied with wars, famine, disease, natural disasters, slave trafficking, and Las Vegas that he doesn't have the time or emotional energy to notice what's going on in their wee corners of the world, much less care about it.

I beg to differ. I'm more convinced now than ever before that we matter to God. He is intimately involved and infinitely interested in even the minutia of our lives. I believe it because I keep experiencing his tangible presence in the big and small spaces of my own life. And because of my vocation as a traveling Bible teacher, I've had the privilege of a proverbial box seat when it comes to watching our heavenly Father lovingly insert himself into the lives of his unsuspecting children.

The truth is, God doesn't just see us; he gazes adoringly at us. He doesn't simply notice us; he moves heaven and earth on our behalf.

—Lisa Harper

July 9

The Rescuers

> The Lord will rescue his servants; no one who takes refuge in him will be condemned.
>
> —Psalm 34:22 NIV

I consider my life a journey along and over the edge of the divine, a continuum that includes the profound as well as the trivial. Many times we have to work through challenges to get past the edge that separates us from the blessings God wants to give us. Amid those challenges, large or small, our best hope is to accept the aid of the rescuers he sends our way.

For me, they're my friends and family and colleagues in the music world. But all of them work alongside the greatest Rescuer of us all. Since the dawn of time, God has offered to put the pieces of our lives back together again when we heed and accept the help he's offered us through so many voices.

The prophet's voice: "Thus says the Lord . . . : 'Call to Me, and I will answer you, and show you great and mighty things, which you do now know'" (Jeremiah 33:2).

The psalmist's voice: "He heals the heartbroken and bandages their wounds. . . . God puts the fallen on their feet again" (Psalm 147:2, 6 MSG).

Jesus' voice: "Come to Me, all you who labor and are heavy laden, and I will give you rest. . . . For My yoke is easy and My burden is light" (Matthew 11:28, 30).

The apostle Paul's voice: "Don't fret or worry. Instead of worrying, pray. Let petitions and praises shape your worries into prayers, letting God know your concerns. Before you know it, a sense of God's wholeness, everything coming together for good, will come and settle you down. It's wonderful what happens when Christ displaces worry at the center of your life" (Philippians 4:6–7 MSG).

—Sandi Patty

The Lure on the Dangling Hook

Stay alert! Watch out for your great enemy, the devil. He prowls around like a roaring lion, looking for someone to devour. Stand firm against him, and be strong in your faith.

—1 PETER 5:8–9 NLT

The "pleasure center" is a part of the brain that reacts enthusiastically to chocolate, pizza, pasta, and any other favorite food (or activity) that provides us with pleasure. But we need to keep an eye on the pleasure center because it loves the "more is better" lie concocted by the enemy of the soul.

That lie keeps us craving and not satisfied. The enemy baits the hook with "more" and dangles it in front of the pleasure center. If we swallow it, we can lose our balance.

For example, two chocolate buttercreams may seem reasonable. Then the "more" hook swings by, and several more chocolate buttercreams may also seem reasonable until the box is consumed and we feel nauseated as well as guilty.

That hook never tires of dangling those luring enticements. The lure may change, but not the false promise that "more is better." That lie can apply to anything in our lives.

Here's the sobering truth about the pleasure center: It's where the enemy hangs out. It's where the bait is stored and the hooks are sharpened. That does not make the pleasure center evil, but it is the place where the enemy will turn good into evil if given the opportunity.

What are we to do to maintain our balance? Be vigilant as we enjoy the pleasure center and be reminded that God created us to experience pleasure that is found in him and authored by him.

—Marilyn Meberg

July 11

A Stranger's Embrace

> Do not forsake me, O Lord; O my God, be not far from me!
> —Psalm 38:21

Recently I was in the backstage area of an arena when a gal approximately forty-five years old came in to stock the sodas and water. I greeted her and asked her how she was, to which she gave the courtesy reply, "Good, thanks."

I didn't think she sounded convincing, so I asked her if she was really good or just sort of good. She turned and looked at me. "I think it's a miracle I'm walking and talking. My son was murdered three months ago, and sometimes I think I'm going to lose my mind."

What an honest answer. My heart ached for this broken-hearted mother who couldn't make sense of someone shooting her son in the back of his head while he was walking down the street. I knew nothing I said could bring reason to this act of violence, so I asked her if I could just hold her for a minute. Immediately she was in my arms.

Sometimes the most comforting thing we can do is touch the grieving person—with his or her permission, of course. I'm not sure my embrace helped her, but I do know her courage helped me.

That kind of mind-blowing loss not only knocks you off your feet but also has the potential to keep you pinned down for a long time. I was proud of this determined momma for getting up, dressing, and stepping back into the circle of life. She has a long, hard trail of grief ahead, but I know she's going to make it, one difficult step at a time.

—Patsy Clairmont

Grace Makes Connection Safe

As iron sharpens iron, so a man sharpens the countenance of his friend.
—Proverbs 27:17

In my quest to find new, "safe" friends, I've learned to pay attention to whether people are judgmental toward themselves or others. I don't dare risk exposing my humanity with someone if she can't accept my imperfection.

That's why one of my safest friends, Michele, is safe: she has blown it with the Lord big time and understands the gift of grace. She knows how to give it and receive it.

Another friend, Nancy, is safe because, even though she doesn't believe the same way I do, she respects my beliefs and loves that part of me even though she has chosen a different path. She knows how to give me room to be myself, not the person Nancy thinks I should be.

Nancy allows me ample space to make mistakes and mess up without freaking out. We don't go to the same church, but she takes God at his Word when he says that the greatest commandment is to love God and then love your neighbor as yourself.

She does that better than almost anyone I know.

Another trait I look for in a safe friend is someone who doesn't try to fix me. She knows that is God's job, not hers. A safe friend may question and challenge me, in the way described in Proverbs 27:17. This proverb reminds me that a solid, sharp person can solidify and sharpen me but not by tearing me down.

A safe friend will live her life before you and trust God to move on your heart in his time and in his way.

Certainly we are more influenced by who a person is than by what he or she says. Sometimes God chooses to use us to speak through, but mostly he likes to live through us.

—Lisa Whelchel

July 13

Trust Betrayed

> Be still before the LORD and wait patiently for him; do not fret when people succeed in their ways, when they carry out their wicked schemes.
>
> —PSALM 37:7 NIV

Forgiveness means we surrender our right to know the outcome. That is hard. We want to know that if we forgive, then the person will be sorry and never hurt us again. When we forgive someone and he turns right around and does the same thing again, not only are we wounded afresh, but we feel so foolish. That never sits well with us.

I was at my bank a few days ago, waiting in line to deposit a check, when I became aware of negotiations taking place between two brothers just ahead of me. One must have been about six and the other, four. It went a little like this:

"Come on, Sam, let me hold your sucker. I promise I won't eat it."

"But you said that last time."

"I know, but I mean it this time."

"All right."

And then soon after:

"Mom! He ate my sucker!"

"Well, why did you give it to him?"

Not only had he trusted his brother a second time, but he had been made to feel that it was his fault for believing the best. Life is hard! But we have access to a Father who can comfort us when we feel like dunces for the mistakes we make. It may take time for trust and healing to begin . . . or finish.

But God is patient. He never said life would be easy; he said he would be there for us—in the good decisions and the bad.

—Sheila Walsh

Changed by the Heat

My brothers and sisters, make every effort to confirm your calling and election. For if you do these things, you will never stumble.

—2 Peter 1:10 NIV

When you bake apple muffins, you blend together flour, butter, baking powder, eggs, milk, apples, cinnamon, vanilla, and so on. But this blending doesn't make the muffins; it only makes the mixture, the goop. You spoon the goop into muffin tins and then put the tins in the oven.

There a strange metamorphosis takes place. The heat from the oven changes the mixture into edible food. In the bowl, the muffin mixture is just dead weight. But the mixture changes with the addition of heat; when the time is right, voilà: irresistible apple muffins.

My professional life is a mixture of hard work and hours of time, concentration, discipline, and sacrifice. To be a working woman demands that I use my head and my heart. It requires different ingredients: delegation, relegation, deferment, courage, humor, a pinch of craziness, a spoonful of sugar.

But all this without heat is just lifeless goop—dead weight.

The hungry person who comes in contact with my mixture of traits won't be satisfied with lifelessness. She wants my blend, hot out of the oven. Only the heat of life and testing and experience can give the one in need the taste that satisfies. The energy of the Holy Spirit comes through my enduring the heat. It's the most important element in being irresistible.

We can give ourselves to people around us in a meaningful, eternal, fulfilling way when we permit ourselves to be transformed by God's energy. We've got to stay hot, tasty, and fresh if we're to be food for the hungry.

—Luci Swindoll

July 15

Successful in God's Eyes

> Remember the LORD in all you do, and he will give you success.
> —PROVERBS 3:6 NCV

Many of us attempt to recreate ourselves daily by focusing on outward appearance or by pursuing personal achievements that bring awards, relationships, and so on. Our identity becomes wrapped up in trying to be what society defines as successful instead of what God deems as successful.

> The world says, "Look out for yourself." God says, "Serve others."
> The world says, "Beauty is important." God says, "I look at your heart."
> The world says, "Be first in line." God says, "The last shall be first."

As life rolls along, it's hard for us to stay in the passenger seat; we must choose to follow Christ. Letting him lead isn't easy, but it's essential to finding ourselves and fulfilling our destiny.

As your insecurities and hidden fears come bubbling to the surface, embrace them, knowing that as you do, healing will come as you find yourself in Christ.

You're an original with a God-sized destiny. So move over because he's the only one with a license to drive your life.

Here's a truth for the journey ahead: "You made my whole being; you formed me in my mother's body. I praise you because you made me in an amazing and wonderful way. What you have done is wonderful. I know this very well" (Psalm 139:13–14 NCV).

Maybe you're not convinced yet, but hang in there; with God's help, you can be.

—Natalie Grant

The Longevity of God's Love

I keep my eyes always on the Lord.
—Psalm 16:8 niv

Pursuing new experiences and achievements is exhilarating and healthy. But there's always the possibility of blind striving, an inability to see the limitations of that for which we strive.

Many of us are slow to learn the obvious. We continually fall into the trap of thinking, *If I just had . . . I would be much more content.* Possessions and life itself have meaning only when I come to terms with the God who created all things. When he is my foundation, the Being around whom my life revolves, only then will I have a sense of purpose. When that purpose becomes well defined, I recognize that everything I strive for is limited in its potential to produce fulfillment. That does not mean I can't, shouldn't, or won't seek after those experiences. But it does mean I must realize that my ultimate joy will never come from things or persons. It will only come from a personal knowledge of and commitment to God.

In the midst of all his resplendent living, the writer of Ecclesiastes concludes: "I know that everything God does will endure forever; nothing can be added to it and nothing taken from it" (3:14 niv). The lack of permanence so common to the affairs of the heart directly contrasts with the longevity of the love we receive from God.

—Marilyn Meberg

July 17

Getting to the Place of Forgiveness

> If you bring your gift to the altar, and there remember that your brother has something against you, leave your gift there before the altar, and go your way. First be reconciled to your brother, and then come and offer your gift.
> —Matthew 5:23–24

One reason we struggle with forgiveness is that we have cheapened what forgiveness really is. There is an element of sentimentality among many in the evangelical church who would suggest forgiveness is easy and quick. People apply forgiveness like a Band-Aid over a wound, without recognizing the wound has to be addressed, acknowledged, grieved over, and owned before forgiveness can ever be real and lasting. To minimize someone's pain with a "Hey, I'm sorry, friend" and even a quick prayer—without truly acknowledging any wrongdoing and its heartfelt consequences—is an offense in itself.

In reality, we may never receive a true apology from our offender. Honestly, though, what good is gained in allowing our wound to fester? Do we feel better for having wrapped ourselves up in our anger? More important, does it enhance our relationships with others and with God?

Jesus said, "In prayer there is a connection between what God does and what you do. You can't get forgiveness from God, for instance, without also forgiving others. If you refuse to do your part, you cut yourself off from God's part" (Matthew 6:14–15 MSG).

The message is very clear: if we want to live free in Christ's love, we must forgive.

—Sheila Walsh

Truth in Its Barest Form

Charm is deceitful and beauty is passing, but a woman who fears the LORD, she shall be praised.
—PROVERBS 31:30

One of the things I find so appealing about the book of Proverbs is how direct it is. I don't have to struggle to get it. Proverbs is an in-your-face kind of book. No easing you into truth, just bottom line. There it is—truth in its barest form: "He who hates correction is stupid" (Proverbs 12:1).

See what I mean? No easy way to hide from that tumble with truth.

Or how about . . . "He who trusts in his own heart is a fool" (Proverbs 28:26)?

Nope, I don't need to search through commentaries, wondering what those verses are trying to say. I get the gist without even having to think.

I'm not a Bible scholar; I don't know Greek or Hebrew. And don't squeal on me, but I can even forget to read my daily devotional. Yet here is what I know for sure: my heart has been changed through the straightforward counsel of Proverbs. I find joy in those colorful verses with their direct wisdom, clear understanding, and their snappy offering of divine instruction. Take yourself on a stroll through these pithy passages and see if you don't agree.

—Patsy Clairmont

July 19

Praying the Prayer of Jesus

Your will be done on earth as it is in heaven.
—Matthew 6:10

Many years ago I was traveling with a group to the People's Republic of China on a special project as part of our work with students. Our trip required a flight to Hong Kong where we spent one night, and then we headed to the dock to board a ship for mainland China. Our driver told us it would be best if we could take the Thai boat and definitely not the China boat.

So we began to pray for the Thai boat. Finally, as we were dropped off at the dock, one of the guys with us jogged ahead. As soon as he reached the end of the dock, he turned back and yelled, "It's the Thai boat!" We all let out a whoop. It was our dream, our desire, the answer to our prayers.

The boarding ramp took us through the kitchen. I held my breath and knew I would not be dining on the Thai boat. As we made our way into the China Sea, the waters were never smooth, but they got worse and worse as the night wore on. As I struggled to hang onto my top bunk, I eventually got very sick. Most of us had the same struggle. The word *miserable* doesn't do justice to my experience that night.

Isn't that life? We set our hearts and minds on something we think will be *exactly* what we want, what is best for us, what will make us happier and better than anything else possibly could. We long for that perfect provision and pray with all our hearts. And then. Then we discover it's not at all what we wanted it to be.

Not just because of the Thai boat but because of years of walking with Christ, I keep learning to pray the prayer of Jesus: Father, not my will but thine be done.

—Mary Graham

Be Careful to See What's Really There

The LORD saves his servants' lives; no one who trusts him will be judged guilty.
—PSALM 34:22 NCV

When I was touring Tiberias, everyone in our group was asked to pick up a small rock before we boarded boats and sailed to the middle of the Sea of Galilee, where we heard Pastor Chuck Swindoll deliver an inspiring sermon. He concluded by asking us to let our rock represent something we needed to let go of. When we were ready, we were to say to God, "I release this" and drop the rock into the sea.

Seated near me was a scowling woman who evidently didn't like the assignment. Throughout the sermon her brow was furrowed, and she couldn't sit still. I secretly wondered why she had come if she was going to close off her spirit to life-giving truth.

Dismissing thoughts about her, I dropped my rock and heard it drown in the sea. For a brief time the Sea of Galilee became the Sea of Sorrows as it drank in our pain. Then it became the Sea of Celebration as we felt the relief of release.

My furrow-browed "friend" held on to her rock, turning it over and over in her hand. Then suddenly she tossed it with gusto into the brink. A smile smoothed her brow as she murmured to her husband, "We may need to get me some more rocks."

And here I thought she wasn't responding! Instead of disinterest, her brow may have been furrowed by realizing that one rock wasn't adequate for her accumulated miseries. I had totally misread that burdened woman.

Ever happen to you? When have you misjudged a situation, forgetting that God's hand might be at work in ways you can't see and don't expect?

—Patsy Clairmont

July 21

Checkout Furor

> Peter came to Him and said, "Lord, how often shall my brother sin against me, and I forgive him? Up to seven times?" Jesus said to him, "I do not say to you, up to seven times, but up to seventy times seven."
> —Matthew 18:21–22

I was at the supermarket, standing in the "ten items or less" line—which, as we all know, is trouble waiting to happen. The man at the front of the line had eleven items in his cart. I only know that because the woman standing immediately behind him counted them out loud. The man offered to put something back, but the checkout girl had the common decency to tell him that wasn't necessary. This only further ignited the fury of the offended one.

I wonder what might have been taking place inside that woman that led her to unload on this unsuspecting shopper. What if she had been piling up grievances over the days, weeks, and years? What if not all of them are small? Perhaps at some point in her life, she had been seriously wronged by someone but had never received the healing of forgiveness—was never able to let her pain go for fear it would diminish the wrongs against her.

When negativity begins to take over, transgressions big and small can pile up until something trivial is enough to put you over the edge.

How many times, dear reader, have you found yourself grousing at someone, knowing full well the real reason for your discontent is another matter entirely?

I know I have. Sometimes I fire off at little things because there is something far deeper going on that I have not dealt with.

If we are going to forgive—if we're going to bring our pain to Christ—we *have* to relinquish the right to "get even." We have to let go.

—Sheila Walsh

Striving for Authenticity

The stone which the builders rejected has
become the chief cornerstone.
—Psalm 118:22

There are so many days when I would love to take an airbrush to the canvas of my life and fix all the mistakes. But humans aren't perfect, and if we pretend to be, we're faking it. I strive to be real and authentic, even if it means letting my flaws and imperfections show.

Think of the apostle Paul, who prayed three times for the "thorn in [his] flesh, a messenger of Satan" to be taken away (2 Corinthians 12:7 NIV). We don't know what that "thorn" was, but it was obviously some blemish in Paul's physical body or emotional makeup.

As he prayed and processed and wrestled with what he knew to be true, he was able to come to a place where he finally said, "OK, here is the secret of contentment that I have found. I know what it is like to be flawed, to be hungry and poor. I know what it is like to be needy and to have nothing. I even know what it is like to have stuff—good stuff in my life. But that is not what brings contentment." (I am seriously paraphrasing Philippians 4:12–13 here.) "Here it is. Here is the secret, the key to abundant life: I can do everything—*everything*—through him who gives me the strength to do so."

I pray today that, as you embrace your flaws and imperfections, you will remember and know in your deepest "knower" that God is the master artist. You have been touched by his hand, and his touch makes you authentic, flaws and all. Don't be afraid to let those flaws show.

—Sandi Patty

July 23

My Devoted Secret Keeper

> Cast your burden on the LORD, and He shall sustain you;
> He shall never permit the righteous to be moved.
> —PSALM 55:22

The gospel writer with whom I most identify is Luke. He kept a journal. It's called "Acts." And isn't that what we do every day, alone or with somebody else—act? While Matthew, Mark, and John give us amazing insight into the life of Christ, Luke gives us detail.

I love detail! I love knowing who went where, who came along, who sat by whom, what they ate, and where they went immediately following dinner. Luke gives us all that information. I just know he kept a journal.

I come from a long line of journal keepers. My mother, grandmother, aunts, and cousins kept little books in which they recorded time and events. Many are filled with pictures and drawings. I scan these treasured volumes from time to time and get insight into my heritage.

Besides God himself, I have no more devoted friend or companion in my life than my journal. I take her everywhere I go, pour out my heart to her, share my burdens and cares, let her see me at my best and worst. She guards my secrets and lovingly holds my heart. She knows all the dreams I ever dared to entertain.

When I go back to her years later, she's not forgotten a single word. She reflects where I've come from, where I am, and where I want to go. As I look back, I can see how I've changed and grown.

The private contemplation that journaling provides gives us a place to examine what life really means to us. Every time we chronicle our thoughts and activities, we are verifying our existence and silently thanking God we're alive.

—Luci Swindoll

The Power of a Father's Focus

You're beautiful from head to toe, my dear love, beautiful beyond compare, absolutely flawless.

—Song of Solomon 4:7 msg

Growing up, I watched my friend Liz get comfortable in the shade. But I'm not talking about the quiet shade of an old oak tree. Liz was in the shade of the perfect shadow her older sister had cast with her four-point GPA, her skill in music, her scholarship to a prestigious university, her achieved goal of a PhD, not to mention her natural beauty.

Meanwhile Liz struggled in school. She jumped from one college to the next, not knowing what she wanted to do, always hanging out in groups of people whose motivation in life was nonexistent. She struggled with insecurities about her weight and frizzy hair. And instead of having a father who encouraged her and her uniqueness, she had a dad who focused on her flaws.

I remember sitting down with Liz one day after another lost battle to drugs. She had already cycled through drug rehab multiple times. During our conversation, I remember her saying that she was finally trying to forgive her dad. I wish we could have talked about it more, but mentally and emotionally, she wasn't ready.

I can't help but wonder if years of not living up to her dad's standards and watching her sister receive all the praise had built insecurity on top of insecurity, contributing to the broken path that she fights to get off of every day.

The way your dad loves or doesn't love you directly impacts how you feel about yourself.

—Jenna Lucado

July 25

Becoming a Safe Person

An honest answer is like a warm hug.

—Proverbs 24:26 MSG

Even more than wanting to find safe people to be my friends, I want to be a safe person to others. These wants work hand in hand: we inevitably seek out friends with the same level of brokenness. That is one of the reasons it is so important to deal with our own issues. We want to have safe friends and be safe friends, but the truth is, hurt people hurt people.

In my life, my distorted thinking tells me that if I make a mistake I will not only get in bad trouble, but I will also be cut off from my source of love and life. Therefore, I must be perfect in order to avoid disconnection. Until I deal with this lie, I will unconsciously seek out close friends who have unattainable standards, and I will desperately try to be perfect in order to keep a connection that feels like my very life depends upon it.

For me, this is happening in many of my relationships, but one, in particular, showed me how safe friendships are *supposed* to work. At first, whenever I made a mistake or an unchristian remark sneaked out or a negative emotion crept up and spilled over, I would brace myself for judgment and correction from this friend. I would then pull back emotionally from her in order to protect myself from the pain of rejection and disconnection.

But time and time again, my display of humanity caused her to step in a little closer, talk a little gentler, smile a little sweeter, open her heart a little more, and reveal a little more of her own struggles.

She showed me that dealing with our past and learning new ways of relating are very important if we want to be safe friends to others.

—Lisa Whelchel

Guide Our Steps, Lord

Guide my steps as you promised; don't let any sin control me.
—Psalm 119:133 NCV

We were living with friends while looking for a house after moving to Oklahoma. We knew the neighborhood we wanted, but despite lots of looking we couldn't find a house that suited our needs.

One morning, I poured out my feelings to God. "Lord, I know you have the right house for us. *You* know you have the right house for us. Can you just tell us? Can you just guide our steps? Literally, God, I ask you to guide our steps as we move throughout each day. Help us find that house you have for us. And, Lord, for our host and hostess's sake, please hurry."

Later that morning, I set out on my fitness walk. But inexplicably I set off in a different direction from the usual route.

Off I went, one step after another, until I reached the opposite end of the subdivision, an area I'd never walked in before. And suddenly there it was, *the* house, with a For Sale sign.

Hmm. Three bedrooms, a small yard, in the neighborhood we loved. I hurriedly called the Realtor to get the details on the house. As I read over her emailed reply, one word came to mind.

Perfect.

Here's what I love about God's sense of humor. I hadn't said, "Lord, guide our *path*" or "*Direct* us the right way."

I had said, "Guide our *steps*," and, wouldn't you know, I *walked* right by the house we ended up getting.

We had arrived in Oklahoma on January 12, 2008, and we moved into our new house on February 9. Because the house was empty, we could close the deal and move right in.

Amazing, right? You would almost think it was the house God had meant for us to have.

—Sandi Patty

July 27

The Many Colors of Forgiveness

> Vengeance is Mine, and recompense; their foot shall slip in due time; for the day of their calamity is at hand, and the things to come hasten upon them.
> —Deuteronomy 32:35

When we are wronged by someone, we sometimes hold on to unforgiveness because we just can't relinquish the idea of retribution. But, as we know, God claims vengeance for himself, so it's not really up to us to expect a feel-good ending for all our woes. We simply have to trust that justice will take its God-ordained course.

That doesn't mean Christians should be wishy-washy when it comes to what is right and what is wrong. We are called to stand up for righteousness. We don't excuse the behavior of the offender, nor do we expect that forgiveness removes the consequences of a person's actions.

A friend who is unjustly maligned can choose to let bygones be bygones, but that doesn't mean the transgressor should be allowed to continue with a hurtful attitude. A battered wife can choose for the sake of her soul to forgive, but that does not mean he should go unpunished under the laws of our country. I believe that forgiveness is offered to set us free, not to put a Band-Aid over the gross sin of another.

Forgiveness unclenches our fists and allows us to let go. It says to God, "I cannot change what happened, although everything inside me cries out for justice. I am placing this unspeakable situation into your hands. I don't have to make offenders suffer, and I don't have to make them feel better about themselves. I relinquish them to you, and today, right now in Jesus' name, I choose life."

—Sheila Walsh

Living "in the Meantime"

Having been justified by faith, we have peace with God through our Lord Jesus Christ.

—Romans 5:1

Some of the struggles Mary the mother of Jesus encountered are similar to what many of us face today—escalating taxes resulting in financial challenges, political unrest, fears for the safety of family members, and conflicts within our houses of worship.

The need to persevere in the face of personal, financial, church, and family challenges is as prevalent now as it was then. There are moments in our lives when giving up on a person or a situation would be much easier than being in an indefinite period of waiting and not knowing what the end result will be.

The physical and mental exhaustion of living "in the meantime"—somewhere between an old and a new normal—creates the need for resolution. We ask questions: How long will I wait for change? What other options do I have? Does God care about the anxiety this limbo is creating in my life?

The Bible says that "tribulation produces perseverance; and perseverance, character; and character, hope. Now hope does not disappoint, because the love of God has been poured out in our hearts by the Holy Spirit who was given to us" (Romans 5:3–5).

Have you experienced that progression in your life—a time when perseverance led to character and character led to hope? Maybe you're still struggling with the "waiting" part of perseverance, or perhaps you've moved into a time of character development. Or you may now be in that place where you have experienced hope that you can communicate to others.

If you're not there yet, it's okay. This process doesn't usually happen overnight, but the Bible tells us it *will* happen.

—Carol Kent

July 29

Securely Embraced by Endless Love

> Who shall separate us from the love of Christ? Shall tribulation, or distress, or persecution, or famine, or nakedness, or peril, or sword? . . . I am persuaded that neither death nor life, nor angels nor principalities nor powers, nor things present nor things to come, nor height nor depth, nor any other created thing, shall be able to separate us from the love of God which is in Christ Jesus our Lord.
>
> —Romans 8:35, 38–39

God's love is the glue that holds our lives together and holds us close to him. It's the promise that guarantees us a heavenly future. And the best thing is . . . *nothing* can keep us from it. Not even death.

That fact was beautifully reinforced for me a few years ago when I attended the memorial service for a close friend who had died at the peak of his career.

Many of us were called upon to speak that day. Then, instead of sharing warm memories or offering her own words of comfort, as the rest of us had done, one friend simply opened her Bible to Romans 8 and read the ageless, empowering words in a strong, defiant voice.

Her voice rang out with confidence and power to remind all of us—maybe even the devil himself—that our friend was with God and so were we, and *nothing* could change that fact.

He holds us in his loving embrace, and nothing can come between us. Absolutely nothing. Not today; not tomorrow. Not in this life or the next. There are no words, no forces, no feelings, no actions—there is *nothing* that can separate us from his love.

Securely embraced by that endless love, we can face any kind of hardship here on earth with courage and faith.

—Barbara Johnson

Whom Do We Follow?

Righteous are You, O Lord, and upright
are Your judgments.
—Psalm 119:137

Sometimes I've made good decisions for the wrong reasons. When I entered junior high, I wanted to play in the band. Several of my friends wanted to as well, and we knew that if we did, we would go places. Literally. The band took band trips, marched in parades, had competitions, and as far as I could tell, had the world on a string.

My mother wanted me to play the clarinet. Fine with me. My uncle had played clarinet in a band as had my older sister. The band was the issue for me, not the clarinet, until I realized my mother wanted me to play the same clarinet the others in the family had played. Huh? It was so old. The kids in my band were playing bright shiny new plastic clarinets. I didn't want a vintage wooden instrument.

Not only did I not want it, it embarrassed me. So, I changed my mind about being in the band. I didn't want to be the only kid with an old instrument. I now know the old instrument was (and is) much more valuable and had an incredible sound that those plastic clarinets didn't. But sometimes perception trumps reality.

Regrettably, false judgments come fairly easily to me. I decide I want to do this, or that; go here, or there; be friends with him, or her; and it's all momentary and for the wrong reason. Psalm 23 says so simply, "He leads me." And God does. He leads me to make wise decisions, judgments, and choices based in reality and truth.

—Mary Graham

July 31

The Gift of *With*ness

He has sent me to bind up the brokenhearted, . . . to bestow on them a crown of beauty instead of ashes.

—Isaiah 61:1, 3 NIV

I'll never forget the time one of my dearest friends called me and could hear the distress in my voice. She insisted I didn't need to experience what I was going through alone. Although she was in the middle of shopping, she left her basket full of items in the store, got in her car, and came straight to my house. I needed her with me, and she knew it.

True friends understand the difference between the times they can say, "If you ever need anything, don't hesitate to ask," and the other times when it says more to just show up.

My friend Angela and I experienced this. When she received some devastating news, she called to share it with me through tears of confusion. As foolhardy as it sounds, I used my airline miles and booked a flight departing first thing the next morning; then I called her and declared, "I am on my way to be with you through this, unless you tell me no. I arrive at 10:30."

That same year, at an especially low point for me, Angela couldn't hop on a plane, so she sent me the gift of being with me through the mail. She put together one large box containing many tiny, individually wrapped presents. One was a cookbook with her favorite handwritten recipes along with a note that said, "When you love someone, you cook for them. Until I can cook for you, enjoy my famous waffles." Another gift was an angel along with a card that said, "Friends are like angels. Thanks for being my angel on earth."

I had so much fun opening each gift and knowing she was so *with* me. My favorite present was a cheap rhinestone tiara with Isaiah 61:3 attached.

Yes, there is such a thing as *withness*, and it can be sent FedEx.

—Lisa Whelchel

Jesus' Agony in Gethsemane

> O My Father, if it is possible, let this cup pass from Me; nevertheless, not as I will, but as You will.
>
> —Matthew 26:39

Jesus was desperate in the Garden of Gethsemane. In Matthew's account of those dark hours, it says Jesus was so troubled he told the disciples, "My heart is full of sorrow, to the point of death" (Matthew 26:38 NCV), and Dr. Luke adds the medical note that the Messiah was under such extreme stress that "his sweat was like drops of blood falling to the ground" (Luke 22:44 NCV).

Jesus didn't square his shoulders and face the cross with unblinking fortitude. He wasn't a stoic martyr; he experienced distress. Not because he was afraid of death but because he dreaded being separated from his Father and receiving his wrath. But he endured that unimaginable ache alone.

Even mouthy, well-intentioned Peter, who'd vowed to stick to Jesus like Velcro, fell asleep while the Messiah mourned under those gnarled trees. Our Savior was bereft of companionship.

No one dropped by with a pint of chicken soup. No one wrote him a note expressing his or her condolences. Every single person abandoned him during his time of deepest need.

That's why the author of Hebrews was able to preach, "God is the One who made all things, and all things are for his glory. He wanted to have many children share his glory, so he made the One who leads people to salvation perfect through suffering. . . . And now he can help those who are tempted, because he himself suffered and was tempted" (Hebrews 2:10, 18 NCV).

Jesus didn't supernaturally skip to the front of the pain line. He chose instead to be an empathetic Hero, sharing perfectly in the frailty and loneliness of our humanity.

—Lisa Harper

August 2

Persisting Priorities

> But seek first the kingdom of God and His righteousness, and all these things shall be added to you.
> —Matthew 6:33–34

In a 1990 journal, I wrote a list of ten things that are important to me. I love rereading it because even after all this time, everything in it still holds true. It's a good touchstone for me when my value system gets out of whack. Here's an abbreviated version:

> It's important that I maintain a strong relationship with God.
>
> It's important that the people I love know that I love them by my generosity and kindness.
>
> It's important that I feel safe. I want to take risks and exercise my faith, but to the degree I'm able, I should keep myself healthy.
>
> It's important that I am always learning, growing, and enlarging my boundaries.
>
> It's important that I work on the areas of my temperament and behavior that I don't like.
>
> It's important always to be engaged in a project.
>
> It's important that I open my heart more and more to the arts.
>
> It's important to have fun.
>
> It's important that my time alone be quality, whether or not I'm resting.
>
> It's important to hold things loosely—relationships, money, possessions, etc.—because God can always take them away.

—Luci Swindoll

Are You Velcro or Teflon?

You have also given me the shield of Your salvation; Your gentleness has made me great.
—2 Samuel 22:36

In my relationship with friends, I struggle with all-or-nothing reactions—a learned behavior from my past when bonding was inconsistent. I needed a stable connection in order to live, but it wasn't always available. So I learned not to need a bond with anyone in order to survive the pain of disconnection.

Today I want to live vulnerably and openhandedly with my friends, and to do that, I need to experience healthy separateness in a safe relationship in which I neither sever nor cling.

It's hard for me to take an honest look at how many times I've unintentionally caused other people pain because I hadn't dealt with my own. Now I'm learning how to deal with my own broken places so I don't inadvertently break other people's hearts. It's difficult to really touch someone with God's love and healing if we're wearing a coat of armor to protect our wounds rather than exposing them and finding healing for them.

I've always operated under the mistaken notion that the more perfect I was, the more others would like me and want to connect with me. So I kept a slick, glossy finish on my layers of protection.

Ultimately, I learned that my very shininess acted like Teflon and prevented any kind of lasting bond. On the other hand, there is very little that holds more tightly than Velcro, with its loops, holes, and fuzz-catching texture. Not particularly attractive, Velcro will certainly stick, just like a true friend.

When I drop my shiny Teflon shield and let my holes, loopiness, and messy layers show, people can get close to me, and I am able to form solid attachments.

—Lisa Whelchel

August 4

Flaws Make Us Real

> I am the true God. There was no God before me, and there will be no God after me.
> —Isaiah 43:10 NCV

I was shopping in a small island town during a cruise, a captivating painting in the window drew me into an art shop. Inside I saw copies of that same painting displayed all over the store—fifty or more of them, all depicting that same Caribbean seascape at sunset.

Then something else caught my eye. It was the same picture, but this one was slightly different. It was a little rougher, a little less polished; you could see a smudge here and there that the other pictures didn't have. There was no frame; it was just a stretched canvas with frayed edges. It looked downright tacky compared with the other pictures that were so perfect.

I remember thinking, *Wow, if the others are only twenty-five dollars, this one must just cost two or three.* But to my surprise, it cost *two thousand* dollars! I couldn't believe it.

The clerk quickly explained. "Oh, that's because the artist actually touched this canvas with his own hands. The others are just reproductions; their flaws have been airbrushed out," she said.

She explained that the imperfections made the picture authentic. That's how you could tell it was the real thing, the work of the master artist.

I stood there looking at that store clerk as if she had just told me the priceless secret to contentment and peace—because she had! You never know where you're going to run into an inspiring sermon in your everyday life, do you?

I came away from that art shop vowing to always strive to be real and authentic, even if it means letting my flaws and imperfections show.

—Sandi Patty

Reflections of Divine Practicality

The LORD gives wisdom; from His mouth come knowledge and understanding.
—PROVERBS 2:6

The book of Proverbs is like a four-mirrored kaleidoscope that gives a parade of images. On first glance, it appears to be an unorganized shopping list for parents, counselors, teachers, singles, wives—why, there's even a bunch of verses cautioning one from becoming a full-time, card-carrying fool. But in truth the parade of topics helps us see reflections of divine yet practical insights for daily living, regardless of profession.

What I personally find helpful when I twirl the proverbial kaleidoscope are the verses about "mouth" that I often need to roll around in my head before my words spill out all over someone. For instance . . . "There is one who speaks like the piercings of a sword, but the tongue of the wise promotes health" (Proverbs 12:18).

Ouch! Are your words cutting-edge? When you slice through to the bottom line of an issue, is it at the expense of someone's feelings? I know I'm guilty. I'm thankful that, in this comparison, we are reminded that we have a choice, that our words can have life-giving potential.

What words will *you* share today?

—Patsy Clairmont

August 6

Becoming a Conduit of Love

> The generous soul will be made rich, and he who waters will also be watered himself.
>
> —Proverbs 11:25

Shortly after I was diagnosed with a malignant brain tumor and underwent surgery and chemotherapy, my doctor called with an update on recent tests. "I see no activity in your brain," he said in his quick, clipped voice.

"W-w-what does that mean?"

"It means we've slowed the tumor," he answered quickly. "This is such good news, I'm calling to ask a favor."

"What could I possibly do for *you*?" I asked.

The doctor wanted me to speak at the next meeting of the local cancer-survivors group.

"I don't know," I stalled, not wanting to do it. "There must be others who know more about cancer than I do."

But the doctor persisted, and I reluctantly agreed. My husband, Bill, helped me copy some cartoons and jokes onto colored paper to hand out to the group. We enjoyed making our plans.

When the day came, I wore a bright outfit, made sure my wig was on straight, and happily headed out the door. Suddenly I remembered how powerful sharing kindness could be.

Standing at the podium that day, I felt a wonderful surge of energy and joy. It was the Proverbs 11:25 boomerang effect at work: "He who waters will also be watered himself." When we share God's grace and goodness with others, the blessing and grace boomerang back to us.

In the midst of whatever hurtful experience you find yourself in, reach out to help others, and you will feel God's love and grace flowing through you as you become a conduit of his love.

—Barbara Johnson

The High Calling of Marriage

Your Maker is your husband—the LORD
Almighty is his name.
—ISAIAH 54:5 NIV

I was raised to believe marriage is a big deal to God and not to be entered into lightly. For those reasons, the idea of marriage scared me when I married Ken in 1961. I felt insecure about my ability to live up to its high calling.

I also feared being swallowed up, losing my identity. I soon learned Ken loved and took pleasure in my identity and had no intention of swallowing me up. He supported my desires until death did indeed "do us part."

From Genesis to Revelation, God tirelessly speaks of the marriage relationship as his supreme illustration of love and partnership. Interestingly, God places himself in the role of loving husband. For example, consider Jeremiah 3:14: "'Return, O backsliding children,' says the Lord; 'for I am married to you.'"

Why does God say he is married to us? He wants his beloved to know how to be a husband, so he set the example for Adam, intending that modeling to be continued for all generations. That modeling included these components: (1) God as husband thoroughly knows us, (2) God as husband loves us no matter what, (3) God as husband forgives us when we ask, and (4) God as husband will never leave us.

Obviously, we women need to pay attention to God's model because those behavioral standards apply to wives as well. When both husbands and wives know, love, forgive, and stay with each other, the marriage bond reflects God's modeling.

—Marilyn Meberg

August 8

Being an Encouraging Person

Behold, I have put My words in your mouth.
—Jeremiah 1:9

A good church is one that does more than offer its members a place to worship. A good church supports its members in their lives outside the church as well, providing support groups and organized volunteer services that reach out to those in need.

I urge you to be aware of others in your congregation who are going through problems, especially difficult situations you've been through yourself. Reach out to them. By helping others, you will help yourself.

I have a friend who went through a painful divorce, and she said that she felt as though she had become invisible within her church. "A lot of people knew what was happening, but no one mentioned it. It would have meant so much to me if someone had touched my shoulder and said, 'I know you're probably going through a hard time. I'm thinking of you and keeping you in my prayers. And if you need to talk, I'm here for you,'" she said. "Now I try to be that encouraging person, and it's been a blessing to me to know that I'm helping someone who's hurting."

Communication is so important when we find ourselves swirling around in the blender of life. We have to find ways to keep talking to each other and to those who can help us.

Of course the most important communication of all is between us and the one who created communication! He has given us a marvelous gift that can help us survive life in the blender.

Whenever you're struggling to communicate with those around you, turn to him. Talk to him. You'll find he will give you the right words when you need them, just as he said he would do.

—Sandi Patty

Parenting from the Inside Out

Don't fret or worry. Instead of worrying, pray.
—PHILIPPIANS 4:6 MSG

To be honest, I felt like I was a pretty good parent as long as I was bigger than my kids. As my children have gotten older, though, being a good mom has gotten harder. Like most moms, I felt much safer when I believed (rightly or wrongly) that I had more control over my children's lives. The faster my kids grow up, the harder it is for me to convince myself that I can truly "direct" their lives.

I, probably like you, firmly believe that I know what's best for my children, and I want to help them avoid unnecessary pain (which, of course, I firmly believe they can do if they listen to my advice and obey my instructions!). But part of parenting teenagers is letting them grow up and make independent decisions—even if those choices are wrong. It's terrifying knowing there is no guarantee that my children will choose to follow Jesus and his ways. So I've learned to redirect my parenting passion. Now, when I'm tempted to lecture my children, I try to pray for them instead.

The power of prayer. These words are so familiar that sometimes we forget what they mean. Prayer is a powerful tool that allows us to communicate with the living God! It's not to be taken lightly or used occasionally.

After all, I can only do so much parenting from the outside in. In contrast, God does *his* work from the inside out. It's heartening to see him work in my kids' lives, and I'm so thankful I can help.

Make no mistake: the quality of your spiritual life will have a direct impact on the quality of your family life. Prayer changes people, including your children. So pray constantly for your youngsters. God is listening.

—Lisa Whelchel

Finding Freedom Behind Bars

> If we say that we have no sin, we deceive ourselves, and the truth is not in us. If we confess our sins, He is faithful and just to forgive us our sins and to cleanse us from all unrighteousness.
>
> —1 John 1:8–9

I will never forget the night I spoke to a group of inmates enrolled in a Prison Fellowship program, Freedom Initiative, at a women's prison in Arkansas.

Two of the inmates were assigned to help run my CD track so I could sing a couple of songs as well. They were sweet, kind women with quite a sense of humor. When I saw there were candles sitting on the podium, I asked one of the inmates if I should light them.

She replied, "Don't ask me. I'm in here for arson!"

I spoke that night on freedom and forgiveness—that true freedom is not the absence of bars but the very real presence of Christ. As the theme verse for the Freedom Initiative's ministry states, "Therefore, if anyone is in Christ, he is a new creation; old things have passed away; behold, all things have become new" (2 Corinthians 5:17). These women were living examples. As I sang at the end of my message, women stood with their arms stretched out to God in worship, tears pouring down their faces. The presence of Christ was so apparent in these broken women, I couldn't help but think of the psalmist's words: "The sacrifices of God are a broken spirit, a broken and a contrite heart—These, O God, You will not despise" (Psalm 51:17).

Afterward, as I listened to their stories, two things became very clear: (1) forgiveness has the power to heal the most brutal of wounds, and (2) the most difficult person to forgive can be the one we see in the mirror every morning.

—Sheila Walsh

Tomorrow Will Take Care of Itself

Look at the birds of the air, for they neither sow nor reap nor gather into barns; yet your heavenly Father feeds them.
—Matthew 6:26

Sometimes I worry. I don't believe in worrying, and I'm absolutely convinced it's not the right thing to do. But I worry nevertheless. I remember my mother was a worrier, and so was my grandmother. However, worry is wrong. It is a lack of trust in the God who loves me, provides for me, protects me, and meets my *every* need. God's Word assures me of that, and additionally, the Word convicts me that worry is wrong.

I have a friend whom I often call when I'm worried. I explain how something *might* happen, something *could* go wrong, or it's *possible* I will make a mistake. She always reminds me not to worry. She often says, "Mary, don't think about that yet. Even if the worst happens, you don't have grace for it yet."

Scripture tells us in 2 Corinthians 12:9 that God's grace is sufficient. When we ponder that, it's clear we experience God's grace *in the moment*, when the need is there.

At any given moment, we could spend our emotional energy thinking about what might happen next, what could happen in the future, or even what did happen in the past. God's grace, I've learned, is in the here and now. That's why Jesus said (and we can say) with confidence, "Don't worry about tomorrow. Tomorrow will take care of itself." By the time we step into all of our tomorrows, his grace will already be there. In the present tense.

—Mary Graham

August 12

Lambs Grazing on God's Love

> Keep falsehood and lies far from me; give me neither poverty nor riches, but give me only my daily bread.
> —Proverbs 30:8 NIV

When, as a young adult, I first cried out to Christ to rescue and forgive me, I soon recognized my need to study the Bible. As I did, life-giving words tumbled out: *peace, prayer, power,* and *provision,* among others.

I was a desperate woman with a heart full of brokenness and too little biblical enlightenment to know what to do with it. So I did a lot of word studies in the light-bearing Scriptures during those emotionally spinning years as I searched for steadying answers. Initially my study style was splintered at best, but because of God's heart for his seeking children, he helped this wobbly lamb find pasture in his stabilizing Word.

It took me years of grazing to realize God's Word was its own commentary. The more I read and studied, the more I saw how one portion of Scripture defines other portions. I found that exciting. That isn't to say I'm not aware of the benefits of researching what others have learned through their lifetimes of education and efforts in biblical studies. I'm a fan of Spurgeon, Chambers, Moody, and others.

Maybe you too are a lamb in search of good pasture, wanting to graze on the hillside of God's love. I pray that as we feed on his Word, our Shepherd will give us hearts full of wisdom so that we may face the choices that come to us daily.

Life is textured. May we be sturdy people, up to the task of living with joyful integrity.

—Patsy Clairmont

Let's Talk

Do what the LORD says is good and right so that things will go well for you.
—DEUTERONOMY 6:18 NCV

A wife's simple statement, "We've got to talk," strikes panic in most men. Why? Most men are not sure what they feel. At the risk of alienating every man on the planet, I'd venture that many men are more inclined to be hunters who want to come home to a clean cave and a good meal. Top that off with sex, and it's a good day. As author Anne Lamott says in her book, *Operating Instructions: A Journal of My Son's First Year,* as much as we may love and respect men, they are "embarrassingly incompetent at life and in love" and have to be taught "the very basics of emotional literacy."

Studies devoted to the differences between men and women indicate women are better able to verbalize their feelings than men, but that does not mean men do not need emotional satisfaction as well. Some studies say boys are inherently little warriors who must live out of their primitive instincts. Others say we are living in an era of insecure men who have been so dominated by strong women they have retreated somewhere with the TV remote.

We may never totally understand the many differences between the sexes, but we can understand that the two sexes need to talk. When talk leads to understanding and understanding leads to acceptance, we've just laid the foundation for emotional connection.

What is acceptance? It is "to believe in." When we, through conversation and understanding, reach the point of "believing" in each other, intimacy can follow. That's God's ideal.

—Marilyn Meberg

August 14

The Girl Who Said Yes to God

> The angel said to her, "Do not be afraid, Mary, you have found favor with God. You will conceive and give birth to a son, and you are to call him Jesus."
> —Luke 1:30–31 NIV

Mary, the mother of Jesus, was only about thirteen years old when the angel of the Lord told her she would give birth to the Son of God.

"How can this be?" Mary asked, confused because she was a virgin.

The angel replied, "The Holy Spirit will come upon you, and the power of the Most High will overshadow you. So the Holy One to be born will be called the Son of God."

Mary swallowed her fear and then answered the angel with all the faith she had within her: "I am the Lord's servant. Let it be to me as you have said" (Luke 1:34–38, paraphrased).

She knew this strange and wonderful announcement from God could mean trouble for her. After all, Mary was engaged.

Young Mary must have been afraid, but instead of rejecting the marvelous promise of God that she would bear his Son, she praised God for all she didn't understand. Her words, recorded in Luke 1, are read by millions now.

She said, "My soul glorifies the Lord and my spirit rejoices in God my Savior, for he has been mindful of the humble state of his servant. From now on all generations will call me blessed" (vv. 46–48 NIV).

Mary's faith sustained her despite all the risks. God went before her and revealed his plan to Joseph. Her life was saved, and she gave birth to Jesus. All around the world, we know her as the one who said yes to God, and her example gives us hope that we can do the same.

—Natalie Grant

The Power of Believing

> Still others had trial of mockings and scourgings, yes, and of chains and imprisonment. They were stoned, they were sawn in two, were tempted, were slain with the sword. They wandered about in sheepskins and goatskins, being destitute, afflicted, torments—of whom the world was not worthy.
>
> —Hebrews 11:36–38

The Bible is alive with stories of men and women who chose to believe in God despite much harsher circumstances than those we face today. One of my favorites is told in Luke 8:43–48. The main character is a woman who had a debilitating health problem. She'd tried every remedy she'd heard of, gone to every doctor she could find, spent all her money trying to find a way back to healthiness, but nothing had worked.

Then she heard about a man who was performing miracles and changing lives. Some people even said he was the Messiah.

Maybe she'd managed to attend some of the gatherings where he spoke. Maybe she simply pondered stories of others who shared what they'd heard and seen. We don't know anything about her life until that day when she fought her way through the crowd in Galilee.

Maybe the crowd was too big, too boisterous, for her to meet Jesus face-to-face. Maybe she was too sick, too weak, to get any farther. Maybe she'd been knocked down, trampled by the throng. Maybe she was simply shy, afraid to call attention to herself and her embarrassing problem.

We don't know how she ended up behind Jesus that day. All we know is that *she believed*. And with that belief burning in her heart, she reached through the crowd and touched the edge of his robe. And that was enough.

It's enough for each of us too.

—Sandi Patty

August 16

Recording What Makes Me Tick

> Those who trust in the LORD are like Mount Zion, which cannot be shaken but endures forever.
>
> —PSALM 125:1 NIV

Since all of life is a journey, why not write about it along the way? When I considered Emerson's observation that "the unrecorded life is not worth examining," I took that injunction to heart. I want my life to be both recorded and examined. I want to know what makes me tick.

I want to live fully every moment. If I don't live in this moment, I'll lose it, and it'll never come again. How does one remember what happens as the years come and go? What can one do to keep the memories from fading? Keep a journal!

I want to record not only my activities but also my feelings in my journal. If I can get my feelings on paper, it helps me deal with them.

All my journals are in my library. Not long ago I took a picture of them with a digital camera and made it into a screen saver for my computer. My whole life is in those books. When that picture flashes on the screen, it represents years and years of the adventure of living. I'm glad the Holy Spirit nudged me a long time ago to start writing things down.

I know few people who take adequate time for reflection—and many who regret that they don't. Who said, "The important always gets sacrificed on the altar of the urgent"? Taking time is a better way to live. Rather than racing from one activity to another, let's take our time. Let's reflect on who we are, where we're going, and the life God has given us. Let's live a life worth recording—and record it! Who knows what we'll learn and who will learn from our enlightenment in years to come?

—Luci Swindoll

Anchored by Grace

For the law was given through Moses, but grace and truth came through Jesus Christ.
—John 1:17

I've been a Christian for more than thirty-five years, but I wasn't able to comprehend God's radical grace until I opened my life up to friendships with safe people.

Before, I preferred the law, playing at life by rules, measuring my worth by how godly a life I could live, trying to earn God's love. Rules always felt safer. There was right and wrong, black and white, lines to stay behind and never to cross. The law was something I could hold on to that made me feel like I had some control in the midst of tumultuous emotions and circumstances.

Yet deep down I wanted someone bigger and stronger to hold on to me during the frightening times of living in this world. What God ultimately gave me was better than something safe to hold on to and even better than someone safe to hold on to me. He rooted me and grounded me in his love. He strengthened me in my inner being. As Ephesians 3:16–21 explains, he anchored my heart to his in an exceedingly abundant relationship of grace.

As children of God, we are to grow closer to grace, not more deeply bound to Law. The law is important, foundational even. We can't just skip law and go straight to grace. Then we wouldn't appreciate the gift or the cost to the Giver of the gift. The law is the beautiful box in which the gift came wrapped. But we are to let God out of the box, out of our containing ideas of him, to know him personally in all his majesty and mystery.

Only babies prefer playing with the box and paper a gift comes wrapped in. With understanding, there is enjoyment of the gift.

—Lisa Whelchel

August 18

The Value of the Written Word

Let love and faithfulness never leave you; bind them around your neck, write them on the tablet of your heart.
—Proverbs 3:3 NIV

For years I insisted that all of our big family's activities had to be recorded on a bulletin board and a dry-erase marker board in the kitchen—I called it Grand Central. Everyone was ordered to leave me notes there, either tacked to the cork board or written on the marker board. Then I added their events to the calendar I kept on my computer, where it was easily updated. I would print out a new copy of the month's activities every time something was added and post it on Grand Central.

At least that's how it was supposed to work.

After one memorable failure of the system, I called a family meeting to announce that I was tired of being told at the last minute that someone had an event that night and we all needed to be there. Or that they had forgotten to tell me about an appointment or a meeting or something that required a parent's signature—*right now.*

"That stuff drives me crazy," I said. "So remember: if there is something important I should know about, *put it in writing* and leave it at Grand Central. You've gotta give me some advance warning. Got it? If it's something I need to know, put it in writing!"

Later that night, when the house was quiet, I happened to walk by Grand Central and saw a tiny piece of paper folded into a square and tacked up in the corner. On the outside of it, someone had written, "Mom."

When I unfolded it, this is what I read: "Mom, I love you. Sam."

That's what our youngest son thought I needed to know.

Obviously, having things written out can be very beneficial, not to mention rewarding.

—Sandi Patty

By Faith, in Faith, and Through Faith

My grace is sufficient for you, for My strength is made perfect in weakness.
—2 Corinthians 12:9

When you receive that bad medical report or you are the object of others' abuse or scorn, when your reputation is unfairly slandered or you are confronted with a life-altering disability, you are driven to your knees in weakness and frailty.

You are driven there not only *by* faith but *in* and *through* faith. By faith because you have nowhere else to turn. In faith because you must trust the One who holds your hardships in his hands. And through faith because you are able to rise from your knees and go forth in hope and confidence.

Even though the Lord does not spread before you the blueprint of your life, explaining his plans and purposes, you can still come to him by faith. Begin by dropping to your knees before the cross of Christ and laying all your questions at Jesus' feet. Yield any stiff-necked, stubborn rebellion—call it sin, if you will—that you might have toward him.

It only takes faith the size of a mustard seed to do this. But—hey—give God an inch, and he'll take a mile, encouraging and strengthening you each step of the way.

—Joni Eareckson Tada

August 20

Free to Be Friends

> A friend loves at all times, and a brother is born for adversity.
> —Proverbs 17:17

Freedom is an essential element to friendship. We find ourselves hurt if our friends do things with other people and we're not included. But if we don't encourage them to be free (even of us), there is no real friendship. When we hold on to anything too tightly, it dies. We kill it in the grip of our will.

Learning to let people be free has been hard for me—especially when I was younger and insecure about myself. I was afraid that if I allowed my friends to fly, pursue their own dreams, differ with me in basic tenets, then we couldn't remain friends. I feared they would find somebody they loved more, and I'd be left in the lurch. But I was completely wrong. Actually, the opposite is true. I've learned that when we open our hands, our arms, and our hearts and let freedom ring, those we love will want to be with us—because we don't demand it of them.

When Scripture tells us "a friend loves at all times," we may want that, but the ability to do it has to come from the Lord. The human heart is selfish, prefers its own way, fights being molded by God, and doesn't want to give in when we don't get what is "rightfully ours." We're stubborn, prideful, and strong willed, and these unbecoming characteristics are most starkly revealed in our relationships.

When I think of my closest friendships—those in which I've grown, learned to compromise and negotiate, established boundaries—I notice that in every case they were built on a mutual ability to let each other be free. Free to investigate, explore, or embrace something that did not necessarily appeal to both persons. And I've learned this lesson from my friends—by their tender truthfulness to me.

—Luci Swindoll

God Uses the Least Likely

Jesus said to them, "Have you never read in the Scriptures: 'The stone which the builders rejected has become the chief cornerstone. This was the LORD's doing, and it is marvelous in our eyes'?"

—MATTHEW 21:42

Through the ages, God has delighted in making helpers out of the unlikeliest candidates—people who seem to be the least qualified for the job.

The book of Joshua describes how God used Rahab, a prostitute in Jericho, to help the Israelites during the time of Moses. Rahab had heard the stories of how God had delivered the Israelites out of Pharaoh's hands in Egypt and how God had brought low all those who opposed them. When Israelite spies appeared at her door, Rahab knew Jericho's walls would eventually fall to their God. She hid the spies from her king and helped them secretly escape in order to ensure the survival of her family.

Her obedience to the mighty God of Israel saved Rahab. And this same God took care of her family for generations to come. In the New Testament, she is listed in the lineage of Jesus himself (see Matthew 1).

The book of Hebrews also mentions her act of faith: "By faith the harlot Rahab perished not with them that believed not, when she had received the spies with peace" (11:31 KJV).

God did not look at Rahab as a prostitute or even as a sinner. He simply saw her as someone who recognized who he was and who his people were.

She was just one of the "least likely" whom God drafted into his service. The Bible teems with stories of others.

Do you think you're not qualified to be used by God to fulfill his purposes? Think again!

—Natalie Grant

All Puffed Up and No Place to Go

> Do not boast about tomorrow, for you do not know what a day may bring forth.
>
> —Proverbs 27:1

You've probably seen the puffer fish swim by on the National Geographic channel. He's a fish that, in the presence of a threat, puffs up to make others think he's bigger than he is.

We all have puffer tendencies—a fake-it-until-you-make-it theology: hoity-toity about our kids, snobby over a job promotion, snooty over a new home . . .

In my case, I was puffed up over a little weight loss. I had dropped two pounds and was ready to tell other people what they ought to do to lose weight. I was making my new eating plan a lifelong lifestyle. Yessiree, I was going to eat sensibly forevermore, and I could tell you how to do it too.

But my weight-loss puffer-moment didn't last long. Long story short, it was a lemon-meringue pie a generous conference attendee sent to the green room. To say I flung myself face-first into that sea of delight would not be much of an overstatement.

The pie incident slung open the doors of my appetite, and over the next four weeks, I ate wildly, finding the two pounds I'd lost plus three more to keep them company.

The Message puts Proverbs' instruction this way: "Don't brashly announce what you're going to do tomorrow; you don't know the first thing about tomorrow" (27:1). It turns out only puffer fish can exaggerate accomplishments without consequences.

—Patsy Clairmont

Nothing Goes to Waste

> I will instruct you and teach you in the way you should go; I will guide you with My eye.
>
> —Psalm 32:8

When I married Ken in 1961, I thought I was embarking on a random journey to a destination of its own determination. In the years since then, I've learned that my life is *not* a random trail. There is nothing random about any aspect of my life, and I'm not in charge of its destination. God is. He is sovereign, not random. Therefore, my life path is sovereignly superintended by a loving God.

Some of you may be in a marriage that does not feel like the "best path." You wonder how you can possibly believe God had anything to do with that path because everything on it feels so wrong. I encourage you to be aware of the ways in which God is guiding you to places and persons who can come alongside you and help. That help may come from a friend, a pastor, marriage counseling, or all three.

I've also learned my greatest spiritual growth has sprung from my deepest human pain. Nothing in our lives goes to waste. All experiences, even a marital calamity, will ultimately work together for our good.

I've also learned to be patient about not knowing what God knows. I have to trust him to take care of what I can't see and ultimately make sense of what I do see.

Your marriage may not make sense to you right now. Do what you can and trust God's way, which is to work out his plans for your life. His faithful love endures forever (see Psalm 138:8).

—Marilyn Meberg

August 24

Layers of False Protection Beneath the Layers

> I bow my knees to the Father of our Lord Jesus Christ . . . that He would grant you, according to the riches of His glory, to be strengthened with might through His Spirit in the inner man, that Christ may dwell in your hearts through faith.
> —Ephesians 3:14–17

When something profoundly hurts us—something we may not even remember fully as adults yet can't quite forget—we may build up layers of physical or emotional protection to keep us from getting hurt again.

The hurt may be caused by something small, like an obnoxious schoolmate loudly scoffing at the holes in our shoes or our poor grade on the math test. Or it can be something big, such as abandonment, physical injury, or sexual abuse. Whatever hurts us can cause us to pull on layers that we hope, consciously or subconsciously, will protect us or keep the hurt from happening again. These layers may be visible in our physical bodies (like layers of fat or fingernails bitten to the quick). Or they may exist as outward behaviors (like layers of compulsiveness or unprovoked anger) that push others away from us. We may add layers to protect ourselves from other kinds of situations or scenarios or secrets we've hidden even from ourselves.

Maybe you're carrying layers of fear, hiding the false belief that you're not good enough, smart enough, slim enough, or interesting enough. Whatever layers are weighing you down, my prayer is that God will deal with you the same way he's dealing with me. Tenderly, graciously, lovingly, he's helping me peel those layers away to find and celebrate the original me he created.

—Sandi Patty

Embracing Grace

The grace of our Lord Jesus Christ be with you.
—ROMANS 16:20

In *The Message* paraphrase of Galatians 4, the apostle Paul's teaching presents the law as being like a tutor when we are children. It tells us what to do and what not to do. It keeps us safe from harm. But when we grow up and act like dearly beloved children of God, we follow him from our hearts because we love him, or even more truthfully, because he first loved us.

We know we are safe because we are close to our Father—he is within us. This is the difference between living from the inside out of love and living from the outside out of fear. Paul says in 1 Corinthians 13:11, "When I was a child I talked like a child, I thought like a child, I reasoned like a child. When I became a man, I put the ways of childhood behind me" (NIV).

I am learning that the Bible actually says that we are to let go of the law and embrace grace or, better yet, be embraced by grace. Of course, my first thought upon realizing what this meant was, "Yeah, but then what's going to keep me from sinning?"

Maybe not sinning isn't the primary goal. Maybe staying close to the Father is the goal.

You see, it's all upside down. I thought if I didn't sin then I would stay close to my Father. Instead, it's the other way around! If I stay close to the Father, I'm less likely to sin.

If you really want to be confused, then join me as I ponder the truth that if I'm really, really close to the Father—as in "Christ is in me"—then he sees me as if I haven't ever sinned and never will. Talk about risky freedom and dangerous grace!

—Lisa Whelchel

August 26

Remorse as Clear as Day

> When Saul had come to Jerusalem, he tried to join the disciples; but they were all afraid of him, and did not believe that he was a disciple.
>
> —Acts 9:26

One of the greatest saints of Christian history began as one of its greatest persecutors—Saul of Tarsus, who became Paul the apostle. Acts 8:3 says Saul "made havoc of the church . . . dragging off men and women, committing them to prison." It was Saul's committed intent to destroy the church.

Saul had no idea he was about to be knocked from his horse by the blinding light of the living Christ, but that's what happened. One day on the way to Damascus, he heard a voice saying, "Saul, Saul, why are you persecuting Me?" (9:4).

Saul was greatly confounded. He asked, "Who are You, Lord?" Saul knew this had to be a message from God, but God's question made no sense. As far as Saul was concerned, he wasn't persecuting God but rather was defending true Judaism.

Then the voice answered, "I am Jesus, whom you are persecuting" (Acts 9:5). Can you even begin to imagine the shock? Saul had just been told Jesus Christ really was the Messiah and he, Saul, was destroying Jesus' people. After his conversion, Saul had to come face-to-face with those whose families he had devastated through his actions. How could they forgive such a grievous wound? It had to be a huge hurdle to embrace this man, known for his hatred and cruelty against Christians, as a brother.

But a brother in Christ he was. And Saul—now named Paul—went on to become a great leader and hero of the early church. The passion that had once led him to persecute now led him to love.

—Sheila Walsh

What Have You Done with God?

While Samuel was lying down . . . the LORD called Samuel. And he answered, "Here I am!" . . . Now the LORD came and stood and called . . . "Samuel! Samuel!" And Samuel answered, "Speak, for your servant hears."

—1 SAMUEL 3:3–4, 10–11

Two little boys, ages eight and ten, were always getting into trouble. If any mischief occurred in their town, everyone assumed the two boys were probably involved.

The boys' mother heard about a preacher in town who had been successful in disciplining children. She asked if he would speak with her boys. He agreed but insisted he see them individually. The agreement was that he would see the eight-year-old in the morning and the older boy in the afternoon.

The preacher, a huge man with a deep booming voice, sat the younger boy down and sternly asked, "Do you know where God is, son?" The boy's mouth dropped open; he stared silently at the preacher with a look of wide-eyed terror. The preacher repeated the question in an even louder voice, "Where is God?" Still the boy did not answer.

The preacher raised his voice even more, shook his finger in the boy's face, and bellowed, "Where is God?"

With that, the boy bolted out of the room, ran home, and dove into his closet, slamming the door behind him. His older brother, after finding him, asked, "What happened?"

The little boy, gasping for breath, said, "We are really in big trouble this time. God is missing, and they think we did it!"

I hope that today, and every day, God is fully present in your life—and never goes missing.

—Marilyn Meberg

August 28

Who Packed *Your* Suitcase?

> You do not know what will happen tomorrow. For what is your life? It is even a vapor that appears for a little time and then vanishes away.
>
> —James 4:14

My husband was a stunned participant in a little adventure of mine. I kidnapped him from his job, and I had packed a suitcase for him that awaited in the car's trunk. Everything in his luggage was new and unknown to him, so when we arrived at our destination, he was surprised by the case's contents. He couldn't have guessed beyond a general theme what was inside. The details were revealed upon the arrival.

The same is true for us. We don't know until a day is unpacked how it will look. None of us could have foreseen the tragedy of 9/11, or that a fierce storm could hit our rich country and that we would not immediately be there for the victims, or that our investments would be wiped out, or that banks would close, or that young people across our land would riddle their classmates with revenge in the form of bullets. Who knew? Not us.

All the more reason to pack our lives full to bursting with the One who flung the stars across the sky at creation's dawn and who holds all of our tomorrows in his hands.

—Patsy Clairmont

Uncovering the Person God Created

Put on the whole armor of God, that you may be able to stand against the wiles of the devil.

—Ephesians 6:11

We all have layers that we hide behind at one time or another. They may feel imprisoning—or protective. They may start out as something good and turn into something bad. Or we may decide they're something that's always bad—and then find out they're sometimes necessary for emotional or even physical survival.

The thing about layers is we need to recognize them for what they are and learn that we can *choose* how we deal with them. Some of them need to be done away with entirely. Others, like those described in Ephesians 6:11, are needed to protect us when we're genuinely threatened by physical, emotional, or spiritual harm.

The important thing, though, is that *nothing* should stand between us and the God who created us. To enjoy his richest blessings for our lives, we must come to him constantly as our real selves, even when it's not what *we* consider pretty.

It's certainly nothing to brag about, but I know all about layers from personal experience. They were created through my many failures over the years. But God unwrapped the *real* person he created me to be. He can do the same for you.

Once you discover the wonderful creation he created *you* to be, I think you'll also realize that the layer all of us need most is the wonderful gift of His grace. That grace means he wraps our vulnerable, failure-prone selves in his eternal love and promises to forgive us, no matter how many layers of sin and mistakes we try to cling to.

—Sandi Patty

Stop and Fly a Kite

> I know that nothing is better for them than to rejoice, and to do good in their lives, and also that every man should eat and drink and enjoy the good of all his labor—it is the gift of God.
>
> —Ecclesiastes 3:12–13

Some people never stop. They are busy all the time. I'm one of those people. I was born that way as far as I know, and I'm constantly looking for the cure.

My friend Luci Swindoll has been good medicine for me in that regard. Many years ago she stepped in at just the right time to do just the right thing. I was working away in my office like a little beaver, deep into a job that felt like it would never end, and somewhat overwhelmed by the magnitude of it all.

As I was sitting at my desk, Luci phoned to say hello. I responded with words that included: too much to do, too little time, too overwhelming. I remember Luci's response exactly: "You need a break. Let's go fly a kite."

I protested, but before long she arrived at my office with a kite. We drove up the mountain, and she taught me how to fly a kite. It had never occurred to me that it would be good medicine for my soul.

The fresh mountain air, the laughter, the sheer fun of seeing that kite blowing freely in the wind were exactly what I needed not only to give myself a little break but also to refresh my spirit. And when I got back to my project, it was a breeze. I felt like the kite.

And I remembered, God has given us all things to enjoy. All we have to do is remember to take the time. Or to be sure we have someone in our circle of friends who helps us remember—and knows how to fly a kite.

—Mary Graham

Stepping into the Unknown by Faith

I will give you a wise and discerning heart, so that there will never have been anyone like you.

—1 KINGS 3:12 NIV

It's strange, because with the gift of years, I always thought I'd be slowing down somewhat due to aging. But instead, the momentum of my life has seemingly picked up, and the rewards of God's grace have been almost mind-boggling at times.

He is giving me more and more capacity to have an even richer life in my seventies. Who knew that would happen? I stepped into the unknown by faith, and he blessed and honored that step in a million ways.

When I take time to look carefully at my life, I often think of 1 Corinthians 2:9: "No one's ever seen or heard anything like this, never so much as imagined anything quite like it—what God has arranged for those who love him" (MSG).

And here's the best part—God will do the same for anyone. He'll do it for you. I grew up wanting a big, huge, wonderful life. But what I didn't realize was that my dream was small compared to the one God had for me. His avenues of discovery were so much greater than I could have imagined. I took a baby step, trusting God to open doors for me, only to discover that my tiny imagination was the tip of the iceberg compared to what he had planned.

His dream continues to unfold, while I stand around being amazed! And when I thought it couldn't get any better than this, it did, and it does. The unfolding of his dream is not because of me and what I do; it's totally because of him and what he does.

It's because of who he is.

—Luci Swindoll

September 1

The Blessing of a Good Fit

> Let the words of my mouth and the meditation of my heart be acceptable in Your sight, O LORD, my strength and my Redeemer.
>
> —PSALM 19:14

How many times, in an attempt to describe something to someone, have you tried to define the item by comparing it to something you and the listener both knew? Perhaps you were describing a color: "The orange is like pumpkins in the fall." Or you might explain how the mother of the neighbor children is like a roaring lion. Or you might emphasize that the latest jab from your mother-in-law is like . . . well, never mind. You get the idea.

The "proverbist" (yes, I made up that word) used *is like* to help us grasp the value attached to a well-placed word, as well as to enlarge our definition.

Is like is a window to help us gain a clearer view.

Is like helps us see what we are hearing.

Is like is morning sunlight filling a shadowed corner.

So here it comes . . . "A word fitly spoken is like apples of gold in settings of silver" (Proverbs 25:11).

What a picturesque scene that paints! Imagine yourself entering a room and finding a splendid, golden gleam and a sterling glimmer coming from golden apples and silver settings that are yours. All yours; you get to take them home.

That's how we can show care and affection for others, by choosing to use words that gleam with love, sparkle with authenticity, and shimmer with truth long after the conversation is over. Oh, Lord, give us such words to share!

—Patsy Clairmont

Everyday Prayers

Though your sins are like scarlet, they shall be as white as snow.
—Isaiah 1:18

I love using everyday tasks and sights to remind me to pray for specific people, things, and issues throughout the day. Maybe these ideas will help you find ways to enrich your prayer life too.

While sorting laundry, ask the Lord to sort out your life, showing you areas that need to be reprioritized, changed, or thrown away.

When adding the softener (or dryer sheets), ask the Lord to soften your heart and give you a teachable spirit.

While folding the laundry, pray for the person whose clothes you are folding. For instance, integrity for your husband, protection and purity for your children.

While cleaning the family room, pray for harmony among family members.

While working in the kitchen, thank God for daily bread.

While cleaning bedrooms, pray for sweet sleep, good study habits for your children, and unity in your marriage.

Pray for our country's leaders every time you see an American flag.

Pray for the lost. Since my children were tiny, whenever we found a penny on the ground, we would pick it up and pray specifically for someone to receive salvation.

Remember to pray. A simple prayer reminder is to pray for your children, one by one, any time you see a digital clock displaying the same number, for instance, when you see 1:11, 2:22, 3:33, and so on. It's amazing how many times the Lord has used this to prompt me to pray for my children.

—Lisa Whelchel

September 3

Gifts That Money Can't Buy

> Receiving a gift is like getting a rare gemstone; any way you look at it, you see beauty refracted.
>
> —Proverbs 17:8 MSG

A few years ago, I decided to count all the projects I have around the house that could be built with existing materials. I asked myself how long I could stay home without having to buy anything—anything at all—to add to what I had on hand, and it turned out to be seven years. That is pack-ratting to the max!

All my life I've bought the makings for hobbies, crafts, baskets, birdhouses, jewelry, models, and books like most women buy salad greens. And this doesn't count the number of things I'd like to make from apple crates, pinecones, Popsicle sticks, wine corks, watercolors, mosaics, and old furniture.

Several years ago a friend was unwrapping a gift I had given her as she said over and over, "I hope this is handmade. Is it handmade?"

Knowing I hadn't made it and fearing she would be disappointed, I finally asked, "What if it isn't handmade? What'll happen then? Will you keep it anyway?"

She looked me straight in the face and said in all seriousness, "I'll give you another chance."

I thought that was hilarious, but it stuck with me. It made me wish I had made the gift, and it also made me realize how much people love handmade gifts. Because when you give them that gift you're not only giving them the object, you're giving them something money can't buy—your time and creativity.

The joy of taking the time, doing things carefully, making something with our hands to give to someone else—even if it's nothing more than a greeting card or a delicious meal—evokes a thrill in us that's hard to describe.

—Luci Swindoll

The Overcoming Power of Jesus

These things I have spoken to you, that in Me you may have peace. In the world you will have tribulation; but be of good cheer, I have overcome the world.
—John 16:33

Children grow emotionally when they see parents managing their own emotions. This is especially true during divorce. Parents who serve as models of survivor behavior let their kids see the value of grieving and managing the pain, and then learning that joy truly can come in the morning. God ultimately provides that joy and invites us to remember that his ear is ever inclined toward our voices.

Life hurts and disappoints us. Jesus said that we would have trials and sorrows but by believing in his power to "overcome the world," we could have peace and "good cheer." Certainly divorce, when it occurs, is a trial that produces sorrow for parents and kids. Jesus offers us hope by saying he overcame not only the sorrow of divorce but all earthly sorrow. Not that we won't experience it, but that we need not be defeated by it.

Jesus is the Overcomer, and he lives within us. That means we, too, are overcomers. There is then power for our personal healing and power for the healing of our kids.

No amount of psychology can do what God intends to do in the lives of his beloved. He uses and blesses psychology, divorce recovery workshops, books, and sincere efforts to make wise decisions. But in the end, our survival and victory are enabled by the indwelling Jesus who has "overcome the world."

—Marilyn Meberg

September 5

Getting Acquainted with the Real You

> Seek first the kingdom of God and His righteousness, and all these things shall be added to you.
> —Matthew 6:33

The more we get reacquainted with the original person God created us to be, the easier it gets to see through the destructive layers we've created that prevent us from living the abundantly rewarding life he wants us to have. He told us that in Matthew 6:33.

I realize now that's where I must begin as I begin to peel away those destructive layers—to seek him first and foremost. Then the other things will fall into place.

I desire to know Christ. I *want* to know Christ. I want to know him the way the apostle Paul did when he wrote to the Philippians, "I gave up all that inferior stuff so I could know Christ personally, experience his resurrection power, be a partner in his suffering, and go all the way with him to death itself" (3:10 MSG).

If I begin there, partnering with Jesus, knowing him personally, and constantly keeping my eye on that goal, then everything else makes more sense. It is the cornerstone of who I am; it is the very foundation upon which everything else lies. If I *don't* begin there, with Christ, the rest of my world makes no sense.

It is a daily, sometimes hourly, decision, desire, and choice to say, "I seek you *first* today, Lord." It is a version of what Jesus himself prayed: "This is the real and eternal life: That they know you, the one and only true God, and Jesus Christ, whom you sent" (John 17:3 MSG).

—Sandi Patty

Saved by the Friends' Truth

Lord, who may abide in Your tabernacle? . . . He who does not backbite with his tongue, nor does evil to his neighbor, nor does he take up a reproach against his friend.

—Psalm 15:1, 3

I believe I'll always have times that I behave badly because I don't get my way, and I'll have to fight against acting like the jerk I really am. I'll have to count to ten and unload my gun at the foot of the cross. Otherwise, who'll be able to stand being around me?

For me, one of the hardest things is being told what to do. How I should change. That I should get over it, grow up, back off, or just shut up. Truth hurts. But there's a way to dispense it that is acceptable—and biblical.

"As iron sharpens iron, so one person sharpens another," says Proverbs 27:17 (NIV). What a great verse. It came to mind not long ago when I was sharpening a knife in the kitchen. I'd been trying to slice a tomato and had almost hacked the thing to mush. Finally, it hit my numb skull that the knife needed a good sharpening. Duh. I took out a whetstone and had at it. In no time it was a razor, slicing that tomato beautifully.

That's friendship whetted by truth. Without a willingness to recognize our own shortcomings, to value correction, or to set about changing and growing up, friendship will simply die. Of dullness! It will have no value.

I don't know where I would be today if my friends hadn't loved me enough to point out inappropriate things in me that needed attention. If we're not willing to rely on the love, honesty, and caring of our friends and loved ones to "sharpen" us, we'll wind up a menace to the human race. And we'll drive ourselves into a corner of loneliness because no one will want to be with us unless they're planning to kill us. Trust me on this!

—Luci Swindoll

September 7

Meeting Christ in the Darkness

> He has not dealt with us according to our sins, nor punished us according to our iniquities. . . . As far as the east is from the west, so far has He removed our transgressions from us.
>
> —Psalm 103:10–12

I believe when we have been deeply wounded by someone—including someone who is not remotely remorseful—forgiveness is the salve that heals us. We don't even need to voice it to the person. It can be a transaction between God and us.

When I spoke to a group of inmates at a women's prison, one of them gave me a letter that told her story about the terrible sexual and physical abuse she had endured. She concluded by saying, "God took me to a prison to set me free."

Many times I've used that same phrase when explaining what a gift my voluntary one-month stay in a psychiatric hospital was for me. In a place of confinement, I had to stop running and throw myself into the arms of God's love. To hear a dear sister, scarred physically and emotionally, describe her journey in the same ten words was beyond humbling.

And yet just as I met the risen Christ in the midst of my darkest night, so did she. Some of the people who wounded her are gone from this earth. Some refuse to acknowledge their guilt. But she is no longer a slave to any of them. Even as Christ forgave her for her sins, she forgave those who had sinned against her. And because of that she has been set free—healed from the most brutal of wounds.

I will always remember her face. Although it was lined around the eyes, there was a quiet beauty and calm there. It was the lightness of one whose wings had been broken but who now soars again.

—Sheila Walsh

Grace and the Body

We believe that through the grace of the Lord Jesus Christ we shall be saved.
—Acts 15:11

For a long time, God's gift of grace felt too good to be true. I was afraid to trust it. On the other hand, I felt comfortable with the law. It felt less risky than grace. Just tell me what to do so I can do it right and earn love and acceptance.

Grace felt all backward to me: tell me what to do so I can do it wrong and realize I can't earn love but can accept it.

Don't get me wrong, the law does work. At the beginning of my quest to seek out friendship and faith, I wrote to a friend, "I feel like I am having a Damascus Road experience. This feels more like being born again than when, as a little girl, I took that first leap of faith and first trusted Christ as my Savior. I feel like all the right and good things I have done in my life have been blessed because God's ways work. Obedience works! But it is nothing compared to the blessing of knowing Jesus through his suffering and grace!"

When I'm honest, I have to admit that I'm afraid, if I let go of the law, I might fall. To me, transitioning from law to grace is terrifying. There is that point in the middle when I wonder if grace is really true, and, if not, I think that could mean certain death.

Grace requires such radical trust, and trust is almost impossible if most of your experiences have been of others letting you go or letting you down.

It all comes back to the truth that growth and healing happen within the context of relationship. *We* are the body of Christ, and we will most often experience his love through the hands and heart of his body.

—Lisa Whelchel

September 9

Standing on God's Promises

> For He Himself has said, "I will never leave you nor forsake you."
> —HEBREWS 13:5

Yesterday my niece and her husband dropped by my house for a visit. In tow were her four small children (three boys and a little girl, Kaylee). My little cockapoo, Bailey, doesn't love having four small children in his space, but neither does he mind it.

The boys love Bailey—they have him perform little tricks we've taught him and reward him with little treats, both acceptable and forbidden. But Kaylee is scared to death of Bailey for no reason that any of us can imagine. Although Kaylee is a big talker at five years old, she cannot put words around her fear of the dog. Bailey is innocent of any wrongdoing, and she has never been attacked or frightened by another dog. For some unknown reason, she's dreadfully afraid of dogs. As a result, she enjoys none of the benefits of a soft, sweet, furry creature who finds licking your face while wagging his tail his greatest delight.

It reminds me of myself. There are so many truly frightful things in the world, and few of them scare me. At all. But the imaginary fears? I fear losing my mind, or my way, or my place in someone else's life. I fear running out of, low on, or away from anything I need. I fear feeling alone, lost, or afraid. And, like Kaylee with Bailey, I have absolutely no reason to fear anything. Not one thing needs to frighten me.

If I can only remember to stand on the promises of God. He will never leave me or forsake me. He will be with me. Always. He loves me perfectly. And perfect love casts out fear. I have nothing to fear but fear itself. Neither does Kaylee.

—Mary Graham

Crafting a Conversation of Divinely Appointed Words

I will give you the words I want you to say.
—Isaiah 51:16 NCV

A few years ago I had the delight of having dinner in the home of a well-known personality. I felt like a scullery maid who had slipped in undetected to dine with the queen's court. Her dining room had been transformed into an elegant French café, with multiple tables draped in floor-length tablecloths, the chairs bedecked in fabric and tulle, and stupendous arrangements centered on each table. As you can imagine we, her guests, were thrilled.

But even more impressive than the elaborate setting were our hostess's well-designed words . . . words carefully chosen to honor her guests, to make even scullery maids feel welcome.

We have the opportunity daily to consider the guests who enter our circle of influence—the gal at the cash register, the man at the post office, the kid in our flower beds, the neighbor in our business, the teen in our faces.

We can fashion words to fit each heart that will be easy for the recipient to receive, words that stay with him or her and continue to build equanimity. With God's help, we can choose words that fit each person perfectly.

I can't think of a better way to share the cross of Christ than in a conversation full of divinely appointed words spoken at the precise moment they need to be said.

Let's talk!

—Patsy Clairmont

September 11

We're Beautiful

> He has made everything beautiful in its time. Also He has put eternity in their hearts.
>
> —Ecclesiastes 3:11

I learned a lot of valuable lessons as I worked through the emotional layers I had built up through the years. For one, I know now without a doubt that God thinks I am wonderful. He thinks you're wonderful too. We share that status with all of creation, including the ancient psalmist, who wrote, "I will praise You, for I am fearfully and wonderfully made; marvelous are Your works" (139:14).

When I look in the mirror with Sandi's eyes, I may see a weary woman with a puffy face and droopy flesh. But when I look at my reflection with God's eyes, I recognize myself as one of his works and remember that all his works are wonderful.

So what if I *choose*—ah, there's a powerful word—to be a reflection of his grace and his love, instead of—or in addition to—what I see in the mirror? That's where real beauty resides. Deep inside, I know that to be true. Now I want to *live* it as intensely as I *believe* it.

And then there are those other earthly eyes that find me beautiful, and, oh, what a blessing they are to me. My husband, Don, thinks I'm gorgeous; he has told me so many times over the years—told me so sweetly and sincerely that I fully believe him. When I'm around him, my spirit soars, my confidence skyrockets, and all those ugly imaginary layers just seem to melt away.

I used to think God gave him special eyes to see me that way. Now I'm beginning to believe that not only am I beautiful in Don's eyes, I am beautiful, period!—in a sassy kind of way. So are you, sister!

—Sandi Patty

Building a Foundation on Truth

This is the victory that has overcome the world, even our faith. Who is it that overcomes the world? Only the one who believes that Jesus is the Son of God.

—1 John 5:4–5 NIV

One benefit of growing up in a Christian home was an early exposure to God's Word. I can hardly remember a day when somebody in the family wasn't reading the Bible or talking about it.

The Bible is an amazing volume of work—like no other! In sixty-six books, there is perfect historical continuity from the creation of the world to the new heaven and new earth. Truths constantly unfold, prophecy is fulfilled, and the most perfect Person on earth or in heaven is anticipated, presented, realized, and exalted.

This collection of authors—kings, peasants, philosophers, physicians, fishermen, statesmen, poets, and plowmen—couldn't have known much about each other because they lived in various countries and their writings extended over sixty generations of human history, representing sixteen hundred years—yet the Bible all fits together.

The Book is utterly inexhaustible. It sweeps across the heights of heaven to the depths of hell, tracing the works of God from beginning to end. And the Bible endures. And its truth continues to transform lives.

Although all that is true, it wasn't until I was a young adult that I realized this Book offers a great deal more than just the plan for salvation. It incorporates everything I need to live a meaningful, rich life, and it explains the benefits that are mine simply because I put my faith in Jesus Christ.

—Luci Swindoll

September 13

Being Held by Grace

> Though your sins are like scarlet, they shall be as white as snow; Though they are red like crimson, they shall be as wool.
>
> —Isaiah 1:18

To understand God's grace, we need to see it in the face of another human being. This thought was proven to me one morning when my younger daughter, Clancy, came downstairs and sat on the couch beside me.

I could tell she was upset even before she said, "Mama, you taught me that if we bring sin into the light, that it takes away its power. I can't keep this inside me anymore. I need to get it out."

Clancy proceeded to confess her struggle and failure in an area of her life.

Although she was a teenager at the time, I scooped her up, put her in my lap, and held on tightly. I kissed the top of her head and thanked her for trusting me enough to invite me into her hidden places. I assured her that her imperfection only made me love her more.

She looked at me with tears in her eyes and said, "I think some mothers think they give birth to angels, and then when they mess up they think they are more like fallen angels. I'm glad that you know you gave birth to a human."

That touched my heart deeply. Isn't that what we all want? To be seen, in all our glory, for better or for worse; for the good, the bad, and the ugly—and to still be embraced and kissed and held?

—Lisa Whelchel

Fussing at God

> You've kept track of my every toss and turn through the sleepless nights, each tear entered in your ledger, each ache written in your book.
>
> —Psalm 56:8 msg

I have experienced four major deaths of loved ones, and with each one I have fussed at God. I felt personally betrayed. How could he let them die? He could have prevented it; why didn't he?

Such "fussings" bring no consolation to the soul. But our negative emotions absolutely must be released and vented. If they are not released, they can take up lodging in the body where they're capable of causing such problems as colitis, back pain, headaches, insomnia, digestive complaints, and a host of other ailments.

Healing begins when we understand that God receives our fussing. We see that in how Jesus responded to the emotional venting of Mary and Martha when Jesus was "late" arriving after their call for help as their beloved brother, Lazarus, was dying.

Jesus did not tell them that, because they were behaving badly, they would be punished by joining Lazarus in the family tomb. Instead, he cried with them! There was no judgment; there were tears of empathy.

Empathy provides incredible consolation. When someone actually cries with me, I know she is not only responding to my words expressing my loss, but she is actually feeling my loss, sharing it with me.

The consolation for the soul that has just vented it all to God is the loving, nonjudgmental extension of empathy we see Jesus offering to Mary and Martha. He honored their emotions by not only receiving their accusations but by *feeling* the intense loss of their brother, Lazarus.

—Marilyn Meberg

September 15

Loving Home

> From the place of His dwelling He looks
> On all the inhabitants of the earth.
> —Psalm 33:14

Before I bought the house I'm living in now in Texas, I lived in a 1,547-square-foot condo and loved it. My favorite spot in the house was my walk-in closet that was only forty-two square feet. I took out the bars for hanging clothes, added shelves, painted the whole thing a wonderful Matisse yellow, changed sliding wooden doors into bifold louvered doors, and converted the whole thing into an itsy-bitsy art studio.

All my how-to books were on the shelves. There was a drafting table and chair, a cabinet with cute, narrow drawers—all of which I built. From the ceiling I hung two mobiles. A small toy bear rode along a string on a unicycle from one wall to the other.

One reason I love my home is because I was sixty-one before I owned one. I spent my money on travel. Because I didn't have enough for both, I chose to see the world first. Now, late in life, I own a home that's filled with memorabilia collected from my trips around the world.

The place where I live has my whole life in it, so to speak—artwork, books, music, photographs, furnishings. Everything speaks of the life I dreamed about when I was growing up. Having a little place that reflects my history, character, travels, tastes, and preferences is more important to me than filling it with expensive furnishings chosen by a decorator.

When the world is pulling at me to do more, be more, acquire more, my home says to me, "Enough already. Everything I need is here."

—Luci Swindoll

The Hardest Battle of All

Then Saul arose from the ground, and when his eyes were opened he saw no one. . . . And he was three days without sight, and neither ate nor drank.

—Acts 9:8–9

Most of us find it hard to forgive ourselves. Regret is a brutal taskmaster. We lie in bed at night, beating ourselves up with what-ifs and if-onlys and despising our weak natures.

While I don't think we need to castigate ourselves with unnecessary guilt, I don't think it's always a bad thing when we find it hard to forgive ourselves. I don't think it should be easy. When I have done something to wound another or to offend God, I think it is only appropriate that I should wrestle with that. Grace is free, but it is not cheap. It cost Christ everything. So when I am in need of forgiveness, I should not come skipping in like it's no skin off my back.

We live in a world of quick fixes and instant gratification. But what works well for drive-through restaurants does not serve our spirits well. Jesus told his followers they would know the truth, and the truth would set them free (John 8:32). It is tempting to rush straight to the freedom part and miss out knowing the truth. But if I want to experience true freedom from whatever wrongs I have committed, I need to face what I did and then separate it from who I am.

The only door to true freedom and forgiveness is to face what we did square in the eye and own it to its full extent. Saul was given three days to sit with his sin before his sight was restored.

When we are able by God's grace to face the worst that is true about us, we no longer have to fear what might be exposed at any minute.

—Sheila Walsh

September 17

Learning by Watching Dad

> As a father has compassion on his children, so the LORD has compassion on those who fear him.
> —PSALM 103:13 NIV

Whether for good or bad, watching how our dads live teaches us how to live, how to have relationships, how to love ourselves.

So many of our life accessories—like confidence, contentment and loving others—come from our relationship with dad. But there are no guarantees. Not having a good dad doesn't mean all our relationships are doomed. And having a great dad doesn't mean all our relationships will be perfect. Our dads *are* going to let us down. So why did God design us to need a dad's love if that love is not guaranteed to heal all of life's hurts? Big mistake?

Nope. Perfect plan.

When your earthly father fails you, your heavenly Father finds you. That's how God's plan stands perfect—no matter what kind of dad you have.

Love from a father doesn't *just* include love from a dad who snores on the couch and pays the cell phone bill. Love from a father includes love from one more dad—the perfect Dad.

He's a Dad who will never make a mistake, never leave us. A Dad who is always kind, patient, and loving—and who never breaks a promise. Nothing, and I mean *nothing*, will ever separate us from his love.

Though our earthly dads will impact who we are, it's only our heavenly Dad's love that can *define* who we are. It's only this Dad's love that can make us complete and fill every need in our hearts.

And it's only this Dad's love that can determine whether we see ourselves, others, and God according to the standards of a new kind of beauty—a beauty we may have never known existed.

—Jenna Lucado

God Vacuums Up Our Sin

Blessed is he whose transgression is forgiven, whose sin is covered. . . . I acknowledged my sin to You, and my iniquity I have not hidden. I said, "I will confess my transgressions to the LORD," and You forgave the iniquity of my sin.

—PSALM 32:1, 5

Bill was a wonderful husband but also a talented joy robber. When we were enjoying a rare clear day in Southern California—the smog was gone and the air was crystal clear—I exclaimed, "Oh, Bill, isn't it beautiful! It looks like God has vacuumed the sky."

"Yeah," Bill grumbled, "but he'll probably dump the sweeper bag tomorrow."

Somehow, joy robbers have a tendency to make us feel guilty about focusing on the brighter side of life, as though we're unaware of our past mistakes or the problems that haunt our lives.

When I feel that guilt creeping into my mind again, I remember the guilt-free phrases in Psalm 32:1–5: "Blessed is he whose transgression is forgiven. . . . The LORD does not impute iniquity. . . . You forgave the iniquity of my sin." Reading those verses, it feels like God has vacuumed up my mistakes—and they're gone forever!

—Barbara Johnson

September 19

Winning the Battle

> The mind governed by the flesh is death, but the mind governed by the Spirit is life and peace.
> —ROMANS 8:6 NIV

Even though there will always be a battle between what we know to do and what we prefer to do, there *are* ways to have a full, meaningful, adventuresome, rich life and—trust me on this—lots of fun. It lies in overcoming the addiction of doing only what feels good.

Proverbs 14:12–13 says, "There is a way that appears to be right, but in the end it leads to death. Even in laughter the heart may ache, and rejoicing may end in grief" (NIV). Doing certain things to relieve the agonies of the spirit can feel so right at the time, fulfilling and fun, but when we go that route, there is hell to pay in the end because we have gotten out of sync with God. So here's what I've done in place of the but-it-feels-so-good scenario:

Instead of taking a lover, I've chosen to believe God's love is more satisfying than any other.

Instead of running up debt and hanging with the "right people," I try very hard to rely on the fact that God isn't interested in my image; he's concerned with my heart.

Instead of taking matters into my own hands and telling off the person who hurt me, I wait and let God handle it his way.

Nothing about these choices is easy. Sinful behavior never fully satisfies the heart. There are momentary pleasures, but the end is death—death of a friendship, of one's health, of one's finances, of a romance, of a dream, and ultimately, of the body.

God knows I'm not speaking from some lofty place. I know this from experience. I've had lots of heartache because I, like every human being, have made foolish choices and suffered the consequences.

—Luci Swindoll

Feel It to Heal It

Do you want to be made well?
—John 5:6

Fourteen months passed between my husband Ken's cancer diagnosis and his death. When he quietly went into eternity, I was flooded with peace, knowing he was out of pain. As time went by, I thought I had grieved fully and deeply. But I had not.

Perhaps you've heard the pithy little phrase "You have to feel it to heal it." Late one afternoon, during a walk on the beach, I was suddenly overwhelmed with the feeling that Ken was never coming back. I felt alone, disconnected, and utterly abandoned. The desperation of my feelings poured out with such racking sobs, I shocked myself.

There on the beach I began to experience the truth of that pithy little phrase. I truly had to feel it to heal it.

Feeling my pain so intensely released the buildup of energy that had accumulated over Ken's last fourteen months. I needed to give myself loving permission to take time off and spend some time alone, to journal about my thoughts, and to nestle in the support of a few select friends who harbored me no matter how I expressed my feelings. All of that took time.

Each of us has a different timetable for healing, and it is crucial that we kindly allow ourselves to heal without someone telling us, "You should be feeling better by now."

They don't know. You do.

—Marilyn Meberg

September 21

The Opinion That Counts

> If we love one another, God abides in us, and His love has been perfected in us.
>
> —1 John 4:12

Reading God's Word and absorbing what it says makes me feel better about myself. Sure, I value the positive opinions my husband and my children have about my looks. But beneath all the layers of my life, at the core of my being, the opinion that really matters is God's.

The question is, will I choose to receive what God says about me? After all, it's not what *they* think of me that counts; 1 John 4:12 says it's *his* love and strength that perfect me.

Second Samuel 22:33 reminds us, "It is God who arms me with strength and keeps my way secure" (NIV). When I set my mind on him, he makes me "completely whole" (Isaiah 26:3 MSG).

And the truth is, often people will see the person I am *choosing* to reflect. So if I move through this life feeling unloved, fat, unhealthy, stupid, or whatever, that is how people are going to unconsciously see me. But when I truly choose to reflect the beautiful-and-beloved-princess attitude, people unconsciously see me that way as well.

I have a lot to do with how others see me—and not just what I do to myself (good or bad) physically, but also mentally. Proverbs 23:7 reminds us that what we think, we become.

I need to memorize Psalm 118:23 and repeat it to myself each time I look in the mirror: "This is God's work. We rub our eyes—we can hardly believe it!" (MSG).

—Sandi Patty

Let's Get Real

Let the morning bring me word of your unfailing love,
for I have put my trust in you.
—Psalm 143:8 NIV

When we feel like we must be perfect to live up to the law, it's very tempting to wear a mask and put on a show. When I first learned that the word *hypocrite* originally meant "actor," I was only a tiny bit surprised and offended.

I never thought of myself as a hypocrite until recently. As a matter of fact, I thought I was the opposite. I was trying very hard to practice what I preach. The irony was, in order not to be thought of as a hypocrite, I often pretended to be someone I wasn't—someone who didn't have problems and struggles, stinky attitudes, and sinful inclinations.

It wasn't until more recently, as I have begun learning about grace in friendships and transferring that experience to the Lord, that I found the freedom to be not so perfect, to take off the mask. Again, I have only really learned through friendship how to let this truth make its way down from my head to my heart.

Would you rather have a friend who is imperfect but real, or would you rather be in relationship with a perfect robot? Most of us want to live authentically, but the reality is more daunting than the proposition. It takes practice, trial and error, making mistakes and learning from them.

This is where we need to have safe people in our lives, people with whom we can be honest and truthful. We want friends we can call and tell, "This is how I'm really feeling; this is the way it really is; this is who I really am." We want friends who will accept us, just like that: all that we are, the good, the bad, the little bit of both. Each of us craves that.

—Lisa Whelchel

September 23

Fly Away

> How precious is Your lovingkindness, O God! Therefore the children of men put their trust under the shadow of Your wings.
>
> —Psalm 36:7–8

God's gift of forgiveness means we don't have to be perfect. We can be comfortable with ourselves, the good and the bad.

I am convinced that forgiveness is the triumph of the believer over the reality that we live on a fallen planet. It is a powerful weapon that overcomes the evil in this world and brings healing to our wounded souls—but we must reach out and accept it. To say that we don't deserve to be forgiven is to make our sin more powerful than the blood of Christ. If God forgives us, then we must forgive ourselves.

When we refuse, we have made the court of our opinion or the opinion of others more powerful than the court of an all-knowing and all-powerful God. It must be a serious wound to the heart of our Father when we will not accept the gift he has given us, because it cost him so dearly. You were bought with a price, dear sister. Every sin was covered by the lifeblood of the Lamb. To refuse such an offering is a pride that must be laid at the foot of the cross.

Accepting forgiveness with a humble heart does not mean that the marks will disappear. The marks will still be there, but I think they can be seen as gifts when we view them as reminders of the grace and mercy of God to us. Our wings may bear a few scars or broken feathers, but by God's grace and freedom, we will fly.

—Sheila Walsh

The Power of Being Vulnerable

Greater is he that is in you, than he that is in the world.
—1 JOHN 4:4 KJV

Sometimes when I'm signing autographs at my book table at a Women of Faith conference, I look up at the line of women waiting to talk to me or to get my autograph, and I feel totally guilt-ridden and incredulous, amazed that anyone would wait in line for *me*.

All those years ago, when I'd made such a huge mess of my life, it was hard to imagine that anyone outside my closest friends and family would ever want to have anything to do with me again. And yet they come, and I'm humbled and amazed that they do.

Inevitably, I look up, and there stands a woman in tears. I sense what she's going to say: "Sandi, I've made such a mess of my life."

It takes a lot of courage to let a stranger peek through your layers of guilt and shame to share something so personal. But broken people like us do it so we can reassure each other, "You're not the only one. You're not alone."

Usually I only have a few seconds, but I want that hurting woman to feel heard and understood. I want her to know she's taken an important first step: she's shared her dark secret.

That's not the time to suddenly start spouting Scripture verses. That can come later when she feels strong enough to work through her guilt with her God and her family and her church. You can't fix broken people with a hammer when what they need is a kind touch and tenderness. It has to be their choice.

And it often starts, I've learned, when they are willing to be a little vulnerable. I've been vulnerable, too, by sharing the worst things about myself. So that's what they tell me in the signing line.

—Sandi Patty

September 25

Seeking Safety

> Whatever is born of God overcomes the world. And this is the victory that has overcome the world—our faith. Who is he who overcomes the world, but he who believes that Jesus is the Son of God?
>
> —1 John 5:4–5

William Palmer, an eighteenth-century man, was hanged for poisoning his best friend. As he stepped out on the shaky trapdoor of the gallows, he looked nervously at the executioner and asked, "Are you sure it's safe?"

The irony of this question is not lost on us, but neither is the universal fear the question implies. We know death is inevitable. But is death safe?

Most people would feel safer staying on earth. It's not a perfect place, but it is at least a known place. What we can know, see, and feel is at least familiar. Change is unsettling to most people. The most unsettling change we experience in life is death: the death of those we love and the death we know will be ours.

As death brings unwanted change, it also brings unwanted emotions. More often than not, those emotions don't feel safe. They cause us to feel out of control and without foundational security. Death causes us to lose our moorings and sets us adrift on a frightening sea of unfamiliarity.

God provides the ultimate consolation when death changes our lives. He defeated death on the cross and offers each of us eternal life in heaven—victory beyond the grave.

Is death safe? We can say that death can feel very unsafe. But what *is* safe is the God-assured promise of the celebration that is ours the moment we are reunited with those we love in a gloriously secure and perfect heaven.

—Marilyn Meberg

I've Apparently Sprung a Leak

They may forget, yet I will not forget you. See, I have inscribed you on the palms of My hands.

—Isaiah 49:15–16

Lately my birthdays seem to be on spin cycle. At the rate they're being slung at me, I'm surprised the icing stays on my cakes. I would like to stay mentally aligned and physically upright for as long as possible, but here's my concern: leakage. Brain cell seepage. I'm, at times, mentally suspect . . . even to myself.

Here's why I think this may be happening. These days when I'm traveling, I'm carrying a large, orange-yellow purse that can be seen from Detroit to Dallas. I call her Bertha. She's approximately one-third my height, and takes considerable strength to lift. When she's slung over my shoulder, I can give the appearance that I'm leaning toward Georgia. I've always loved the South.

Because of all my travel, I need many items, which I have tucked into the folds of Bertha's belly. While I know I've placed them in there, when I actually need an item, finding it becomes a struggle, as well as a mental health issue.

Often, in frustration, I vigorously dump the entire contents onto the airport seat next to me, aware that I'm being watched by nearby passengers waiting to board our flight. Then as I stare down at all my personal litter, I have a revelation: I no longer have any idea what I'm searching for. Zip. Nada.

That's why I'm starting to suspect brain leakage. Well, at least it's one of the reasons. There are others. But right now I can't quite seem to remember them.

—Patsy Clairmont

September 27

Friendship Adventure

> Let us therefore come boldly to the throne of grace, that we may obtain mercy and find grace to help in time of need.
> —Hebrews 4:16

I am on a journey to learn how to connect on an intimate level, to develop authentic friendships, and to learn what it means to be a safe person. Maybe being on a journey means there is always more road ahead; maybe what looks like the destination is simply another corner to turn.

This adventure in friendship has included many bumps in the road. Thankfully, it has also been marked by a few rough patches being made smooth.

I've learned to value my relationships over productivity. I believe with all my heart that, although we may not be able to measure the invisible worth of investing time in people, there are few endeavors of more eternal significance.

I am finally grasping the love of Christ that passes all understanding. It has worked its way down from a head knowledge to a heart experience that is transforming me.

In fact, I barely recognize myself.

Being "good" is no longer more important to me than being connected—with God, myself, and with others. I can be real, even real ugly and selfish and sinful, and then believe the truth that I am still loved and lovable.

This transition happened for me in the throne room of grace. Whenever I find myself in sin, I walk with confidence to "the throne of grace" mentioned in Hebrews 4:16. I don't cower in fear or shame. I choose to believe that nothing I could ever do could change the way God feels about me. He adores me. He delights in me. Even in the middle of my sin.

God feels the same way about you, his precious daughter.

—Lisa Whelchel

Going the Extra Mile

Whoever compels you to go one mile, go with him two.
—Matthew 5:41

When I first started traveling, I had no extra money. But I so wanted to go that I agreed to do it with a friend, and we worked on the details together, splitting the financial load.

That's when I saved twenty-five dollars a month for five years. There wasn't a month it was easy, because I had to sacrifice in other areas to do it. But when the time came to go, not only did I have enough to make the trip, but I also had enough to financially help the sister of my friend. The three of us made that first trip in 1966, and it set in motion trips I have made on a tight budget all my life.

More than thirty years after that first trip to Europe, I went on a cruise around the coast of South America with three of my closest friends. It was our Christmas vacation. I took along about a hundred wooden children's blocks and, from them, built a tiny Christmas tree for our stateroom on top of the television set. I made the tree the first day I was on the cruise, December 14, and we ogled it for fifteen days.

On Christmas Day, after attending a church service on the ship, we had our own little service in our room at the foot of the tiny tree. We prayed together, thanking God for our years of friendship, that wonderful trip, the goodness of the Lord, and the countless blessings that had come to us from the extension of his gracious hand. Then we opened gifts amid lots of laughter. No one can take away that memory from us. It's what going the extra mile is all about.

—Luci Swindoll

September 29

Welcome to the Quiet Zone

> Trust God from the bottom of your heart; don't try to figure out everything on your own. Listen for God's voice in everything you do, everywhere you go; he's the one who will keep you on track.
>
> —Proverbs 3:5 MSG

When I exited the elevator on the sixth floor of the hotel, I noticed a small sign near the one that pointed me toward my room. It said, "Welcome to the Sleep Advantage Quiet Zone." The sign went on to share a pledge to restrict housekeeping or maintenance activities to midday hours and also promised that "No children, leisure groups, marching bands, or circus animals would be assigned to this floor." When I reached my room, I promptly called the front desk and asked if it would be possible to be moved to the floor *with* the circus animals. Who would want to miss an opportunity like that?

It seems harder than ever to maintain any sort of Quiet Zone in one's life. From our constant availability to others by phone or e-mail to the constant availability to us of entertainment through movies, television, or the Internet, when are we ever truly quiet? We hear of the voice of God being a still small voice that speaks to us in the silence of our hearts. While I frequently feel like I struggle to hear the voice of God or to be confident of his leading, I also know that I rarely create a quiet zone in which to hear his voice or to feel his presence. Too often, I'd much prefer the action of the circus animals to the silence of my own heart. But I know that it's only in the quiet when I am seeking God with all my heart, sharing my soul with him, and listening for his presence that I am truly available to hear what I so long to know.

—Lori Robertson

Preoccupied by Whom?

Jesus . . . was led by the Spirit into the wilderness, being tempted for forty days by the devil.

—Luke 4:1–2

Jesus was led by the Spirit into the wilderness to be tested by the vicious enemy of his soul. He overcame that temptation.

Every day we struggle to say no to things that trip us up or yes to things we know are right. Why is that? Simply put, we want what we want, and we'd really like it now. It's human nature, and it harkens back to that tasty morsel of fruit in the garden of Eden. Over time and by God's grace, we learn to temper our selfish nature, but some vestige of it still lurks under the surface.

Of course, different things tempt each of us. For some of us (okay, a lot of us) it's food. We crave food when we are happy, when we are sad, and when we can't quite make up our minds what we are. We gorge ourselves again and again until we can't move.

For others, it is relationships. We search for the perfect person who will fill the empty space inside us. We demand a certain ideal and won't settle for anything less, even if it means we might spend a lot of time alone.

For some, it is the temptation to dwell on the past and not move on to all that God has for us. Perhaps we feel that if we move on, we'll be letting go of something that is part of who we are.

Whatever the temptation, the common thread will be the amount of time and energy involved in dealing with it—which is what Satan wants. A person preoccupied with herself is a person not preoccupied with God.

—Sheila Walsh

October 1

Soaking Up Comfort

> You are my hiding place; You shall preserve me from trouble; You shall surround me with songs of deliverance.
> —Psalm 32:7

A loved one's death sets us upon a sea of frightening unfamiliarity. One of the ways we can navigate that sea is by immersing ourselves in Scripture, soaking up comfort such as Psalm 94:19: "In the multitude of my anxieties within me, Your comforts delight my soul."

Those of us who have experienced the death of loved ones know well "the multitude of . . . anxieties." Thankfully, that psalm takes us beyond our anxiety and points us to a solution for our souls: remembering and then pondering deeply the many consolations God provides for his beloved.

We see anxiety turn to consolation as we read of the death of Lazarus in John 11. Divine consolations were lovingly given to the deeply grieving sisters, Mary and Martha.

One of those consolations was that Jesus allowed the sisters to be real with their feelings. When they fussed at Jesus and blamed him for not coming sooner, he did not chastise the sisters for their feelings. He didn't berate them for their lack of faith in him. He simply let them talk. It is interesting Jesus did not become defensive under their accusations or make excuses for delaying his coming to Bethany. He simply asked them to believe in who he was and who he had always been to them.

He asks us to do the same, believing the reassuring promise of Isaiah 25:8: "He will swallow up death forever, and the Lord God will wipe away tears from all faces."

—Marilyn Meberg

Words as an Accessory

He who has knowledge spares his words.
—Proverbs 17:27

I love words. Always have. They are powerful, important, influential, endearing, instructive, inspiring, and tender. But they also have the tainted potential to be devastating, defeating, derogatory, discriminating, demeaning, and divisive.

Being a word lover, I was relieved to find that Proverbs 17:27 doesn't say that knowledge is silent but rather suggests that knowledge is into selectivity and brevity.

This brings to mind a picture of an old man leaning on the steady cane of knowledge; attached to his belt is a small purse. Inside that purse reside his carefully chosen words for the day. He has counted them out, and he holds them close until needed. Note the contrast in size and purpose between the cane and the purse.

I know from experience that the longer I talk, the more likely I am to regret something I say. Hmm. Maybe that's what this verse is about. I'm grateful we aren't being asked to withhold our words; that *would* be a challenge for me! Instead, we're to allow knowledge to support our existence, accessorized by our wisely filled purse.

—Patsy Clairmont

October 3

It's All Part of the Adventure

> I realize that I don't have what it takes. I can will it, but I can't *do* it. . . . The answer, thank God, is that Jesus Christ can and does.
>
> —Romans 7:18, 25 MSG

Life is hard; no doubt about it. But in it there's lots of depth to be explored and growth to be experienced. That's all part of the adventure. For me personally, exploring, knowing, and experiencing start and end with the fact that Jesus loves me. He tells me so. And it is that divine love that transforms the human heart.

I don't always get God's truth exactly right, and sometimes I'm way off, but I do believe a great part of doing life differently is nourished at the well of having built my foundation on solid doctrinal truth. Apart from that, there is too much emotional pain in life for me to keep going, too much remorse to pick up the pieces, too difficult a path ahead to keep trucking down the road.

In the fourth chapter of Ephesians (one of my favorite books), Paul wrote, "We will no longer be infants, tossed back and forth by the waves, and blown here and there by every wind of teaching and by the cunning and craftiness of people in their deceitful scheming. Instead, speaking the truth in love, we will grow to become in every respect the mature body of him who is the head, that is, Christ" (vv. 14–15 NIV).

What a wonderful mouthful of doctrine! Paul says we're strong adults who know how to tenderly speak the truth. Christ is our leader, and because of that we don't ever have to waver in our beliefs. We are secure in him.

—Luci Swindoll

The Healing Power of Being Heard

May the God of patience and comfort grant you to be like-minded toward one another, according to Christ Jesus, that you may with one mind and one mouth glorify the God and Father of our Lord Jesus Christ.

—Romans 15:5–6

The first necessary quality for authentic friendship is opening up the heart and inviting in another person to look around and see the real you. The second quality is being accepted and understood.

Not too long ago, I received a phone call from a friend I grew up with. She asked if we could just drive around and talk. As soon as I hopped in her car, she broke down. "Lisa, I feel like I'm in a prison," she said. "I don't know if I love my husband anymore. I'm screaming at my children all day. I want out, but I don't want to leave."

We pulled over to the side of the road, and I spent the next few minutes sharing with her times when I have felt the same way. I told her stories of when my kids were smaller, my husband was busy at work, and I felt isolated and alone, like the worst wife and mother in the world. I didn't give her any advice or Scripture verses. I simply gave her empathy and understanding. Mostly, I listened.

A few days later, I called just to check in to see how she was doing. Her circumstances hadn't changed, but she was feeling better. Just getting it off her chest and sharing her burden with someone else made her feel lighter and able to journey on.

I think that is one of the things that makes Alcoholics Anonymous successful. They simply share where they are and receive each other as they are. Then they say, "Thank you," and "Next." There is healing power in being heard.

—Lisa Whelchel

October 5

Practicing a Mind-Set of Gratitude

> The LORD is good to those whose hope is in him, to the one who seeks him; it is good to wait quietly for salvation of the LORD.
>
> —LAMENTATIONS 3:25–26 NIV

I have often wondered if Mary, the mother of Jesus, continued to maintain her attitude of gratitude following her powerful song. Her tender response to an unexpected pregnancy expresses an unwavering faith, resolute trust, and deep thanks to God.

I wonder if she continued to choose gratitude during the bewildering and sorrowful moments when her family feared Jesus was crazy (Mark 3:20–21), at the cross, or after the ascension. I suspect she did, because Luke got his account of the details in chapters 1 and 2 of his gospel from *someone,* and a portion of it appears to be information that nobody alive but Mary possessed. Based on historical research, we are told that Elizabeth, Zechariah, and Joseph all had probably died by the time of the crucifixion.

Several times, Luke mentions that Mary treasured and pondered things in her heart. That means some of this information appears to have come from Mary, perhaps indirectly. If so, it seems likely that her song in Luke 1 remained the theme song of her life. It says, in part, "My soul glorifies the Lord and my spirit rejoices in God my Savior, for he has been mindful of the humble state of his servant" (vv. 46–48 NIV).

Choosing gratitude when current circumstances offer no hint that life will eventually turn out okay does not come naturally or easily. But the attitude of Mary—so full of praise and the steadfast confidence that God is at work in ways we cannot see—gives me an example I long to follow.

—Carol Kent

Mothering a Mob

You've given me a staggering task, ruling this mob of people. Yes, give me wisdom and knowledge as I come and go among this people—for who on his own is capable of leading these, your glorious people?

—2 CHRONICLES 1:9–10 MSG

I can empathize with King Solomon as he looked out over his "mob of people" and considered the "staggering task" he'd been given. As the mother of a blended family of eight children, there were times when the task of parenting our "mob" of kids seemed absolutely overwhelming.

No matter how many children you have, parenting can be exhausting. Years ago, I heard an expert on *Oprah* say that raising two children and being a stay-at-home mom is equivalent to *three* full-time jobs.

In bigger families, we parents don't get a lot of "my time" when we can relax and recoup our strength for the next go-round. Someone's always intruding into those precious moments with a runny nose, a forgotten backpack, or a need to talk. But there's a lot of fun to be had in our families, large or small, even in our exhaustion.

To find that fun, we need to ask God for "wisdom and knowledge," as King Solomon did, and we need to keep a positive perspective. Our home is a crazy place, but I love being there. My big, blended family is exhausting, but it's exhilarating too. Somehow I actually seem to thrive amid this strange chaos. Actually, it doesn't happen "somehow."

It happens because I've chosen to find the joy in the midst of mayhem.

—Sandi Patty

October 7

Everything's a Gift

> The devil said to Him, "If You are the Son of God, command this stone to become bread."
>
> —Luke 4:3

In the desert, Satan's temptation of Jesus was real and understandable. Jesus would have been very hungry at the end of forty days without food, and Satan tempted him with something very basic—something we can all understand at gut level.

I think that's significant, if for no other reason than it shows us how sneaky Satan is. Rather than tempt Jesus with something overtly evil like lust or murder, Satan appealed to what would seem innocent, innocuous. We all need food to live, and Satan was just offering a little something to tide Jesus over.

Jesus replied, saying, "It is written, 'Man shall not live on bread alone, but by every word of God'" (Luke 4:4). His response showed an undivided heart. Jesus knew that physical hunger and release are only temporary, but God's plan is eternal.

In a restaurant recently, after my family gave thanks for our food, our waitress said, "It's been a long time since I've seen anyone do that in here." What an interesting comment. It's as if, in our culture, we have separated the physical and the spiritual rather than seeing all of life as a gift from God.

Cravings reveal to us what is true and what is false. How many times have you found yourself thinking, *This is what I really need to feel better about myself.* Whether the "this" is food or a new dress or a new relationship, the gratification of the craving reveals that we were longing for something more, because the satisfaction is so short-lived. Jesus told Satan that bread might satisfy for a moment but, to really live, we need the Word of God.

—Sheila Walsh

Our Perfect Dad

Behold what manner of love the Father has bestowed on us, that we should be called children of God!
—1 John 3:1

God is the best Dad in the world! Getting to know him as our Dad will redefine our look inside and out, making us more and more beautiful. *We* are his beautiful daughters. That's all that matters! That's what God sees when he sees you and me, his beautiful creations!

So we shouldn't let anyone else define who we are or whether or not we are beautiful. The only One worthy of telling us who we are is our perfect Dad.

God knows exactly what each one of us needs to be the person he created us to be, and he wants to provide every essential for that look. Only he can give us what it takes to be truly beautiful.

Not having a good relationship with her parents can be a really difficult thing for a girl to overcome, but thankfully, our God is able to make any relationship good if we let him.

No dad is perfect, but God sets the perfect example for how we should look at our relationships and ourselves. So bring your perfect Dad into the relationship picture. Because, in order for God to make our relationships with boys, friends, and ourselves more beautiful, we have to make sure to chat with him about the relationship that matters the most: us and God.

Remember that he is the first and primary authority in your life who can tell you exactly who you are and where you are going. Who does he say you are? His! And where does he say you are going? Wherever he sends you.

And girl, he's got *big* plans for you (check out Jeremiah 29:11)!

—Jenna Lucado

October 9

God *Will* Find You

> I remind you, my dear children: Your sins are forgiven in Jesus' name.
>
> —1 JOHN 2:12 MSG

God knows where you are. He will find you no matter how far you've fallen, no matter how many layers you try to put between yourself and him. Wherever you are, whatever you've done, if you'll let him, God will wrap you in his amazing grace that vaporizes all the sins you've committed, no matter how many layers you've piled on to keep from exposing your mistakes.

And here's the best part: whether your mistakes are simply stupid or horribly destructive, if you ask him to, he will forgive you and give you another chance to live your earthly life for him—and your eternal life *with* him.

Girlfriend, it just doesn't get any better than that!

The emotional and behavioral layers of guilt and shame that we pull over ourselves, trying to cover our sin, can be difficult to remove. It takes work to strip away the layers so God's grace can do its best work.

Not that God makes it difficult.

All *he* requires is that we ask his forgiveness—and believe that his Son's death and resurrection make that forgiveness possible . . . even when we ask for it again and again.

And Acts 2:38 quotes the apostle Peter's straightforward directions for how to "change your life. Turn to God and be baptized, each of you, in the name of Jesus Christ, so your sins are forgiven. Receive the gift of the Holy Spirit" (MSG).

God made salvation simple and grace readily available. It is we humans who somehow feel the need to layer his plan with cultural complications.

—Sandi Patty

Give Your Friends a Present

I'm speaking as plainly as I can and with great affection. Open up your lives. Live openly and expansively!

—2 Corinthians 6:11–13 msg

It's interesting to me that when we are really gut-honest with people about our frailties and failures, it makes them feel better about themselves.

You know what I'm talking about. Have you ever gone over to a friend's house and her dirty dishes are in the sink, her kids are fighting, and there is a sticky film of syrup on the kitchen table? Doesn't it make you feel all warm and fuzzy about yourself?

What a gift that is! Give your friends a present. Go without makeup. Wear your comfy jeans to lunch. Invite them over and leave your unfolded laundry on the couch. Trust them with your real self. Maybe they will risk doing the same with you.

One of the sweetest gestures a friend ever made toward me was when she vulnerably confessed an insecurity she felt about a friend in her life who hadn't responded to her last few e-mails. She contacted her friend with a very honest e-mail and then asked me to pray for her because she was nervous about how it would be received. I sent her a note that said, "I appreciate being invited into the behind-the-scenes, under-the-surface, into-the-heart, from-the-inside-out perspective of this girlfriend-drama e-mail exchange. I like being your friend. It is a privilege. You are special, and I feel special that I get to be your friend. . . . Thank you for letting me 'know' you, as in being known."

When people think we have no insecurities or faults, it works against connection. Vulnerability creates connection faster than almost anything.

—Lisa Whelchel

October 11

God Always Hears Our Prayers

> Teach us to number our days, that we may gain a heart of wisdom.
> —Psalm 90:12

As he stood amid the mourners outside the tomb of his friend Lazarus, Jesus prayed, "Father, I thank You that You have heard Me. And I know that You always hear Me, but because of the people who are standing by I said this, that they may believe that You sent Me" (John 11:41–42).

Jesus made that statement not only for the bystanders but for us standing beside our lost loved ones. Perhaps we have prayed for an extension of life, and when our loved one dies, many of us wonder if God really heard our prayer.

Jesus said to God, "You always hear Me." We have the same degree of access to the ear of God. God always hears our prayers. So why does God not always do what we ask?

The timing of what our loving, sovereign God does is determined by him alone.

Job 14:5 states, "Our time is limited. You have given us only so many months to live and have set limits we cannot go beyond" (NCV). The same truth is found in Psalm 139:16: "You saw me before I was born. Every day of my life was recorded in your book. Every moment was laid out before a single day had passed" (NLT).

God took control of the earth at the moment of creation. He will forever be in control. That means he determines the time when we are taken from this earth. There is peace in knowing God is in control of even that.

—Marilyn Meberg

A Mind-Boggling Truth

> The mystery in a nutshell is just this: Christ is in you, so therefore you can look forward to sharing in God's glory. It's that simple. That is the substance of our Message.
>
> —Colossians 1:27 msg

Head knowledge alone does not encompass the essence of what life is all about. Knowing truth alone can never make my heart soft.

As a matter of fact, too much data makes me weary. Even if it's all true. Spare me the loquacious person who goes on and on about anything. As much as I love words, I find people like that tedious. Show me the person who can melt my heart, who is tender and sweet, but not given to maudlin sentimentality and hollow drama. I'll follow him or her to the ends of the earth.

So where's the balance between head and heart? The integration of what we think with how we feel affords a rich, authentic spiritual life and ensures meaningful connections with others. But where do we find the formula?

As simplistic as it sounds, we find it in relationship with God. He created us—will, intellect, and emotions. Scripture says we are complete in him.

Throughout the adventure of living, I've experienced his sturdy hand holding me and directing me. He has consistently proven himself faithful, and because of this, I try to look at everything through the lens of his presence in my life.

The apostle Paul said the same thing in Colossians 1:27. When I take that verse at face value and begin to examine what it says in everyday terms, it's mind-boggling to me that Jesus Christ lives in me. What a concept. The fact that he chooses to commingle with me in this way is unfathomable. The truth that I can be integrated and whole in him both challenges and delights me.

—Luci Swindoll

October 13

The Compelling Quality of Calm

> A man of understanding is of a calm spirit.
> —Proverbs 17:27

I'm drawn to calm people. Not vacant, the-light-is-on-but-nobody's-home people. Not the aloof, arrogant types either. I'm drawn, instead, to those who exude settled centeredness. Their insides aren't churning. Their tongues aren't wagging. They aren't fretting, stewing, or clamoring. They are functioning in their gifts and aren't threatened by yours. They are anchored in Christ, and the sea within them is still. I find that kind of steadiness compelling.

Unfortunately, calm isn't innately who I am. My insides have always been skittish, which I'm sure is why I'm drawn to soft music, gentle rain, and quiet spaces. I need the soothing influences they offer, and I've been working on claiming calm more often.

Some time ago, a friend who hadn't seen me for a couple of years sweetly commented that I was much quieter on the inside than she had known me to be in the past.

I remember being so heartened by her assessment because I felt that God was confirming the work he was doing in me. Like sparks from a flint when they catch soft kindling, the flame of Christ's presence and the work of his Spirit were being seen in my life. I was thrilled.

Today I continue to fan that little flame within me. Oh, I've still got plenty to say, and I do suffer bouts of the fidgets now and then. But each morning, I bless, in Christ's name, my day's journey, and that conscious act helps me to move consciously through my day with calmer purpose.

—Patsy Clairmont

Officially Engaged

He died so that he could give the church to himself
like a bride in all her beauty.
—EPHESIANS 5:27 NCV

If I had control of the pen, I would have written my life differently. I would have added a mate to fuss at and snuggle up to and grow old with. I would have inserted children to read to and cook for and defend in the principal's office. I'd have colored in a real family sitting around the table at Thanksgiving instead of a group of dear single and divorced friends.

But I am not the author of my own life; God is. And the older I get, the more convinced I am that he's the perfect storyteller.

If you're like me and you've put your faith in Jesus Christ, you know we can enjoy deep contentment. We can bask and revel in the reality that we have been completely accepted and are totally adored by the Son of God. We can pick the petals off daisies and say dreamily, "He loves me" with the absolute assurance that "He loves me not" will never, ever apply to us again.

We are officially engaged to the King of kings and Lord of lords. We've been bought with the most costly dowry ever paid. And though this season of betrothal is stretching longer than some of us would like, a wedding more wonderful than we can possibly imagine really is right around the corner.

Therefore, may we seek to be content in the already, sighing as we admire the sparkling rock Jesus slid onto our finger, but conscious of the not yet. Satisfied with our salvation but still eagerly awaiting consummation.

—Lisa Harper

October 15

Blessed by the Gift of Hospitality

> There was once a man who threw a great dinner party and invited many. When it was time for dinner, he sent out his servant to the invited guests, saying, "Come on in; the food's on the table."
>
> —Luke 14:16–17 MSG

One of the best gifts my mother gave me was an appreciation for the fun of hospitality and the joy of friendship. She modeled both in every way. She was a people person who loved big gatherings.

As far back as I can remember, Mother had friends and was constantly inviting them to dinner or parties at our house, to meet at church, come over for coffee, go shopping, or (on occasion) come with us on family vacations. She was always gathering up folks who wanted or needed companionship, and she genuinely enjoyed their company.

Friendship is a wonderful thing. I cannot imagine a day going by without talking with my friends. In fact, as I sit here working, trying to put words together in a meaningful way, it would be a lot easier if I were writing an e-mail to one of my friends. I could just say whatever came to mind. Any way I'd want to put it would be fine with them.

In a beautiful essay on friendship, Ralph Waldo Emerson said there are two cornerstones foundational to friendship. One is truth, the other tenderness.

I agree. To love someone, we must know he or she is truthful with us. Love is built on respect and respect on truth. Truth and tenderness must go hand in hand because, if they try to stand alone, one will be too hard and the other too soft.

—Luci Swindoll

The Blessing of Loving Your Enemies

> But love your enemies, do good, and lend, hoping for nothing in return; and your reward will be great, and you will be sons of the Most High. For He is kind to the unthankful and evil.
>
> —Luke 6:35

One thing God asks of us, that comes with a blessing, is that we love our enemies. A strange request, yet I have found him to be true to his word. It happened some years ago in my life, but the results of that obedience have lingered for a lifetime.

My mother-in-law was dying. She never liked anyone who married her sons, but she particularly disliked me. She called me "one of those Jesus people." When her cancer was diagnosed, the Lord spoke to my heart: "Go and care for her." I couldn't have been more shocked. Although I knew a divorce was imminent with her son and me, God was asking me to go and care for her?

Hard, and yet harder still would be saying no to God, so I packed my bags and moved into her home. Gradually God began to knit us together. My mother-in-law's heart began to soften. She began to reach out to me. When I finally had the nerve to say, "What about God?" She answered, "I guess I knew he is there because you are here."

From that moment on God knit us together in love. My mother-in-law accepted Christ into her heart and asked me to read the Bible to her and to sing hymns. What a beautiful time we had in those last weeks. I will never forget how this brilliant businesswoman became a little child as she prepared to meet Jesus.

I am living proof that God blesses those who will love their enemies, and I will never be the same.

—Lana Bateman

October 17

The Slow, Painful Path to Wholeness

> Unlike the culture around you, always dragging you down to its level of immaturity, God brings the best out of you.
> —Romans 12:2 MSG

Several years ago, a friend of mine had a simple little hangnail that became infected with staph.

Even with powerful antibiotics, the infection grew worse. An X-ray revealed that the infection had traveled dangerously near the bone. The doctor referred him to a surgeon who, every day for two weeks, peeled away layer after layer of dead skin to get to the root of the infection so it could be treated at the source.

It was a very painful process, my friend assured me. But without those hurtful daily peelings, the infection could have spread to the bone, perhaps necessitating amputation, or it could have even entered his bloodstream and eventually killed him.

My friend's experience illustrates how deeply buried our hidden feelings can be and how something ridiculously minor and, at first, inconsequential can become a life-threatening danger.

And even after we've peeled back the guilt, shame, selfishness, addiction, jealousy—whatever prevents a wholesome relationship with God—the healing continues. My friend had to continue to go back to the doctor after the last treatment to have the infected site monitored.

There were probably faster ways to bring about healing—amputation, for instance. Obviously that wasn't the best choice, for several reasons. The best option took the most time but brought about complete healing.

It's the same with us as we seek help with removing the layers that shield us from the life God intends for us to have.

—Sandi Patty

Gaining New Insights from Old Thoughts

The works which the Father has given Me to finish—the very works that I do—bear witness of Me, that the Father has sent Me.

—John 5:36

My mental idle typically revs high, but I've calmed down through the years, thanks to Christ's promise that he will complete the work he begins within us. I still tend to be inwardly jiggly, though. The evidence of that came two years ago when tests revealed that I have stomach ulcers. I wasn't prepared to hear that news. After all, I've always considered ulcers, well, unspiritual.

I thought I had walked with Christ too long to be toting around ulcers. What kind of testimony was that? How could I tell others that Christ was the Prince of Peace and then confess that my insides were riddled with sores?

Understanding often comes as we wade through our own thinking. In doing so (again), I discovered new insights in my old thoughts that were keeping me from the deeper calm I desired. Remembering instead that eternity is where and when Jesus finishes up his work within us definitely calms me. I thought I needed to be fixed before I got there, so I kept dragging myself into the workshop, tightening the vise, and hammering away.

But here's the truth: I don't have to strive. Jesus has things under divine control.

—Patsy Clairmont

October 19

The Laughter Within Us

> A merry heart does good, like medicine, but a broken spirit dries the bones.
> —Proverbs 17:22

One of the richest sources of humor lies within us and our experiences. When we take ourselves too seriously, we miss opportunities for a good laugh, and the tension this produces can kill future laughs before they are even born. A good laugh can make us relax, mellow out, and feel refreshed.

If we can laugh occasionally, we can experience a respite from the burdensome cares and pressures of human existence. The pressures may not go away, but we can possibly view them with less tension. When our tension is relieved, we can get back to the serious business that occupies the majority of our time, and we return with a more relaxed spirit.

We frequently hear statements like, "Oh yes, he has a great sense of humor" or "She is so funny—I love to be around her" as if these favored few were unique and set apart by their capacity to create or appreciate humor. On the contrary, I believe we *all* have the capacity for fun and laughter. We do not all have the same abilities in creating humor—we are not all stand-up comics—but we can all laugh.

Many of us, however, need to be released from the bondage of our circumstances and ourselves so that the inherent capacity to laugh, which lives in us all, can bubble to the surface and carry us through those times that produce tension and break our spirits.

—Marilyn Meberg

Honest Friendship

What you say to one another is eternal. I mean this. When two of you get together on anything at all on earth and make a prayer of it, my Father in heaven goes into action.
—Matthew 18:18–19 MSG

Honesty—the gift of having someone who will be honest with you about you—is an essential quality for authentic friendship. One of my long-distance friends helped me see how that kind of honesty can work when she suggested that whenever we get together in the same town, we could continually strengthen our friendship by asking each other three specific questions.

She went first: "One. What do you see in my life that encourages you?"

I responded, "I see you being willing to ask the hard questions of yourself and of life and, ultimately, of God. You don't want to live in a Pollyanna world of denial. You want the truth, the whole truth, and nothing but the truth, so help you, God."

"Okay, two," she ventured. "What do you see in my life that you would caution me about?"

I had to think a long time about that one, but then, in gentle honesty, I said, "When you write in your journal, be as raw and unfiltered as possible. You may eventually end up using your thoughts and reflections in a future book, but don't journal with an end result in mind."

"Good, thanks," she said. "Three, What else would you like to say?"

"Without hesitation," I said, "that I love getting to be your friend on your journey!"

Since this first conversation, we have asked each other these questions a few more times, and—without fail—they have drawn us closer.

—Lisa Whelchel

October 21

Prayer Changes Me

> Therefore humble yourselves under the mighty hand of God, that He may exalt you in due time, casting all your care upon Him, for He cares for you.
> —1 Peter 5:6–7

Prayer has been one of the sweetest adventures of my life. I believe with all my heart that prayer really does change things.

Prayer also changes me. As I praise God, my burdens lift. The burdens themselves may not change, but they're transferred from my shoulders to God's. As I unload my cares on him, I sense his presence and strength. As I confess my sin and wrong attitudes, I know he forgives me.

No matter how heinous or continuous my sin, or how often I bring it to God for forgiveness, he will and does forgive me. I know that in my head, and I experience it in my heart. This kind of prayer helps me have peace afterward.

Sometimes the hurt and pain of the heart are so deep that one can do nothing more than groan or cry out. Fortunately for us, "the Spirit himself intercedes for us through wordless groans" (Romans 8:26 NIV). The primal heart cry of prayer is invaluable. It cleanses us and sustains us and gives us strength to go on.

There is no escaping the undeniable fact that we need an advocate to go before us as well as run with us. Someone who will fight our battles and cheer us on. Someone who will renew us and strengthen us for the next task. This person is the Savior, Jesus Christ, God and man in one person forever. He knows my need, receives my burden, heals my wound, and sends me on my way with his blessing and power. Knowing this, I can experience his love, forgiveness, and solace because he knows my longing heart so intimately.

—Luci Swindoll

Have You Really Met Him?

Our heart shall rejoice in Him, because we have trusted in His holy name.
—Psalm 33:21

Our initial impression of a person can sometimes make or break a relationship. In the same way we judge people by our early impressions, we often do the same with God. What was your initial impression of God?

When someone says, "God," what characteristics come to mind right away? Some people might say, "Scary" because they picture a God who throws balls of fire and punishes anyone who doesn't floss before going to bed or—worse—has doubts, sins, and struggles.

Others may picture an old guy with a beard. He smiles a lot while he sits on a couch of clouds, but that's about it. He's not very active, and he doesn't really care about being involved in a human being's life. At times, I believe in a genie-in-the-bottle God who should give me anything I want. How we picture God may be based on what other people have said or on what we have imagined him to be like. The real issue is, have you ever truly met him?

If you have never really met the one true God, I would love for you to meet him for the very first time. Some of you may have known God for a while. If so, that's great! Others may not have known you could actually meet God at all. That's okay too!

Wherever you are, whoever you are, do me a favor: open your heart to hearing God tell you who he *really* is.

—Jenna Lucado

October 23

Abiding in Jesus

> Abide in Me, and I in you. As the branch cannot bear fruit of itself, unless it abides in the vine, neither can you, unless you abide in Me.
>
> —John 15:4

I believe that, to be the mothers we want to be, we need the power of Jesus working in us and through us. If we want to see the fruit of the Spirit grow in our children's lives, then we must first make sure we are abiding in him, as he tells us in John 15:4.

When I looked up the word *abide* in my Bible software, I discovered that in the original language it had more to do with simply spending time with Jesus, hanging out with him. Well, it didn't exactly say that in the Greek, but that was the basic idea. And what do people do when they hang out together? Well, obviously, lots of things—but the common denominator is *talk*! To get to know someone, to strengthen a relationship, to connect with each other, you talk. That is what prayer is: talking with God.

Many of you mothers with young children at home are surely thinking: *I don't have enough time for my family, my home, myself, my responsibilities, and everything else as it is! How am I going to find more time to abide in Christ*?

Trust me, our heavenly Father understands the seasons of a mother's life. There are times when a quick "I love you, Lord" first thing in the morning, followed by a "Protect my children" on the way to school to a few random "Bless my husband," "Give me wisdom," "Help!" and "Forgive me" prayers throughout the day are all we can manage because we are so out of breath.

God understands. Relax. Take a breath. I pray that you find ways to carry on a conversation in prayer with your heavenly Father during this season of your life as a mother.

—Lisa Whelchel

Wanting What We Can't Have

God is faithful, who will not allow you to be tempted beyond what you are able, but with the temptation will also make the way of escape, that you may be able to bear it.

—1 Corinthians 10:13

Have you ever been tempted to take an easier path than the one you believe would honor God?

Perhaps you've cheated on a test or lied on a business report or engaged in questionable practices, trying to tell yourself the end justified the means. Perhaps you're in a difficult marriage and find yourself drawn to someone else.

I know what it feels like to be tempted, to grab what seems right or necessary or to take an easy way out of the hard work of being a follower of Christ. Most of us struggle with wanting to avoid pain. It's human nature to want what we can't have—in this case an end to suffering, whether big or small. And yet, in taking things into our own hands, we lose the opportunity to allow God to work on our behalf for the greater good.

A few nights ago, I participated in an online chat (if you don't know what that is, ask your kids!) on the subject of prayer. One woman wrote to say she had been praying for a child who has been seriously ill for three years and yet God seems silent. Her temptation was to quit on God. Why bother praying when he doesn't answer?

In my mind's eye, I could see her standing on top of that mountain with Satan whispering, "Forget God. He's forgotten you. Just worship me."

One of the hardest elements of our walk with God is to keep worshiping him even when it hurts. When the devil tempted Jesus in the desert, Jesus looked at everything Satan offered him and then looked ahead to the cross and the agony he would have to endure.

And then he chose to worship God.

—Sheila Walsh

October 25

We Will Never Be Alone

> Casting all your care upon Him, for He cares for you.
> —1 Peter 5:7

As a little girl, I remember hearing the song, "You'll Never Walk Alone," but the words didn't mean anything to me until I took a trip to Ireland, long after I became an adult.

My partner in Christian ministry for many years, Patty Burgin, had a trip planned to Scotland to do an outreach and invited me to join her. I told Patty I'd go with her if she'd be willing to join me in visiting a friend at the University of Dublin. It was arranged.

On the morning after the conference, we were to catch a train to Glasgow, where we could get a ferry to Ireland, and then we would make a quick hop to Dublin. It looked simple. Suffice it to say I was an inexperienced traveler. In Glasgow we were surprised to find ourselves on the wrong side of the tracks (literally) when the train broke down. When we asked a steward what he might suggest we do, he replied, " Well, Laddie, I'd pu' up a pryr' if I were yew!" So we did. Then we ran to the wharf, made it to the ferry, and made it to northern Ireland—at midnight. What now? It was much too late to take a train anywhere, so we put up another prayer. It wasn't long after that a car drove by the pier, and the driver said he knew a place we could go. In no time we were in front of a pleasant Irish house.

Inside, the most wonderful woman greeted us and gave us hot tea and a warm bed. The next morning, we took the train to Dublin and all was well. I will never forget the experience of staying in that home, however. I said to Patty just before we fell asleep, "No one on earth knows where we are. *No one.* Only God. And he is with us. We are not alone."

And we weren't. We have never been. And we never will be.

—Mary Graham

Laughing at Whatever Is out of Whack

Then Abraham fell on his face and laughed, and said in his heart, "Shall a child be born to a man who is one hundred years old?"
—Genesis 17:17

Theodore S. Geisel, better known as Dr. Seuss, charmed both children and adults with his delightful depiction of a world in which characters and events are exaggeratedly unusual and out of step with the ordinary. Dr. Seuss described his fictional world as illustrations of the "out of whack." An example is the elephant named Horton who appears in one Dr. Seuss book sitting on the top of a spindly tree, enduring the environmental rigors of changing seasons as he determines to hatch a bird egg.

There are times when we might wonder if we have unwittingly wandered into a Dr. Seuss-type world. The events in our lives don't always coincide with our sense of the predictable and expected.

Dr. Seuss was once quoted in a magazine article as saying, "Humor has a tremendous place in a sordid world. It's more than just a laughing matter. If you can see things out of whack, then you can see how things can be in whack."

In other words, our ability to see the distinction between what is out of whack and what is not assures us that we have a handle on what occurrences make up a normal world. Our perspective is clear—in balance. Dr. Seuss speaks profoundly about how we react to the irregularities of life. A key to altering our perspectives and ensuring mental and emotional health lies in our ability to find humor in whatever is out of joint.

—Marilyn Meberg

October 27

Letting Go of Perfectionism

> The Lord will perfect that which concerns me; Your mercy, O Lord, endures forever; do not forsake the works of Your hands.
>
> —Psalm 138:8

For years my friends have told me, almost in unison, that I'm too "cranky" with myself. My expectations, for myself and at times for others, have angelic dust on them because I set them so high. Perfectionism, I know, is a strict taskmaster who offers no free lunches, much less recess.

We will always be less than we hoped at some level until we stand before the only Perfect One. We live in a fallen world, where disease is rampant and imperfections are the rule of the day but where Christ, who understands our frailty, makes provision for us. If we can grasp that, we will not be as wobbly; calm will keep us sane, and we will become like Jesus.

But when?

Just beyond the veil of time when we come into completion.

Until that day when Jesus makes all things new, may we together continue to forgive ourselves, forgive others, and let go, not of worthy goals, but of perfectionism.

—Patsy Clairmont

Healing Is Hard Work

To the pure all things are pure, but to those who are defiled and unbelieving nothing is pure; but even their mind and conscience are defiled.

—Titus 1:15

As we remember that we are God's beloved creations, we gain the goodness of God's healing balm of love. He loves us. He created us. So what's not to like? That's what keeps me running back to him. I constantly want more of his gracious, love-enriched, healing balm.

When I'm able to see myself as he sees me, I also find and embrace the pure and innocent little girl I once was. Back then I thought everyone else in the whole wide world was pure too. I was too young to believe any differently, so when I was corrupted by abuse, my mind and conscience were corrupted, too, like a corrupted computer file that no longer functions properly.

I felt at least one of my emotional layers fall away when I learned enough about abuse victims to look back at the blonde-haired, blue-eyed little girl I used to be and say, "It wasn't your fault. It wasn't because of anything you did or didn't do, said or didn't say. It was because a bad person made evil choices and inflicted hurt upon you. For a long time, you blamed yourself and kept that hurt hidden because you didn't know any better. And eventually the blame and guilt infected all the other parts of your life. But none of it was your fault. You were a victim. But no more."

Believe me; it feels good when those layers begin to fall away and healing starts. But there's another side of letting those layers go. It's the fact that the healing doesn't happen suddenly and then it's done once and for all.

Healing is a process, and it's hard work.

—Sandi Patty

October 29

Be Honest!

> One who has unreliable friends soon comes to ruin.
> —Proverbs 18:24 NIV

Ultimately, I don't want a friend who always says yes or only says what she thinks I want to hear. I want a friend who will tell me where she wants to eat or what she wants to do or not do. I want to know how she feels and what she needs.

It feels much safer to me to have a friend who will speak up and tell me when she is frustrated with me or when I've hurt her feelings than one who merely pretends that everything is okay.

Not that we have to share every fleeting feeling. During a silent retreat, I learned that I don't have to react to all of my emotions. In the quiet, the Holy Spirit revealed a truth that set me free. I wrote this in my journal:

> I've learned . . . that I can allow feelings to surface, feel them deeply and completely, but I don't need to "do" anything with them! If anger were to rise up, . . . I could let it come up, feel it, and let it keep going through me and out of me. . . . I have the choice not to react in anger or say what I'm feeling, unless I decide to. When hurt surfaces, I don't have to run away or withdraw or devise a plan not to feel hurt again. I can feel it, grieve it, let it go, and know that the feeling will eventually go away.

When I do need to vent, I want a friend who can handle my honesty. I want to be the safe person friends come to when they are afraid to be real with anyone else. Remember, your honesty is a gift, and it encourages others to be authentic with you.

—Lisa Whelchel

The Gift of Community

God is building a home. He's using us all—irrespective of how we got here—in what he is building.

—Ephesians 2:22 msg

As far back as I can remember, I've had sweet fellowship and a sense of community with my family and friends. We often talk about spiritual things and the importance of a relationship with God. I well remember my parents praying together about financial concerns, health issues, and various family problems.

Because of this kind of vulnerability in my earliest community, I've always sought out relationships in which I can be real and honest. I don't want anybody to judge me; I want to be myself and know that is okay.

One of the reasons I love working with Women of Faith is the loyalty I feel among this fantastic team of friends whom I deeply love and respect. They don't censure or criticize me. They make me laugh and think and feel and want more and more time with them. For the most part, they consistently model the way I want to be. The fact that they came along at this juncture in my life is almost too good to be true. It is an enormous gift of grace from the Lord, and I never take it for granted.

I'm not saying we don't have occasional conflicts or don't have to work through problems from time to time, but this unique group of pals gives rise to a sweetness I've never quite known before.

I've often thought that this is the kind of community I've yearned for all along my life's journey—one in which there is boundless love, extravagant grace, and outrageous joy. We all give, and we all receive; we care, and we're cared for; we're in it for the long haul. The sweet fellowship we enjoy is born out of knowing that God is using all of us, no matter how we got to this place.

—Luci Swindoll

October 31

Mercy Reigns

> You hem me in behind and before, and you lay your hand upon me.
>
> —Psalm 139:5 NIV

When I consider that the three people who most irked me recently were a woman who talked too loudly and too long, a chunky, claustrophobic flyer, and a lady with bad driving habits, I have to admit I'm getting on my own nerves because all of those aggravating little quirks abound in *me*!

The old adage "When you point out somebody else's flaws, you've got three fingers pointing back at you" comes to mind. That encourages me to be more lethargic when it comes to taking offense and to remember I'm only reading the tiniest paragraph in their stories.

Maybe the verbose woman with too much volume in Starbucks has a hearing problem and rarely gets to converse with other people in social settings. Maybe middle-seat-man really does have issues with small spaces because his mean mama punished him by locking him in a closet when he was a child. Maybe the lady who wouldn't share her lane on I-65 was coming home from the doctor's office and preoccupied with how she was going to tell her husband and children that the lump in her breast was malignant.

Maybe if I knew their whole stories, including the sore spots and sad chapters, I wouldn't be so quick to judge them as inferior.

I'm so glad Jesus isn't irritated by the people who irritate me. If he were, surely he would also roll his eyes in exasperation a million times a day over my gaffes. Yet, instead of making angels guffaw in glory by mocking our foolishness, our Redeemer reigns in mercy.

Jesus never forgets our sore spots or sad chapters.

—Lisa Harper

Refusing to Show Off

I have kept the ways of the LORD, and have not wickedly departed from my God.
—PSALM 18:21

To tempt Jesus, Satan took him to the pinnacle of the temple in Jerusalem and said, "If You are the Son of God, throw Yourself down. For it is written: 'He shall give His angels charge over you,' and, 'In their hands they shall bear you up'" (Matthew 4:6).

In essence, Satan was tempting Jesus to show off. After all, what a sight it would be for Christ to throw himself off the temple! Everyone would see the angels swoop in to rescue the Son of God.

But Jesus refused to give in to the self-indulgent desire to have God respond to risky behavior; instead, he kept his life under the shadow of his Father's wings.

Jesus knew: Miracles don't change hearts. Obedience does.

We so often want miracles—something that will overwhelm and amaze us. We might have right desires at the root of things, but we're blinded by the methods. God has given us his Holy Spirit to guide and direct us. He has given us his Word to be a light to our daily path. He has given us the body of Christ so that together we can work out our salvation with fear and trembling. But so often we want more. We want the feel-good moments when God shows up like a magician and pulls miracles out of a hat.

I say, if you want to feel special, take a good, long look at the cross. There has never been a greater statement made by God than the sight of his Son stretched out on the cross out of love for you and for me.

—Sheila Walsh

November 2

Being Authentic While Setting Boundaries

> Keep your heart with all diligence, for out of it spring the issues of life.
>
> —Proverbs 4:23

I hate conflict. I want everyone to like me, and I don't want anybody to be mad at me. I just don't want to have to be somebody else for that to be possible. I want to be loved and accepted for who I am. To do that, I need to *know* who I am and be brave enough to be different from you.

This is easier said than done. Even saying what I want is a boundary. It separates me from you; it defines me.

A boundary is not a punishment. Learning that simple truth has helped me a lot. Rather, a boundary is a protection. I can simply say, "If you continue to ________ (fill in the blank), then in order to take care of myself, I will have to ________."

This kind of healthy boundary-setting is self-care. It answers the question we would all be wise to ask in unwanted situations: What will I do to take care of myself?

At first, this idea seems to conflict with what I've been taught all my life: I am to prefer others above myself. But God has used a handful of instances to help me find that both of these teachings can coexist.

One time, I felt the need to express my opinion within the context of authentic friendship, even though I knew my friend would be mad at me. And she was.

Later, though, she shared how God had used me to help her experience a deep healing in an area she had been avoiding.

Being true to who I am, God has ultimately used me repeatedly in someone's life to bless her at a much deeper level than if I had laid down my life for her.

—Lisa Whelchel

Diligent Attentiveness

Be diligent to know the state of your flocks,
and attend to your herds.
—Proverbs 27:23

Did you know that if a teacher invests in an unruly child, that teacher can change the direction of the child's life? Former president Jimmy Carter quoted his grade-school teacher in his inaugural address. Why? She had attended her flocks diligently, and students do not soon forget.

I suspect that's the kind of diligence intended in Proverbs 27:23. To be diligent is to esteem and to love. It's seen in one's behavior of steady, constant, earnest, dedicated, energetic, lively effort. *Diligent* also means to discern, to search for, and to give attention to—to set your heart on something or someone.

And the phrase *attend to* means "to know well the face of, as in appearance."

Most moms' diligent attending to their families enables the moms to recognize at a glance when something is up with their herd. Years ago, I walked through the living room and noticed a look on my toddler's face that stopped me in my tracks. He hadn't said a word, but I knew that precious little face. I had memorized every nook and cranny around his mouth, nose, and eyes since his birth, and something that day set off an alarm in my shepherdess's heart.

I questioned him while scanning the surroundings and quickly spotted the evidence: an empty bottle of baby aspirin. Somehow he had knocked it off a high shelf and consumed the contents. Needless to say, emergency activity followed. That story ended well . . . because I knew my little lamb's face.

—Patsy Clairmont

November 4

Whole Again

> Now we look inside, and what we see is that anyone united with the Messiah gets a fresh start, is created new. The old life is gone; a new life burgeons! Look at it!
>
> —2 Corinthians 5:17 msg

First United Methodist Church in Oklahoma City, the city where I was born, is more than one hundred years old. Called "First Church" by its members, it stands across the street from the national memorial marking the site where the Murrah Federal Building was bombed on April 19, 1995.

The violent explosion killed 168 people, including children. While our whole nation grieved over the tragic and senseless loss of life, smaller losses were mourned as well. The blast caused severe damage to the grand old First Church structure and its beautiful stained-glass windows.

Almost before the dust settled, volunteers and church members lovingly collected the fragile shards of glass from the rubble. Over the next five years, they carefully put those pieces together in totally new creations—crafts, decorative items, and mementos that became beautiful and meaningful works of art.

Today, wonderful new stained-glass windows glow on the building's reconstructed façade. One of them, in the chapel, includes a single piece of unbroken glass that miraculously survived the blast. On that unblemished piece is the face of Jesus.

The windows at First Church are especially meaningful for people like me and for families who feel like their lives have gotten all cracked up and glued back together—people who know what it's like to be broken and end up in a totally new creation. We are living out the powerful truth of the inscription on one of the windows: *The Lord takes broken pieces and by his love makes us whole.*

—Sandi Patty

Controlling Circumstances with Humor

A feast is made for laughter.
—ECCLESIASTES 10:19

The ability to laugh over unexpected and unwanted experiences that threaten to get the best of us enables us to change our perspective. When something goes wrong, instead of being victimized by it, we need to lighten up, take the situation less seriously, and see if there isn't a laugh to be found somewhere. When we are able to do this, we are in control of our situation instead of our situation being in control of us.

At the moment that something awkward happens—we chug down someone else's iced tea, thinking it's our own, or notice during church that we're wearing two unmatched shoes, or put our foot in a tub of cement while supervising home-remodeling helpers—the ridiculous thing we've done is not funny but a painfully embarrassing reality. Without the capacity to laugh and appreciate how ludicrous we must have appeared, we might succumb to feelings of abject humiliation. One of the great values in humor is its ability to help us regain control of our circumstances.

Nor is humor limited to our lighter experiences. I believe that even in our pain, in the deepest anguish of our souls, the ability to be less intense and to enjoy some humor can give relief and help bring restoration. I maintain that even if a moment of humor is offset by days or weeks of sadness, remembering that sweet moment can do more to restore our balance than we can imagine.

—Marilyn Meberg

November 6

Admiring God's Creation

> You are the only LORD. You made the heavens, even the highest heavens, with all the stars. . . . The heavenly army worships you.
>
> —NEHEMIAH 9:6 NCV

A few years ago, around Thanksgiving, some of the kids and I were coming home from their show-choir rehearsal. As we drove, we oohed and aahed about how clear the sky was and how many stars we could see. When we got home, one of the kids, Jennifer, stayed outside with me to enjoy the beautiful starlit evening.

We turned off all the outside lights and stood in the driveway a long time, looking up. Just looking and talking. We talked about God and how amazing it is that he created all this. Then, for some reason, Jenn asked, "Mom, which way is north?"

I pointed in the direction I thought it was. As we both turned in that direction, we saw the most beautiful falling star. It was so big and clear. In the past when I've seen falling stars, I've caught a glimpse out of the corner of my eye, making me wonder if I'd really seen it. But not *that* falling star. We watched it fall for a good three seconds. We couldn't believe it. It was so stunning we both whooped and shrieked, prompting our dogs to start barking hysterically, probably thinking we were being attacked by an ax murderer. We laughed and hugged and cried, all at the same time. Then we ran inside in case the neighbors came out to see what all the commotion was.

What a beautiful moment with my beautiful daughter . . . and our wonderful God. It was almost like he knew we had been admiring and appreciating his creation all evening. Isn't it just like God that he would seem to say, "Thanks for noticing. How about a falling star to top off the evening?"

—Sandi Patty

We Are Richer Than We Think

> You know the grace of our Lord Jesus Christ, that though he was rich, yet for your sake he became poor, so that you through his poverty might become rich.
>
> —2 Corinthians 8:9 NIV

The basic principle behind being a good steward is the genuine belief that we are richer than we think. Because of this, our giving becomes greater than we believe to be prudent, since our source of wealth is inexhaustible. Living out of that endowment is what makes us capable of being generous from the heart.

Stewardship is a practice that goes beyond managing our material possessions; I understand it also to include time and energy—anything that is ours to spend. When we share out of the fullness of our being, out of a spirit of openness and flexibility, we are truly rich. We experience a vitality that comes from an inner source.

Os Guinness says, "It all belongs to the Lord anyway. . . . We give because we've been given to." When we look at ourselves as the constant recipients of the continual grace and goodness of God, our generous Father, how can we overdo in giving to others? He is our inexhaustible source.

One of the greatest adventures as God's children is trusting our Father with our finances, our time, and our energy. Giving from our wealth—no matter how small or large—is not a gamble, although we're dealing with the great unknown because of our own limited vision. But God has promised to meet our needs, and he won't go back on his promise. He's got the goods to do it! I could recount story after story of how he has surprised me by replenishing my money, time, and energy.

—Luci Swindoll

November 8

God with Us

> Behold, the virgin shall conceive and bear a Son, and shall call His name Immanuel.
>
> —Isaiah 7:14

Have you ever been with a friend and you know she's not truly present? Instead, she's a million miles away in thought.

What disconnection, even if all the right words are coming out of your mouths. I've been wondering lately if this isn't one of the many reasons God sent his Son to be *with* us. I've been thinking about what it means to be present, and I keep coming to the idea that it is a gift, a gift so important to God that he even named his little boy Immanuel, *God with Us*.

Jesus didn't stay in his own heavenly world. He stepped into ours to be fully present, all there, 100 percent *with* us. Is that not the truest definition of the friendship we have with him? Is that not the model?

I am learning that an easy place to exercise my presence-practicing muscles is within friendships. When I am with a friend, I want to be fully engaged with her. Eyes connected, ears attuned, opinions on hold, mouth in neutral, heart wide open. The more in-the-moment encounters I have on the human level, the easier it is for me to be *with* Immanuel in an incarnational way. Not worrying about the future or regretting the past. Not trying to think the right thoughts or say words that will cause him to act. Just being with him.

I think Jesus really likes that. I know I do. It touches my heart when someone makes room in her busy life to be with me. I know what that costs. Our time is so valuable, and every one of us is spread so thin in a million important ways. In today's economy, to give someone your time is worth much more than money can buy.

—Lisa Whelchel

It's Not for Me to Know

A future awaits those who seek peace.
—Psalm 37:37 NIV

I once bought a nice telescope and couldn't wait to get home with it. It was late October when that big, full autumn moon fills the sky and the heavens are alive with stars. You know the season.

I carefully read the instructions and put it together. Night came, and I set the telescope in front of the picture window in my dining room, working with the lens dial to focus on the moon.

Nothing happened. I couldn't see a thing.

I reread the directions, went through all the steps, double-checked each item, and set it back up. Again, nothing.

Next night, another full, luminescent moon. Gorgeous. I couldn't wait. But the telescope wouldn't work. I simply could not focus the lens. "All I want to do is see something in the distance," I told the telescope. I finally caught a quick glimpse of the moon, like a shadow . . . hazy, oblique. Dissatisfied, I put the telescope away and later took it back to the store and got another one.

I worked with the second telescope off and on for weeks but never saw much of anything. I finally ran out of patience and put it in the bottom of the closet.

Maybe I try too hard to see what's in the distance with everything. Some aspects of my spiritual life are like that too. I wonder what's in the distance, down the road, around the corner, beyond today. What kind of adventure does God have for me next? Will it be hard or easy? Will I recognize that it's from him?

God has left a lot unsaid in the areas where I want to know more, and no matter what I do, I can't figure it out. It's simply not for me to know.

—Luci Swindoll

November 10

Seeking Out Joy

> He made the entire human race and made the earth hospitable, with plenty of time and space for living so we could seek after God, and not just grope around in the dark but actually *find* him.
>
> —Acts 17:24 MSG

After his divorce and before we were married, my now-husband Don and his kids enjoyed a time when it was "just them" living in a little house. He says now that it was an important step, a buffer that gave him, as a newly single parent with custody of his kids, time to help him and his kids adjust to and understand who they were as a family.

That experience prompts him now to offer this advice to others coming out of a divorce or spousal death situation: "Don't rush into a second marriage, especially if you're a parent," he says. "Don't move on to that next step until you and your kids have a good sense of who you really are."

To do that, Don and his children established new traditions, like Super Wind-Down on Friday evenings, when they would push back the furniture, drag out the sleeping bags, rent some movies, pop some popcorn, play board games, and enjoy a lively living-room camp-out. Now they all remember those days as a special time when they spent more time laughing than they did missing what they had lost.

Those weren't necessarily easy days—Don was a single dad with custody of the three kids, working for the YMCA in wellness and also attending college classes to finish his degree. Money was tight, space was limited, and there were many stressful days. They had to look for the joy in their new circumstances; it didn't come searching for them. But together, they found it.

—Sandi Patty

The Cutting Edge

As iron sharpens iron, so a man sharpens the countenance of his friend.
—Proverbs 27:17

If you've watched someone sharpen a knife, you know a lot of grinding goes on, which causes sparks to fly. When I first read Proverbs 27:17, I wondered if it was suggesting that we should grind on each other's nerves.

I've done that. Quite honestly, it didn't seem to help a whit.

Instead, I believe this verse is describing the kind of investments that help us become keener in our perceptions, sharper in our wit, and more directed in our energies.

If you're talking big yet living small, I won't be drawn to the tinkling brass of your verbal offering. But if I know you've paid your dues to learn a truth, you better believe I'm going to lean in to your experiential whetstone to sharpen my perspective. Authenticity is the cutting edge that adds veracity to one's offering.

And there's something else. The sharpest knives I own have sheaths to protect me from being cut when I reach into the drawer. Likewise, I've noted that individuals who have been through the steely rubbings of hardship are sheathed in empathy. Their intentions aren't meant to be cutting. They realize that truth's edge will be severe enough and they need not bear down. They aren't confused; their experiences have taught them that they aren't the Holy Spirit. They offer us the keen truths they've learned, but God's Spirit alone forges our character.

—Patsy Clairmont

November 12

Flipping On the Light

> You, Lord, are my lamp; the Lord turns my darkness into light.
> —2 Samuel 22:29 NIV

I hate having to go to the bathroom in the middle of the night because, well, I'm kind of a sissy at night. I still get a little nervous about shadows and creaking noises. Sometimes I flip on the lamp just to prove to myself there's no scary monster in my room.

One day I was about to walk into my house when no one was home. But before I turned the door handle, I saw a shadow moving inside. I ran to the neighbor's house to ask her to come inside with me. But as soon as we walked toward my door, I realized the ceiling fan was casting a shadow on the wall. So there I was, asking my neighbor to help me fight off a ceiling fan.

It's so easy to live our entire lives thinking we see God for who he really is. We think we have him all figured out. We think we know the type of God he is when, in reality, we haven't allowed him to flip on the light switch. We base our knowledge of him on a distorted shadow rather than on who he says he is.

Sometimes I am too scared to open up my heart to him and see God for who he really is because then my life, my beliefs, and everything I think I know could change.

I would rather hide behind a God I created in my head so I can live my life however I want. Too often I settle for my mistaken impression of what I think God looks like rather than let him show me the surprising truth about himself.

The cool part is, when we do see God for who he really is, amazing things can happen.

—Jenna Lucado

Gassed Up with Laughter

Behold, My servants shall sing for joy of heart.
—Isaiah 65:14

As a friend and I were driving to a speaking engagement, we stopped at a dubious-looking location for gasoline: two padlocked gas pumps stood beside a little store and adjoining restaurant. We waited for someone to unlock the padlocks and pump the gas, but nothing happened.

I hurried into the store, where a nonchalant woman said, "The place to get gas is from the cook in the restaurant."

Failing to notice the humor in her remark, I went next door, where the waiter said the cook was busy slicing roast beef. When I asked if I could pump it myself, he simply walked away.

We decided to wait over a piece of pie. *Forty minutes later* we asked again and were told the cook was looking for a plunger because the toilet had clogged. Sensing my increasing hostility, he offered to pump the gas himself.

As we waited in the car, a dilapidated vehicle stopped next to us, and two filthy, bearded men fell out the door, wrestling.

Finally we drove away, still slightly irritated by the long delay, the beef-slicing, toilet-plungering cook, and the ridiculous wrestlers.

Then the craziness of it all settled on us, and we started to laugh. The farther we drove, the harder we laughed! Tension and irritation evaporated as the laughter rolled. I just wish I had seen the humor sooner—but I hadn't because of my self-absorption and concentration on the task at hand.

—Marilyn Meberg

November 14

Making Yourself Praise God

> Praise be to you, LORD, the God of our father Israel, from everlasting to everlasting.
>
> —1 CHRONICLES 29:10 NIV

I used to think worship and praise were about God. I wouldn't have said this out loud, but I thought it was something he needed—or maybe not needed but at least wanted. I realize now that, in some ways, praise is really about me. That sounds as heretical as my previous observation, doesn't it?

All I know is, whenever I sing about the Lord's awesome power, his faithful goodness, unquestionable sovereignty, and love without measure, I don't think I'm telling him anything new, but I am often reminding myself of something I've temporarily lost sight of.

When we remember God's awesomeness, our challenges look smaller in comparison to his greatness. Admittedly, though, praise is often the last thing we feel like doing when we need it most. Maybe that is why it is often referred to as a *sacrifice.* Hebrews 13:15 says, "Therefore by Him let us continually offer the sacrifice of praise to God, that is, the fruit of our lips, giving thanks to His name."

Let me encourage you to *make* yourself praise the Lord. I know that sounds awful, but if you are anything like I am, then you know what I'm talking about. Whether it is because we are too busy or because we like to do something about our problems or because we don't think we have a very good singing voice or we weren't raised to praise the Lord out loud or any other excuse, we have to get over it and discipline ourselves to proclaim the glory of God's name!

It is worth it because he is worthy.

—Lisa Whelchel

Missing Out on Madness

Like a madman who throws firebrands, arrows, and death, is the man who deceives his neighbor, and says, "I was only joking!"

—Proverbs 26:18–19

If we had a machine that could detect scars on our hearts, I wonder how many of the wounds would have been caused by a piercing arrow of jealousy, a firebrand of envy, or a deadly word of revenge—all forms of anger. If we aren't cautious, we will dress up these familiar emotions in the clothing of our rights. Then we believe we have a rationale for our behavior. That's a slippery slope to long-term madman status.

I'm concerned for our society because of the level of anger and brutality in our entertainment. Vile language seems to be a necessity to receive the ratings that draw folks to the box office. Audiences pay to hear madmen rage and fling violent language into the air, ripping holes in the viewers' dignity, numbing their sensitivities, and smudging their moral decency.

And we wonder why violence and fear are escalating in our world . . .

Anger can fill us up like a container of gasoline, full to the brim. Then the slightest jiggle can cause us to spill over and burst into flames of fury. We all need to check if our pots are seeping over with ire so that we don't become madmen or madwomen hurling words that burn, puncture, and bring death.

—Patsy Clairmont

November 16

Stepping Closer to the Heart of God

> Blessed is every one who fears the LORD,
> who walks in His ways.
> —PSALM 128:1

When Satan urged Jesus to jump off the temple in Jerusalem to demonstrate that God had given "his angels charge over You" (Luke 4:10), he omitted the second part of verse he was quoting (Psalm 91:11), which adds, "to keep you in all your ways."

It was a telling omission.

Satan can and will tempt and test us in many ways. What he does not know is the *way* we will respond. Will we respond in the way modeled for us by Christ? Or will we be like a child at a birthday party who grabs the first piece of cake simply because she's been told not to? Will we pitch a fit, like a child in the grocery store when we don't get the sugar-coated cereal we want it?

Satan doesn't know.

We can give in to his temptation. Or we can look to Jesus, who gave us the perfect responses in his encounters with Satan. He told him, in essence:

- "God is my provider."
- "I will not take the easy way out."
- "I will not seek the spectacular; I will seek God's face."

I don't know what situations you are facing right now, but I know that Christ our Savior has left his footprints in the desert sand for us to follow. What Satan tempts us with is never what we are really longing for. It may appear to meet a need at the moment, but it will just take us deeper and deeper into the wilderness.

Christ's steps keep us close to the heart of God.

—Sheila Walsh

Watching for a Glimmer of Laughter

You have put gladness in my heart.
—Psalm 4:7

I am an only child, and I absolutely adored my mother. When she died in 1984, I was devastated. Of course I'm glad she's in a painless eternity with Jesus. But I miss her still.

Mom had asked that her body be cremated. On the day I picked up the little box that contained her ashes, I struggled to grasp the reality that I would never again see what was visually familiar to me about her. What I carried in my hands was completely foreign.

Ken was waiting in the car. As I opened the door with the box in my hands, he averted his eyes in an attempt to be more casual about that moment than either of us felt. As I placed the box on the seat, there was an awkward moment of silence.

Then I said quietly, "Mom, would you like a seat belt?"

Ken looked startled, and I laughed—not hard and loud—but I laughed, and it felt good. Mom would have understood—in fact, she would have joined me. For a few minutes, my hurt was diminished—less intense. The painful moment was relieved by a quiet laugh.

You may feel there are times when life simply will not yield one ounce of humor. May I suggest that during those seemingly unbearable times of pain, you fight to find a glimmer of light, a reason to laugh, remembering that those moments will not last forever.

—Marilyn Meberg

November 18

Stronger in the Broken Places

> Therefore you shall be perfect, just as your
> Father in heaven is perfect.
> —Matthew 5:48

For years, whenever I read Matthew 5:48, I couldn't think of a single instant in my life when I had been perfect, and there didn't seem to be much chance of it happening in the future. Since then I've come to see it's the journey that's important to God, not that we ever reach the goal and become perfect.

Faith is a compass, not a stopwatch. If you remember that, you can accept that you're living out God's plan for yourself, even if it doesn't seem to be what the rest of the world might consider "perfect" at the time.

When Don and I got married, our pastor gave us a beautiful china cup and saucer. He enclosed a letter, sharing a special story about the special significance that pattern had for him and his wife.

Well, one weekend I came home from a performance somewhere, and the cup's handle was broken off. During one of the kids' rushing passes through the house, it had been accidentally knocked off the shelf where it was displayed.

I cried when I saw it, remembering the meaning it carried, and the kids were crushed. We glued the handle back on as best we could, and yes, we can still see the crack.

But guess what: somehow that cup brings me more joy and seems even more meaningful to me now than it did before, maybe because it helps me remember all that our pastor did to help us put our broken lives back together during the turbulent times surrounding our wedding.

And you know what else? That cup now is the sturdiest piece of china in my house. It's had other tumbles off the shelf, and that handle is still intact. It is, indeed, stronger in the broken places.

—Sandi Patty

The Lord's Special Day

He said to them, "Come aside by yourselves to a deserted place and rest a while."
—Mark 6:31

Isn't it wonderful that God, our best Friend, has already arranged for us to have at least one whole day a week when we can "quit" our other jobs? Okay, I have to admit that I'm one of those people who likes to work, and I find it extremely difficult to relax. Being productive, to me, is fun; I get an adrenaline rush as I'm completing a project. So the Sabbath commandment is tough for me. It is very hard for me to justify giving up a whole day without accomplishing something.

Of course I understand that is the wrong mind-set. And I don't think I'm alone. I find it interesting that we still consider nine of the Ten Commandments to be valid today. We agree that we shouldn't steal, commit adultery, and so on. But "Remember the Sabbath day, to keep it holy" (Exodus 20:8)? Nah, that's old-fashioned, we think.

Now I've come to understand that keeping up the same frantic pace I have the rest of the week is not just a poor personal choice; it's disobeying God and rejecting his thoughtful gift.

What's even more amazing is the observation that this particular commandment is the only one God chooses to illustrate with a personal example: "For in six days the Lord made heaven and earth, the sea, and all that is in them, and rested the seventh day" (Exodus 20:11).

I think God knew it would take nothing short of a command and a personal example to convince us to slow down long enough to take a "still picture" of our family and reflect, *It is good!*

Remember, rest is a key element in God's plan for all of us. Never forget, even God rested!

—Lisa Whelchel

November 20

He's Got It Wired

Eye has not seen, nor ear heard, nor have entered into the heart of man the things which God has prepared for those who love Him.

—1 CORINTHIANS 2:9

My daddy's favorite Bible verse was 1 Corinthians 2:9. He quoted it many times to me, wrote it in letters, and jotted it on gift cards. Now he knows what God prepared for him because he's been in the presence of the Lord for many years.

Gratefully, my own ultimate tomorrow is a given as well. When I put my faith in Jesus Christ as my Savior, I sealed my destiny. The finished work of Christ and his promise about what is to come assure me I'll spend eternity with him.

Frankly, I love the fact that God has a plan for every tomorrow of my life on earth and beyond. Even though I can't figure it all out, he's got it wired. This reassures me that I'm loved and safe.

God knows our course, and he knows us. He loves us. He provides. He plans ahead.

Because the Lord has set this example, I firmly believe I need to plan ahead as well—to consider the tomorrows of my life while still living fully in today. I want tomorrow to be adventuresome, certainly, but I'd also like to avoid as many unpleasant surprises as possible. There is absolutely no way I can know what will happen, but the future will surely come, and to the degree I'm able, I sincerely want to be ready. I believe the Lord will take care of me throughout the course of my life, but I would also like to take care of myself as long as possible, in whatever ways will enhance my physical, mental, and spiritual health.

—Luci Swindoll

Jesus the Overcomer

> Don't let evil get the best of you; get the best of evil by doing good.
>
> —Romans 12:21 MSG

Paul wrote to the church in Thessalonica, "That's why I couldn't quit worrying; I had to know for myself how you were doing in the faith. I didn't want the Tempter getting to you and tearing down everything we had built up together" (1 Thessalonians 3:5 MSG).

God never tempts us or sets a trap to see if we will be faithful. The apostle James wrote, "Let no one say when he is tempted, 'I am tempted by God'; for God cannot be tempted by evil, nor does He Himself tempt anyone" (James 1:13). Yet how many times have you heard people accuse God when disaster strikes? How many times have you fallen prey to that excuse yourself?

God is never the author of evil. Satan is. But Satan's goal is to make you forget that point. When we remember that Satan is the one whose carnivorous smile lies behind the evil he carefully places on our paths, it will be far easier to resist and overcome.

And do you realize that sometimes we believers try to tempt or test God? This happened over and over in Old Testament times as God's people demanded a sign that he was still with them. It's tempting to want to do that today. I can think of many moments in my life when I wanted God to give me some sign that he had heard my prayers.

Perhaps you've tried the old "open your Bible at random and stick your finger on a verse" routine too.

As I think back on those moments in my life when I doubted, I see them now as a lack of trust—and, even more, a lack of belief that I am totally loved by God.

Perhaps that is one of Satan's greatest tricks: to make us question the love of God.

—Sheila Walsh

November 22

Growing Deep Roots of Gratitude

> These are the things I go over and over, emptying out the pockets of my life. . . . Shouting praises, singing thanksgiving—celebrating, all of us, God's feast!
> —Psalm 42:4 MSG

I've been thinking about becoming more grateful. Which is apropos since today is Thanksgiving. I've always loved this particular holiday. I love the crazed grocery store runs late the night before when we realize we need more rolls or forgot to get marshmallows for the sweet potato casserole.

My mom taught me years ago that Thanksgiving is about remembering to focus on good things, even in the presence of bad things. Recent experience has shown me how remembering those bad things can actually bring divine goodness and mercy into sharper focus. In the context of being lost, being found is more wondrous. In the context of being persecuted, finding acceptance is more precious. In the context of being sick, being healed is more miraculous.

So I don't want to forget all the mistake-filled chapters in my story, such as when I ran away from home during a teenage tantrum and got pneumonia after being foolish enough to pout outside during a thunderstorm. Or when I ran away from my senses a few years later and into the arms of a young man who only wanted one thing from me, and it certainly wasn't my undying love.

Apart from Jesus, I'm a faithless prodigal waiting to happen. But I'm learning that the roots of gratitude grow deepest in the sober soil of remembering how hopeless my life is without God.

—Lisa Harper

Learning How to Look at God

> The Lord your God in your midst, the Mighty One, will save; He will rejoice over you with gladness, He will quiet you with His love, He will rejoice over you with singing.
>
> —Zephaniah 3:17

The iPhone can do almost everything these days. It stores music, movies, pictures, and games. It has apps for playing games, checking your fitness level, finding the nearest Wendy's, working out, making the bed, and filing your nails—all of this and a phone too! (Okay, so I stretched a couple of iPhone capabilities, but one day it will happen.)

When my mom first purchased an iPhone, even with all of these applications at her fingertips, the only thing she used her iPhone for was calling and texting.

Now, any time I show her a new trick that her iPhone can do, she gasps, "I didn't know my phone could do that!"

When we let God show us all that he can do—when we stop assuming we know everything about him and let him teach us who he really is—we gasp, "I didn't know my God could do that!"

It's time to turn on the lights, baby! It's time to look beyond the faint shadow of the God you know. It's time to let God teach you and me how he wants us to look at him.

So how does God want us to look at him?

He wants us to see him as our *Dad*.

We cannot comprehend the God of the universe singing over us, delighting in us, and nudging the angels, saying, "That's my girl. Isn't she beautiful?" But that's the kind of Father we have!

—Jenna Lucado

November 24

Laughter, the Joy Intensifier

> Why am I so sad? Why am I so upset? I should put my hope in God and keep praising him, my Savior and my God.
> —Psalm 43:5 NCV

I believe there's a distinction between the experience of joy and the act of laughing. This belief is based on my understanding of Scripture, which teaches there is a wellspring of joy within each believing heart and God means to suffuse our innermost beings with it.

Many people know that joy but do not necessarily express it in overt laughter. A nonlaughing person is not necessarily a nonjoyful person. Cheerfulness and joy are not moral requirements for Christian living, but I do believe they are a consequence, an inevitable result, of our faith in God. When we attempt to generate joy within ourselves apart from God, it is sporadic at best. Ultimately, we sense the inability and depletedness of our own humanity.

On the other hand, when God-sourced joy generates laughter that bubbles up from deep within me, I double my pleasure! Laughter can intensify joy, and shared laughter can intensify joy for others as well. What greater testimony can we give an unbelieving world than a cheerful, joyful demeanor that bespeaks an unshakable faith in the provision of an almighty God? That attitude says far more than any number of words and phrases we might offer in the vain hope that we are being a positive witness. The truth of the cliché, "Your actions speak so loudly I can't hear what you say," is no laughing matter as we consider the attitudes we can reflect to those around us.

—Marilyn Meberg

The Joy of Servanthood

He poured water into a basin and began to wash the disciples' feet, and to wipe them with the towel with which He was girded.

—John 13:5

There is something in our human flesh that doesn't want to be compared with others, but if we are, we want to come out on top. In contrast, one of heaven's most liberating secrets is to pray for the success of those around us.

Satan hates it when we refuse to fall for his theatrics. But I have discovered that it's hard to fall off a pedestal when you are washing someone's feet.

Jesus showed his friends that the new kingdom offered a whole new way to live. "He asked them, 'What were you discussing on the road?' The silence was deafening—they had been arguing with one another over who among them was greatest. He sat down and summoned the Twelve. 'So you want first place? Then take the last place. Be the servant of all'" (Mark 9:33–35 MSG).

One of the greatest advantages of putting down that self-made cross we drag through life is that it frees up our hands. It frees us to worship our Father. It frees us to wash our sisters' feet. It frees us to walk beside each other without whacking each other over the head and getting splinters in our hair! It frees us to be like Jesus.

The longer I am in relationship with him, the simpler life seems. Notice that I said *simpler,* not *easier.* I see now that being an overcomer in Christ is simply doing the things Jesus did. The great news is that what gave Jesus strength to resist the enemy, the internal struggle, or the lack of understanding in others was the Word of God and the fellowship of his Father. We struggle so hard to get it right, but Jesus told us to just follow him and his example.

—Sheila Walsh

Choosing Crinkly over Cranky

> Why are you down in the dumps, dear soul? Why are you crying the blues? Fix my eyes on God—soon I'll be praising again. He puts a smile on my face. He's my God.
> —Psalm 43:5 MSG

Have you noticed that we're less cute when sad settles on our faces? Even wrinkles look fun when we smile; we look crinkly, not cranky. A smile has neon appeal and is a powerful influencer. Haven't you ever been in a not-so-good mood, and then a stranger bebops past you and beams her bright whites, and you find yourself returning the smile? What a great contagion to spread! May it catch on worldwide.

Recently I opened a container of cottage cheese and found these words on the inside peel of plastic: "A smile is a gift anyone can give."

I read it, and guess what? I smiled.

In contrast, when my grandson, Noah, was a toddler, he took full advantage of his position as the baby of the family, which included pouting. He learned to drop his bottom lip halfway down to his Nikes, and when that strategy produced the results Noah intended, he was quick to use it again. A purposed pout needs admirers, or it just isn't worth the lip-sagging effort.

Sometimes I can be so covert in my sadness that it seems appropriate to me, even deserved. I ask the Holy Spirit to spotlight my own pouty intentions. The holy scrutiny of God's Spirit helps me examine the truth within myself and remember that I don't have to wear my sadness like this year's fashion statement. Instead, I can deliberately don kindness and compassion for others. That countenance change helps me to step out of myself and protect others from my poutiness.

—Patsy Clairmont

No Match for God's Love

I will not boast, except in my infirmities. For though I might desire to boast, I will not be a fool; for I will speak the truth.

—2 Corinthians 12:5–6

Evil is very real. But it is no match for the love of God. Even when we are called to walk down a path we would never have chosen, I believe God is in the redeeming business. Nothing we have faced will be lost, and nothing we have lost will be lost forever.

Satan loves to show us our needs and play on our fears, trying to make us think we don't have "enough" strength, money, courage, intelligence . . . whatever.

But Jesus said his grace would be enough. There is nothing you or I will face today or tomorrow that we will face alone. Jesus will be there with us with everything we need to walk through it.

Think of the apostle Paul. In his second letter to the Corinthians, he told them he had some kind of "thorn in the flesh" (2 Corinthians 12:7). He said he had asked God three times to remove it, and God had said no. But hear Paul's words as he responded to that answer:

"Satan's angel did his best to get me down; what he in fact did was push me to my knees. No danger then of walking around high and mighty! At first I didn't think of it as a gift, and begged God to remove it. Three times I did that, and then he told me, 'My grace is enough; it's all you need. My strength comes into its own in your weakness.' Once I heard that, I was glad to let it happen. I quit focusing on the handicap and began appreciating the gift" (vv. 7–9 MSG).

—Sheila Walsh

November 28

Just Ask

If any of you lacks wisdom, let him ask of God, who gives to all liberally and without reproach, and it will be given to him.

—James 1:5

Sometimes I know I need a friend but just hate to ask, especially when I don't really know what I need. I just know that I can't find what I'm looking for all by myself, and I don't want to be alone.

As an example, one morning in the Starbucks drive-through, I sent my friend Kimmie a text message: "Nothing urgent at all, but if you find yourself with a few minutes, could you give me a call when you get a chance?"

Within five minutes, my cell phone rang with her sweet voice on the other end. After making sure I wasn't interrupting anything important, I jumped in: "Kimmie, I don't even know how I'm feeling, but one thing I do know is whenever I'm having a hard time understanding myself, you help me just by listening with your heart and hearing mine. I don't really even want to say the words out loud that I'm thinking because I have a sneaking suspicion that they are very selfish and immature and not at all how Jesus would feel if he were in my situation."

I proceeded to unload every jumbled thought that was strangling my soul on the inside. And as usual, by the end of the conversation, I felt a hundred pounds lighter. It really wasn't anything in particular that Kimmie said. She just has a gift of being with me in the middle of my messiness; she convinces me that she hears what I'm saying and understands how I'm feeling.

And when we can't be together or even talk on the phone, we can always be together in spirit, keeping each other in our prayers.

—Lisa Whelchel

Rifling Through the Trash Pile

You drew near on the day I called on You,
And said "Do not fear!"
—Lamentations 3:57

In the early 1990s, I engaged the services of mental health professionals and went to them for private counseling sessions. It was a very positive experience in the long run, although there were moments I wanted to storm out of the session screaming and drive like a maniac back to my house. Or better yet, kill the therapist.

During those eighteen months, I had two counselors, a man and a woman, and they each did me a world of good. On the poor woman I dumped every negative thing I had ever thought about any human being who ever crossed my path, thus getting it out of my system. And with the man, I began to pick up the scattered debris that was my inner life and put it back together.

There's something very gratifying and healing to one's soul about dumping the truck then rifling through the trash pile, deciding what's important to keep and throwing the rest away. It's sort of a "come-to-Jesus" moment, as Marilyn Meberg calls it—an important, defining time in one's personal growth. When I started to put the pieces back together, I made a list of things I really wanted out of life from then on, through all my tomorrows. The list includes:

a rich, meaningful relationship with the Lord,
a sense of stability wherever I am in the world,
a contentment in all circumstances, and
an abiding knowledge that my life has purpose.

—Luci Swindoll

November 30

Encouraging Through Brokenness

> You, LORD, hear the desire of the afflicted; you encourage them, and you listen to their cry.
>
> —PSALM 10:17 NIV

Hard times can make us miserable, or they can bring out the best in us. Look around you, and you'll see examples of those two extremes every day: dour and bitter complainers who curse the hand life has dealt them; and outward-focused angels who always manage to find the joy and give others a hand, even amid their own hardships.

You may or may not have chosen the circumstances you find yourself facing right now. But either way, you can start to make those difficult circumstances better simply by aiming your attitude toward heaven and seeking out every shred of joy you can find. Often it's found in helping others.

Reaching out to others can be something good that can come from a hurt we've gone through. By remembering our own times of brokenness, we can offer Christ's love and comfort to others whose lives still lie in pieces amid the rubble. We can show them through our actions—and when it's appropriate, through our words.

I don't know about you, but I am so much more encouraged by someone who is willing to share her hurts with me rather than trying to make me believe she has it all together. Aren't you glad Jesus didn't say to us, "Come to me, all you who have your act together"? I would be left out for sure! Instead he says, "Come to Me, all you who *labor* and are *heavy laden*, and I will give you rest" (Matthew 11:28, emphasis mine).

—Sandi Patty

Choosing to Smile

Let those also who love Your name
Be joyful in You.
—Psalm 5:11

In times of turmoil, it's important to remember that whatever it is that threatens to crush your spirit and claim your joy today will not necessarily be there tomorrow, next month, or next year. Life moves forward, and circumstances change. You will not always be in a pit!

That reminder in itself brings a respite to the soul. From there perhaps a glimmer of light can seep through the darkness, enabling you to search out that seemingly elusive but spirit-lifting smile or laugh that helps you regain control. Never forget that God, in his sovereign love and power, holds our lives in his hands and works everything according to his plan.

My security, my rest, my peace, and my joy live always in the sure knowledge of that comforting truth. But God invites my participation in the executing of his divine will for my life. To me, a part of that participation has to do with how I perceive the events of my life. I determine whether I'm going to view my experiences through a negative or a positive lens.

Indeed, if my perceptions are negative, then it stands to reason my life will feel out of whack. Thank God I have a choice. I don't have to pout, fuss, complain, or mope; I have the option to smile, chuckle, laugh, and look for joy in dark places. When I do, in that arena where God invites my participation, I am in control.

—Marilyn Meberg

December 2

There's Always Hope

> He cried with a loud voice, "Lazarus, come forth!" And he who had died came out bound hand and foot with graveclothes.
>
> —John 11:43–44

My only living sibling, Elizabeth, was dying, and no one knew why. The situation looked hopeless. Then, as I sat at her bedside telling her stories of childhood, as mysteriously as she had slipped into the coma, she began to wake up.

The doctors were mystified at her recovery. They couldn't explain it; they just knew it shouldn't have happened. Then, after she was conscious, they said she would be paralyzed, but she isn't. They thought she would be blind, but she isn't. The doctors studied her closely and walked away shaking their perplexed heads.

The slopes of hopelessness are slippery and hard to climb back up once you have slid down the embankment. Albert Einstein said, "There are two ways to live your life. One is as though nothing is a miracle. The other is as though everything is a miracle."

When I arrived at the hospital, Elizabeth's vital signs were dismal, but I didn't whisper my good-byes to her. It never seemed like the right time as I sat beside her day after day. I didn't have a sense that she would be healed, but I didn't have a sense she would die. I pleaded for her recovery and then waited to see what God had planned.

My philosophy on hope is this: If there's any sign of life, there's hope for this life. If there's no sign of life, there's hope for the next life. Either way we win. Christ made sure of that.

—Patsy Clairmont

Welcome Home!

[May you] know the love of Christ which passes knowledge; that you may be filled with all the fullness of God.

—Ephesians 3:19

When I'm away from home, my husband, Don, and I talk on the phone frequently, sometimes several times a day. When the trip is over, I drive home from the airport, often chatting with Don by cell phone on the way, especially if he's not at work.

When I spot our house, more times than not, Don is standing in the driveway, waiting for me, a huge smile on his face. I jump out of the car, and he wraps me in his arms. Honestly, the Prize Patrol bearing a million-dollar check couldn't give a better welcome than Don gives me when I come home from a road trip.

Don isn't one to sit around watching TV, so he was probably working in the house or out in the yard. It would have been much more convenient for him to just look up from whatever he was doing and wave hello to me as I came in, maybe blow me a kiss and tell me to leave my luggage in the car and he'll carry it in later.

But that's not what he does. When he thinks I'm getting close, he stops what he's doing and heads for the driveway. He reminds me of a big ol' puppy dog, waiting for its little girl to come home.

I greet him the same way when he's been gone a day or more. The fact is, we're crazy about each other, and we want our kids to see us showing our love and devotion to each other. Our willingness to stop what we're doing and welcome each other home is symbolic of the way we prioritize our family life. We make time for each other. On a regular basis we set other things aside and make our marriage a priority.

—Sandi Patty

Yes, He Knows Us by Name

> The Lord knows those who are His.
> —2 Timothy 2:19

Several days ago a friend was visiting in my home and said, "Where's the dog?" I was stunned. "I beg your pardon. We don't call him 'the dog.'" It felt disrespectful not to use his proper name.

My family never had pets when I was a child. And the first time I had a dog it was not my idea. I remember thinking we could have her sit on a towel in the den and that might work. Then I fell in love with her. She was named "Corrie ten Boom" because she'd been rescued the day she was scheduled to die in the pound, which reminded me of the real Corrie ten Boom's escape from a prison camp.

When *our* Corrie had puppies, I named the first one Boomer because being from Oklahoma, I had meaning attached to Boomer Sooner. One became Betsy because she was tiny and frail and the sister of Corrie ten Boom. Another was named Casey because it was 1983 and Campus Crusade had an enormous event that year in Kansas City for college students, called KC83. You get the picture.

One of my favorite dogs ever was an adorable cocker spaniel named Mercy because, just as the Bible teaches, she followed her owner all the days of her life.

Names mean something.

The theme song, "Where Everybody Knows Your Name," from the television sitcom *Cheers* is one of my favorites. The thought sounds so inviting, so personal, so real. And how much more that God himself knows us. He knows our name, where we are at any given moment of our lives, what we need, what we long for and love. He would never think of us as "the girl," "the woman," "the one in blue." God knows your name.

—Mary Graham

Living in Christ's Victory

Embracing what God does for you is the best thing you can do for him.
—Romans 12:1 msg

For years I was afraid if I stopped trying so hard to be a "good" Christian, Satan might overtake me. In my flawed thinking, I also believed that if I stopped working so hard, there would be very little in me for God to love.

It has taken me many years to understand that God simply wants us to embrace what he has already done for us and rest in that. When I am trying so hard to live a good life, all the focus is on me, and all I can see are my flaws and failures. When I take my eyes off myself and my performance, and focus instead on the love of God and his companionship, I find amazing joy and peace.

Jesus wants us to live in his victory. He has already overcome the enemy and paid for our sin.

When I was a young girl, I dropped a china plate that had sentimental value for my mom. I was horrified and tried to hide all the pieces, but I felt so guilty I had to tell her. She looked at the pieces, hoping it could be mended, but it had been shattered; she threw the pieces away.

Later that day I retrieved the pieces from the trash and worked for hours trying to glue them back together, to no avail. When Mom heard me crying and saw what I was doing, she said, "Sheila, I've already forgiven you for breaking the plate. It's over. Just let it go."

Resting in the love of God means letting go of all the broken pieces we cling to and clinging instead to him. An overcomer is not someone who has never fallen, but rather someone who knows where her true strength lies.

—Sheila Walsh

December 6

Putting Pride and Fear Aside

> In the world you will have tribulation; but be of good cheer, I have overcome the world.
> —John 16:33

Why do we sometimes hesitate to ask our friends to help us carry our burdens through prayer? I received an e-mail from a friend who apologized for bothering me but said she really needed prayer. She listed three huge things that had happened to her or her family over the previous six weeks. She had carried these burdens all alone, when her friends could have helped carry the load!

I reminded her this is what friends are for and later wrote her a tongue-in-cheek e-mail:

> I hope I'm not bothering you, but could you pray for me? A small F5 tornado ran through our neighborhood last month and ripped our roof off. Thankfully, we only lost the Christmas decorations we had stored in the attic, but it is a bit of a nuisance when it rains. Then our kitten had her wisdom teeth pulled, and she got dry sockets, so it has been a real CATastrophe. Today I discovered that evil hackers hacked into my Web site and added twenty pounds to all the pictures of me! That's when I thought maybe I should ask my friends to pray with me.

Let's put pride and fear aside, and dare to reach out and admit our need for each other. Trust me, a real friend considers it an honor to be there in a time of need. Praying together is one of the highest privileges of friendship, and connection is one of the mightiest privileges of prayer.

—Lisa Whelchel

The Gift of Waiting

Men have not heard nor perceived by the ear, nor has the eye seen any God besides You, who acts for the one who waits for Him.

—Isaiah 64:4

We've heard it many times. Just wait on the Lord. Yet how many of us have realized he promises to act on our behalf when we wait on him? What does it look like to wait on him? While there is no easy answer to this question, we can look at a story Christ told.

Our story opens with a son who has come to demand his share of his father's inheritance. The rebellious boy took the money and went to a far country, squandering it on women, wine, and song. Without a penny, he found himself starving and slopping pigs for a farmer.

Finally, he thought, "I will go home to my father and beg his forgiveness. It would be better to be his servant than to live like this." Still a distance away, his father saw him and went running to embrace him. He shouted for the servants to kill the fatted calf, to cover the young man with a fine robe, and to put a ring on his finger, for this boy, once dead to him, was now alive. He was lost, but now he was found.

What a wonderful story, but let's think about it. In the beginning, the father could have run after the boy and refused to let him go. He could have tried to control him, thereby losing his relationship forever, but he did not. He waited on the Lord. The result: God acted on his behalf, and in God's own way, God brought the boy to himself and turned his heart toward home and toward his father (Luke 15:11–32).

Yes, indeed, God does act on behalf of those who wait for him.

—Lana Bateman

December 8

What Happens When We Rejoice

> A merry heart makes a cheerful countenance, but by sorrow of the heart the spirit is broken.
> —Proverbs 15:13

A scientist who studies the effects of humor on the human body reported that laughter stimulates the brain to produce the alertness hormone, catecholamine. The long-named substance contains epinephrine, norepinephrine, and dopamine and enables us to respond physically to emergencies. When the arousal hormone is released, it in turn stimulates the release of endorphins—the body's natural painkillers. As the brain's level of endorphins increases, the perception of pain decreases. Laughter, then, causes the body to produce its own painkiller.

I love to see the truth of Scripture confirmed by secular sciences. God has prescribed a joyful heart as good medicine (see Proverbs 17:22), and now science confirms that our body's natural painkillers are released when we laugh. The oft-repeated scriptural imperative "rejoice" takes on new significance as we realize what happens physiologically when we do rejoice.

It is not his intent that we suffer from ulcers, migraine headaches, and other stress-related illnesses. God means for us to experience joy, and we find our joy in him. If we are not experiencing joy, perhaps David's prayer in Psalm 51:12 could be ours: "Restore to me the joy of Your salvation, and uphold me by Your generous Spirit." Our salvation is Jesus; because of him, we anticipate an everlasting eternity with the God of the universe. Before that eternity is ours, however, we live out our days on this earth. We want to live them with joy. We want to live them with health.

—Marilyn Meberg

Let There Be Light

God saw the light, that it was good.
—Genesis 1:4

When God said, "Let there be light," there was! But take note that he didn't design the light holders—the sun, moon, and stars—until four days later. During creation, light was bounding about willy-nilly until it was corralled into designated positions.

Recently I was thinking about that sentence, "Let there be light," and it hit me anew that those were God's first recorded words. I don't know if that makes them more important or holier than anything else he said, but that reminder caused me to lean in and listen deeply because I don't want to miss the impact of his proclamations.

As I further explored "Let there be light," I was reminded that not only does Scripture's first book open with light, but the last book also closes with it. The theme throughout the Bible, from beginning to end, cover to cover, from Genesis to Revelation, is Jesus, the Light of the World.

As a matter of fact, we could say that the Bible is bookended in light and a holy fire. For light is the symbol God has chosen to represent the truth, and Jesus is the flame of our faith. Of course, divine insight is full of light, and Christ is that light; so anytime we understand something that's true, something we never had grasped before, Jesus is all over it. Don't you love that?

I can become downright giddy when a fresh truth settles inside me. I want to shout from the rooftop, "I get it! I get it! I finally get it!"

—Patsy Clairmont

December 10

Constant Contentment

> An appetite for good brings much satisfaction.
> —Proverbs 13:25 MSG

I once made a list of things I really wanted out of life. The hardest one of them to achieve was "contentment in all circumstances." Oh, boy. That's a challenge, isn't it?

Let's say something happened where I lost my health and was no longer able to function independently. Could I learn to be content? Good question.

The answer lies in the word *learn*. Of course that would be very difficult for me—one who has known independence my entire adult life. But I know the apostle Paul said he learned to be content in all circumstances (Philippians 4:12).

Learning to be content is an educational process, as is all learning. It takes time, and I'm sure over time at least some measure of contentment would come. It would start with the acceptance of present reality and hopefully move toward genuine contentment.

Funny thing, but when I told my mental-health therapist about this desire on my list, he smiled and said quietly, "Fat chance."

How true. How in the world can I be content in all circumstances? I really don't believe I can, but I'll try. I'll throw my heart into it and ask the Lord for his help.

Hardships, losses, inconveniences, interruptions, relinquishments? I could name twenty things I have to work at to find contentment. Maybe it won't happen in some areas. I don't know. I do know one thing: if I don't want it, it will never come. Never even be a blip on the horizon.

I call God into these dark areas of my life all the time, asking him to illumine me with his wisdom and encouragement then help me follow him into the light.

—Luci Swindoll

A Dad Who Calls Us Beautiful

The Spirit you received brought about your adoption to sonship. And by him we cry, "Abba, Father."
—Romans 8:15 NIV

When we look at God as our Dad, we get a free life makeover. We begin to really see ourselves as his daughters.

We have a Dad who calls us beautiful, so we begin to see ourselves as beautiful too. But not in the way the world defines *beautiful.* What God helps us recognize is an inner beauty accessorized with security, value, love, self-control, peace, joy, and contentment.

We finally see what God sees when he sees us!

And it doesn't stop there. We also start seeing others the way God sees them. Bitterness turns into forgiveness. Unhealthy longings slowly evaporate because of the attention God gives. That's how God starts to redefine for us what relationships are about.

But here's the deal: we can't assume everything will just *instantly* fall into place. God wants us to spend time getting to *know* him as our Dad. He wants a Father-daughter relationship with us. The more we get to know him as our Dad, the more our life changes.

In the Bible, King David tells us to "meditate" on God's Word. That doesn't mean David is asking you to pull out your yoga mat, sit Indian-style, and start humming, "Ooommmm." But King David understood the importance of taking in God's words, thinking about them, applying them to your life, and soaking in them day and night.

As I got to know God this way, he soon became very real and personal to me.

—Jenna Lucado

December 12

Know Thyself

> The Lord is good, a stronghold in the day of trouble; and He knows those who trust in Him.
>
> —Nahum 1:7

I've learned a lot about authentic friendships in the last few years. For instance, I know that before you have deeply connected friendships, you need to embrace your own neediness, shame, fears, insecurities, hopes, and longings for those relationships. I've learned that recognizing your own weakness is the perfect starting place for growing in intimacy with others.

Value intimacy with yourself as much as intimacy with God and others. When you talk to yourself, please be both honest and gentle. I needed help to know myself. Consider inviting a trusted counselor, guide, pastor, or mentor into your secret places, perhaps even ones you've hidden from your own sight.

Gaining close friendship means opening yourself to being more vulnerable with old friends and taking the risk to reach out and develop new friends. But first, please make sure you know how to discern safe people in whom to entrust your heart. Listen carefully and watch them without judgment but with wide-open eyes before you open wide your life.

I wish for you authentic relationships where you can dare to tell and hear the truth—where conflict is merely a precursor to your next step of growth and more intimate connection. And as you realize this, you can initiate difficult conversations in order to understand each other's perspective, to feel and then forgive, and to begin again at a deeper level.

My desire is that you will find friends who love to be with you and with whom you can connect, whether you're in the same room together or far apart.

—Lisa Whelchel

Let Christ Displace Worry

> Be strong and of good courage, do not fear nor be afraid of them; for the LORD your God, He is the One who goes with you. He will not leave you nor forsake you.
>
> —DEUTERONOMY 31:6

One of Satan's favorite tricks is to tempt us with some attractive lure and then decorate the tempting package with fear. Think of how he tempted Jesus in the desert, when Jesus was literally beginning to starve.

Can you see how Satan uses fear to tempt us away from trusting God?

- Look at your bank balance. You're not going to make it this month.
- Look at how exhausted you are. You don't have the energy to do what you need to do.
- You've splurged again and ruined your diet. You may as well quit.
- Your child is walking away from faith? She'll never come back. You blew it.

Jesus' short and powerful reply to Satan points us back to the Word of God to counter what might seem true at the moment with what is always true. "Don't fret or worry," he said. "Instead of worrying, pray. Let petitions and praises shape your worries into prayers, letting God know your concerns. Before you know it, a sense of God's wholeness, everything coming together for good, will come and settle you down. It's wonderful what happens when Christ displaces worry at the center of your life" (Philippians 4:6–7 MSG).

I love the phrase "when Christ displaces worry at the center of your life." That is how Jesus resisted temptation, and so can we.

—Sheila Walsh

December 14

Sorry, Wrong Number!

Do not sorrow, for the joy of the LORD is your strength.
—NEHEMIAH 8:10

I attract strange and funny incidents the way refrigerators attract magnets. For instance, last December, I had a phone conversation that went something like this:

"Mrs. Johnson?"

"Yes."

"This is Fred from Real-Life Prostheses, and . . ."

"I think you have the wrong number, Fred."

"I just wanted to let you know that your new breasts aren't ready yet."

"My new what?"

"Your husband called and asked us if we could do a rush job and have your new breasts ready before Christmas. The other guy told him yes and promised to have them ready tomorrow, but then we realized you were an extra-large, and they have to be special ordered. The other guy should have checked with me. I'm so sorry."

"Fred, I . . ."

"Oh, dear. He probably wanted it to be a surprise. He said you were going somewhere special for Christmas, and he knew you would want to look your best."

"Fred, I'm so sorry to argue with you, but I really don't think my husband called you. He died three years ago, and I just checked—yes, I still have my own breasts. And by the way, they're not what you would call extra—"

"Oh, my! Oh, dear! I am *so* sorry. I can't imagine how this happened. I . . . well . . . I. Uh, have a nice day."

Isn't God good? On any given day, he might have a stranger call you unexpectedly and give you a laugh that lasts a lifetime.

—Barbara Johnson

God's Faith-Bolstering Word

Are not two sparrows sold for a copper coin? And not one of them falls to the ground apart from your Father's will. But the very hairs of your head are all numbered.

—Matthew 10:29–30

Our joy, our ability to laugh in the face of difficulties, has more to do with how we view God than how he views us. Sometimes we fear maybe God isn't all that interested in our daily lives. We've been taught the his-eye-is-on-the-sparrow-so-we-know-he-watches-us mentality, but we aren't convinced. Sometimes we see our lives running counter to our prayers, and we assume God doesn't care. That prompts us to feel a growing fear that God is unaware of our trials and circumstances. When this happens, we need bolstering, and there's no better source for faith-bolstering than God's living Word.

Reading God's words to Jeremiah (and to us) invariably renews my vigor as well as my faith. When he reminds us that he has a hope-filled future for us (see Jeremiah 29:11–13), I feel like David when he said, "By my God, I can leap over a wall" (Psalm 18:29).

To feel assured of God's plan for us, we need to be convinced that he is aware of us as individuals. That's why I love Matthew 10:30, which says the very hairs of our heads are numbered. What mind-boggling personal awareness!

I am not on a haphazard course of my own poor choosing. Psalm 16:11 assures me "You will show me the path of life." I choose to believe God will indeed make life's path known to me and that where I am on that path is no surprise to him.

—Marilyn Meberg

December 16

Awaking My Imagination

> There shall be no night there: They need no lamp nor light of the sun, for the Lord God gives them light.
> —Revelation 22:5

Getting up in the wee hours to experience the first rays of light conquering darkness heartens me. I watch the ebony melt from the sky and drizzle behind the distant stand of trees, and my senses awaken. Those first morning moments when the sun seems to ignite a horizon of hope—a new dawn, a new day, a new beginning—who doesn't need that? Genesis 1:4 tells us God himself found it pleasing: "And God saw the light, that it was good; and God divided the light from the darkness."

Yesterday can't be altered, tomorrow can't be predicted, and today can't be controlled any more than I can adjust the sun's path. While this knowledge could make us feel helpless, I find a deep comfort in the knowledge that the one who placed the sun on its course has lit a distinct path for us. The path is filled with purpose and with the potential for interior prosperity: "You will show me the path of life" (Psalm 16:11).

While on earth, we will encounter both darkness and light, but that will not always be so. A day will come when Christ in all his glory and light will fill every shaded nook and every shadowed cranny, and darkness will be no more. Nothing will be as we now know it, and earth and God's people will experience full redemption.

Imagine that. Just imagine!

—Patsy Clairmont

Even Anger Is a Gift

Be angry, and do not sin.
—Psalm 4:4

In so many ways, I grew up in a perfect family, reared by loving parents who worked in music and ministry all their lives. Mom and Dad gave my two brothers and me the most wonderfully stable and encouraging upbringing any child could hope for.

I don't have a single memory of them arguing. If they ever said a harsh word to each other, it was out of my hearing. What a blessing it was to grow up in that family. And yet . . .

My parents tell me now that they did argue occasionally. They did get irritated with each other from time to time. They didn't have a perfect marriage, but they hid its imperfections from their children, wanting to shield us from their private disputes.

As a result, I grew up without seeing how adults' normal conflicts were resolved. I didn't learn how to respond appropriately when someone I loved did or said something hurtful, whether it was accidental or intentional.

Because I never saw my parents show anger, I grew up thinking I must be flawed somehow whenever I got mad. I'd like to say I figured this out by myself, but most of these revelations came during the time I spent in a residential therapy center during those dark days after my first marriage had ended and the music world was poised to (rightfully) condemn me as a sinner and a hypocrite.

I am so thankful for the skilled and Scripture-guided professionals there who helped me see that *all* our emotions—even anguish, even anger—are gifts God gives us to deal with the pressures and pleasures of our lives.

—Sandi Patty

December 18

Bathroom Conversations with God

> The LORD is near to all who call upon Him, to all who call upon Him in truth. He will fulfill the desire of those who fear Him; He also will hear their cry and save them.
> —PSALM 145:18–19

A turning point in my life came when I was a teenager and I changed the way I approached prayer. Up to that point, my prayer life had closely resembled frequent chats with a department-store Santa Claus: "Dear God, I need this and that, and please bless him and her, and thank you for all these gifts. Amen."

Not that God doesn't want to hear and answer our needs and bless our loved ones and give us gifts, but that is such a tiny sliver of the relationship he longs to have with us. He offers us friendship, guidance, revelation, peace, and so much more.

Now, this may sound a bit sacrilegious, and I don't want to offend anyone. But this really did help me. Maybe it will help you. I decided not to close my eyes when I prayed. I also ruled out bowing my head. I wanted prayer to be more like a conversation than a spiritual discipline.

With that in mind, I got up every morning, walked down the hall to the bathroom (which is where I had my daily devotions), sat down on the toilet (the lid was down!), and imagined that Jesus was sitting across from me . . . on the rim of the bathtub. (I guess we should have traded places, considering I was sitting on the throne, but I didn't think about that at the time.) I could look straight into Jesus' eyes and pour my heart out to him.

This new perspective changed my morning quiet time from religious routine to heart-to-heart conversations with my Abba Father.

—Lisa Whelchel

"Why Not?" Instead of "Why Me?"

Be transformed by the renewing of your mind.
—Romans 12:2

The ability to think is a wonderful gift. We take it for granted, yet what would it be like if we couldn't remember, evaluate, determine, make plans, decide right from wrong, or change our minds?

When I ask myself hypothetical questions—"If I had the chance, would I do that again?" "Could I learn to fly a hot air balloon?" "Should I have been a mud wrestler?"—in effect I reestablish who I am and validate the fact that it's okay to be me. I've done this kind of thing all my life at various stages. The mind is like a compass, and I want mine set at true north.

It has been said that sixty-five thousand thoughts float through our minds each day. Every one of those thoughts has the seed of possibility in it. We choose with our will what we'll do with that thought. Will we stay stuck in "If only . . ." or "Why me?"—or will we open our minds to "What if?" and "Why not?"

Let's never stop asking questions. Questions give us a harbor to remember where we once lived mentally. They remind us of the possibilities that can be born out of thoughts and musings, and they link together patterns that define our lives. Asking questions keeps us open-minded and openhearted to what was and is and might be in the years to come. Questions send us on our way into all sorts of journeys in search of adventure.

—Luci Swindoll

December 20

Bad Shame Versus Good Guilt

> Let us hold fast the confession of our hope without wavering, for He who promised is faithful.
> —Hebrews 10:23

Cheap perfume. That's how shame feels to me. It's like the cheap, cloying perfume I used to get as a child at Christmastime. Mine came in a little bottle in the shape of a dog, which I loved, but the fragrance inside was terrible.

One Christmas, as I opened the container and sniffed, hoping this year the manufacturer had come up with something more pleasant smelling, my little brother ran past me with his new robot. He rammed into me at full throttle, and the whole bottle poured out onto my sweater. The smell was atrocious!

I took my sweater off, took a bath, and then I took another bath. But I smelled of that cheap perfume until Easter!

Shame is like that—nauseating, heavy. It's like a ravenous, demanding monster, and no matter how much you feed it to quiet the noise, it is never enough. It sits in the pit of your stomach or wraps its cold arms around your shoulders. And it doesn't let go. Shame tells me I *am* something wrong. There is no hope there.

Guilt, on the other hand, is something different. Guilt has a purpose. It is there to (hopefully) teach you, and it has a point of beginning and ending. Shame is not as clearly defined as guilt. It doesn't seem to have a beginning or an end; it just is.

Guilt tells me I have done something wrong. With that awareness, there is hope. I can go to the person I have hurt and ask him or her to forgive me. Or I can work to right an injustice I committed.

—Sheila Walsh

He Likes Me!

I have inscribed you on the palms of My hands.
—Isaiah 49:16

My concept of Jesus used to be so big that it lacked the personal. Instead of focusing on a close connection with him, I had worked long and hard on those relationships I could manipulate through my "Look at me, aren't I great!" mentality.

That is why bulimia had seemed like such a good option for me for so long—I believed it kept me thin, and I thought people accepted me more readily when I looked a certain way.

I cannot begin to explain how freeing it was when I embraced Christ as my real Friend. For so long he was simply a gigantic *idea* to me. Although I believed them to be true, the unfathomable images of Savior, Redeemer, and the ultimate Sacrifice for mankind made God so big in my mind that what I knew of him didn't translate to what was going on in my everyday life.

I had always been told of God's great love, and somewhere inside I believed it. But what completely melted my heart, what completely liberated me from choking insecurity, wasn't just the truth that Jesus loved me but that Jesus *liked* me. Exactly as I was. I didn't have to pretend; I didn't have to be a certain size or wear the right jeans. I could have a bad-hair day, and he would still like me.

It wasn't just my obedience and righteousness he was interested in. He was interested in me. He autographed me on his hand, not because I was born into a great family or because of any of my successes or my attempts at being "cool" or even because he loves me, but because he likes me just as I am.

—Natalie Grant

December 22

On Stage, Living a Dream

> Sing to the Lord, all the earth; proclaim the good news of His salvation from day to day.
>
> —1 Chronicles 16:23

On my journey back to good health after bariatric surgery, I regained something wonderful. I fell in love with music all over again. Now my joyful heart is full to bursting as I think of the times music spoke for me when I couldn't find the words. Music has been a gift to me all my life.

Never were those feelings stronger than when I stepped onto the stage at Carnegie Hall for a series of Christmas concerts a couple of years ago with the New York Pops orchestra. Stepping onto that stage was one of the most thrilling things I've ever done as a musician. It represented so much more than a sold-out concert. Not so much "look at me, I've finally made it," but an acknowledgment of my long season of experience.

I've done this singing thing in tiny churches and grand settings. But to perform in Carnegie Hall is every musician's dream, at the top of the wish list. Carnegie's stage is not where you refine your work. It's the place where you'd better be prepared.

We have a little saying in our family: "Go big or go home." For me, standing on that edge at Carnegie Hall incorporated both the recognition of my past experience and an edge, defined as where "something is likely to begin."

It felt like the celebration of a new beginning: A new, healthier body. A new chapter of my work as a performer. And, an all-encompassing thankfulness to the One who has made it all possible, a closer relationship to my Savior.

—Sandi Patty

Posting Path Lighters

These words which I command you today shall be in your heart. You shall . . . talk of them . . . when you walk by the way, when you lie down, and when you rise up. . . . You shall write them on the doorposts of your house and on your gates.

—Deuteronomy 6:6–9

Have you ever read all 176 verses of Psalm 119? C'mon now, honestly? Every verse? If not, I dare you. Here's why: those verses are like sticky-note reminders for our zany emotions. But because Psalm 119 is so cotton-pickin' long, we're tempted to start reading but not finish.

About halfway through this psalm, you may think to yourself, *This is repetitious.*

Exactly. It's meant to be. It's a way to secure our minds with the protective counsel offered in Scripture. If you have had children or pets, you know how many times you have to repeat important instructions. ("If I've told you once, I've told you a hundred times: float your sailboat in the sink, not the commode!") Psalm 119 is full of necessary reminders to keep us on the narrow yet lit path.

To remind myself to think often of God's Word, I like to place it, like memos, first inside, then outside of myself. Want to join me? We'll memorize it. Study it. Sing it. Rehearse it. Teach it. Post it.

Write your favorite verses in your journal, pen them in calligraphy and frame them for your walls, tape them to your mirror, magnetize them to your fridge, and most importantly, walk in the light they will add to your path.

—Patsy Clairmont

December 24

It's Not How We *Start*

> I have fought the good fight, I have finished the race, I have kept the faith.
>
> —2 Timothy 4:7

I have yet to meet someone who has not struggled with his or her self-esteem at some point. We all struggle to different degrees and handle our insecurities in widely ranging ways. I handled mine the only way I knew how: with a damaging eating disorder.

Many of you struggle daily in that same prison, fighting that same psychological disease.

Others of you are coping with insecurities, fears, and lack of self-worth by experimenting with drugs and alcohol. Some of you are medicating your pain with sexual promiscuity, seeking love, affection, and acceptance wherever you can find it. You may even be dealing with your problems by cutting yourself because you are full of so much depression, anger, sadness, and rage that slicing your flesh brings you a strange release and a sense of control. Still others of you may not be "acting out" at all, but on the inside, you constantly rip away at your self-image, inflicting horrible emotional wounds on yourself with words sharper than any blade.

If you're coping with whatever is going on in your head by using one of these (or other) dysfunctional and dangerous methods, you feel tossed out—discarded and rejected. You are ashamed, and you feel alone. Shipwrecked on a deserted island with no rescue in sight.

I know that island well: been there, done that, wrote the tour guide.

Now I know that success is not about how you start; it's about how you finish. This journey through life can be hard and get really messy at times. We're bound to fall down. But each time we get up again, we learn another valuable lesson.

—Natalie Grant

The Hope of Christmas

The Word became flesh and made his dwelling among us.
We have seen his glory, the glory of the one and only Son,
who came from the Father, full of grace and truth.
—John 1:14 NIV

As the song says, "In the air, there's the feeling of Christmas." I love Christmas because I get to see it through the eyes of my three young children. They turn Christmas music on first thing in the morning and make a date with their grandma to make sugar cookies. They work at my side in our local food pantry and are continually awed at how much *more* food is on the shelves *this* time of year. Even now they are discovering that Christmas brings the best out in people. They pick out their "angels" for Project Angel Tree and gather shoe boxes for Operation Christmas Child.

I love Christmas because I get to try new candy, cookie, and goody recipes for my family!

I love Christmas because the bell ringers are faithful in their gentle reminder that someone needs me, us, you. We do make a difference. One dollar at a time.

I love Christmas because, despite massive commercialism and all the political correctness in saying "Happy Holidays" and stripping courthouse lawns of nativity scenes, somehow we still haven't managed to ruin the spirit of Christmas.

I love Christmas because of the joy and hope that *is* Christmas. It was at this time that the Word became flesh and made his dwelling among us.

I love Christmas because Christmas is love. I don't say that to trivialize anyone's pain but rather because love and hope are still alive. If we are quiet or still long enough we *can* feel that love in the air.

—Donna VanLiere

December 26

Breathing in God

> Let patience have its perfect work, that you may be perfect and complete, lacking nothing.
>
> —James 1:4

As a mom, I believe it's critical that I "live and breathe" Jesus because what I inhale is what I'll exhale. Proverbs 23:7 says that our outward actions are prompted by our inner thoughts: "For as he thinks in his heart, so is he."

I've found that most moms have an easier time giving than receiving. It's very important that we learn how to receive so we have more to give. It is equally if not more important to discern the right and healthy things to receive so we can give wisdom and life to our family.

Be intentionally aware of everything you allow to enter through your eyes, ears, and heart. What are you watching on television and movies? What are you reading? What kind of music are you listening to? Are you surrounded by friends who fill you up or friends who tear you down? It isn't just about you. What you allow inside your heart and mind is what will inevitably be poured out on your family. What you receive is, most likely, what you will give.

So what should we be receiving? Jesus told his disciples, "Receive the Holy Spirit" (John 20:22). Some of the practical ways we receive the Spirit are through praise, Bible study, meditation, prayer, and rest. By taking time to receive from God, we learn to take care of ourselves.

The truth is, my only hope for being a good mother is receiving the power of Jesus to parent through me. That is why I must breathe in Jesus all through the day so I may impart life to my family.

—Lisa Whelchel

A Welcomed Vision

To everything there is a season, a time for every purpose under heaven: . . . a time to weep, and a time to laugh.

—Ecclesiastes 3:1, 4

Eleven or twelve hours after my mother's death, I was in the shower, which often serves as my sanctuary, thinking about my mom. Trying to internalize the enormity of what had happened that day, I pondered her arrival in heaven. What was it like?

As I tried to visualize her in her new surroundings, I became lost to my own. Gradually, I saw her in the arms of Jesus. He was holding her as one would a child, cradling her against his body. Her face was radiant, and as Jesus held her, he began to gently swing her back and forth in his arms, back and forth.

In the vision, Mom laughed and laughed, until her head was thrown back in total abandonment. At first I was a bit startled. Mom hadn't laughed in two years—hadn't even smiled in six months. But as joy and relief flooded over me I thought, *Well, of course. She can laugh now. God has wiped away all her tears, and now it is my mother's time to laugh again.*

I don't believe I'd ever had a vision before. I'm not even sure what I think about people who claim to have them! But that evening, the image of my mother's carefree laughing not only comforted me but also inspired a concept I love: In life we encounter pain, heartache, and sorrow. But as believers in Christ, who conquered death, we have the last laugh!

—Marilyn Meberg

December 28

A Sovereign God

> The Lord will perfect that which concerns me.
> —Psalm 138:8

Psalm 138:8 gives us a powerful word from God, one that David understood quite well. But do we? This expression of the sovereignty of God should give us great peace. Notice that it does not say, "If I don't fail God or disappoint him, he will accomplish what concerns me." It doesn't say, "If I don't ever sin again, he will accomplish what concerns me." Nor does it say, he *might* accomplish . . . or he *could* accomplish . . ." David's words simply say, "He *will* accomplish what concerns me."

What are you worried about today? Is it your children, the salvation of those you love, your job, your friendships, your home, or your church? Whatever your concerns might be, God is addressing them.

Some of us feel this can't be true because we have prayed so long for something so very important. However, we don't have a timeline with David's words, do we? He simply says it will be done. Can we trust, as David did, in what we cannot yet see?

Can we trust that God is addressing what concerns us in exactly the way we would like, or as quickly as we would like? Not always. Sometimes he is about to place his hand on our lives in ways we could never have dreamed or imagined, but we can trust that our God is fully alive in all that is happening—even the delays.

We have a God who is after our highest good. His great love could do no less. He knows our hearts, our longings, and our needs. His love will not allow anything to touch our lives that will bring more pain or struggle than it takes to make us all we have prayed to be and all he desires for us to be.

—Lana Bateman

Why God Tests His People

> The Lord your God led you all the way these forty years in the wilderness, to humble you and test you, to know what was in your heart, whether you would keep His commandments or not.
>
> —Deuteronomy 8:2

The Israelites were tested many times early in their history. First, they were enslaved by the Egyptians and held captive for 430 years. After Pharaoh finally let them go, he changed his mind and sent soldiers to attack God's people. Then, because of their choices, they were lost in the desert for forty years, pushed to the limits of their ability, and crying out to God for answers, wondering if they'd made the wrong decision to leave Egypt.

Why were they put through so much? To learn the heart of their God. To understand that they were loved and treasured. To appreciate and accept the need to put their complete faith in God. And to see how capable they really were when they did put their faith in Him.

I believe that one of the most powerful fruits of testing is to begin to finally grasp that, although we are weak, in Christ's strength we are strong. Each time we are tested and by God's grace we stand, we grow in our knowledge of him and in our confidence that, indeed, "I can do all things through Christ who strengthens me" (Philippians 4:13).

When Satan tests us or when we try to test God, it serves no purpose. But when God tests us, the testing is for *us*—to show us what is in us. He doesn't test us to shame us. I believe it has to be a gift of love—his own divine show-and-tell. He's showing us we're strong . . . in him.

—Sheila Walsh

December 30

Amazing Connection

> Be strong. Take courage. Don't be intimidated. Don't give them a second thought because God, your God, is striding ahead of you. He's right there with you. He won't let you down; he won't leave you.
>
> —Deuteronomy 31:6 msg

My husband was taking our six-year-old son for his vaccinations the next day.

At first, our little boy expressed concern that Daddy wouldn't accompany him into the exam room. When I told him that I knew Daddy never did, or would, send him to the exam room by himself, he sighed and said, "Well, you're just more supportive."

Now, *that* I could understand. Moms and dads are supportive in different ways, and "mom support" probably felt a little more meaningful to a six-year-old in a doctor's office.

Isn't it amazing how God created us for connection—to need one another? Did you know that science has shown that simply the presence of another person in a stressful situation decreases the levels of one's stress hormones by 50 percent?

I've always believed that one of the most effective lies of the enemy is the one that whispers, *You're the only one*. It's easy to believe you're the only one who's ever been in that situation or made that bad choice or been victimized in that way.

But the truth is, God sent his Son to live a human life and to experience human challenges and heartbreaks. He understands how we feel. And the fact is, no matter where you've been, what you've done, or what's happened to you, God was there. You've never lived an unloved moment, and you've never experienced anything that hasn't passed through his hands.

—Lori Roberson

Taking Hold of the Kite String

If I go up to the heavens, you are there; if I make my bed in the depths, you are there.
—Psalm 139:8 niv

I read an article about a woman who, at the age of eighty-seven, finished college and got her degree. Her name was Anne Martindell. She started classes at Smith College in 1932 as a freshman. But after a year, her father, a federal judge, forced her to leave because he was afraid she'd be too educated to find a husband. Can you beat that?

In the interim, she served as U.S. ambassador to New Zealand, a New Jersey state senator, and head of the U.S. Office of Foreign Disaster Assistance. She married and divorced twice, had four children, nine grandchildren, and two great-grandchildren. In 1996, feeling a void in her life, she decided to take the advice of a loved one and enroll in Smith's educational program designed for older women who wanted to return to class. She earned her diploma in 2002 and received an honorary doctorate at the same time.

The program's founding director told the reporter that when Mrs. Martindell first came back to campus, she walked with a cane, but within weeks it disappeared, and in no time she was revitalized. "There was a spring in her step and a gleam in her eye," the director said.

What better describes adventure? It's letting your personal vision and dreams take you to new heights and new beginnings. Lauren Bacall once said, "Imagination is the highest kite one can fly"—so true. Let's take hold of the string, fly away to where it takes us, and who knows? We might wind up on the moon.

—Luci Swindoll

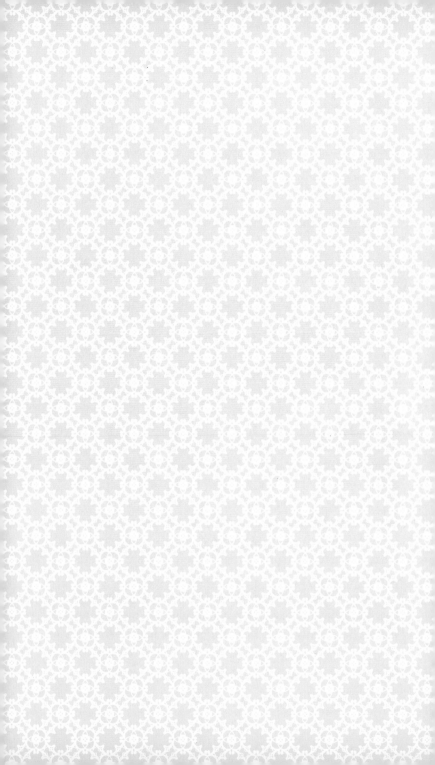

Sources

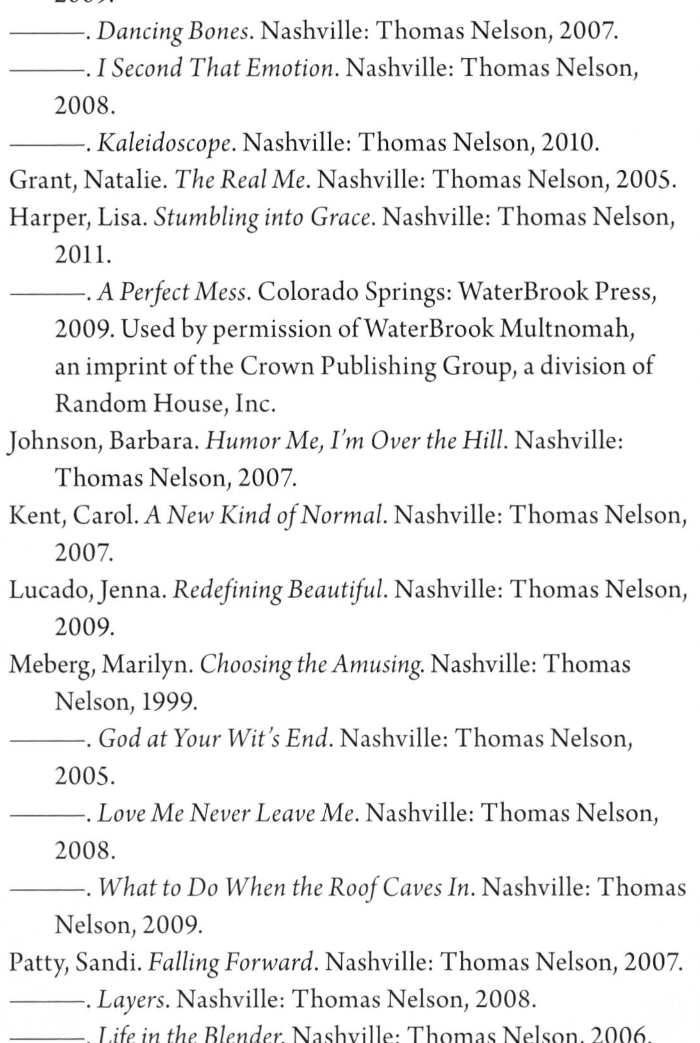

Clairmont, Patsy. *Catching Fireflies*. Nashville: Thomas Nelson, 2009.

———. *Dancing Bones*. Nashville: Thomas Nelson, 2007.

———. *I Second That Emotion*. Nashville: Thomas Nelson, 2008.

———. *Kaleidoscope*. Nashville: Thomas Nelson, 2010.

Grant, Natalie. *The Real Me*. Nashville: Thomas Nelson, 2005.

Harper, Lisa. *Stumbling into Grace*. Nashville: Thomas Nelson, 2011.

———. *A Perfect Mess*. Colorado Springs: WaterBrook Press, 2009. Used by permission of WaterBrook Multnomah, an imprint of the Crown Publishing Group, a division of Random House, Inc.

Johnson, Barbara. *Humor Me, I'm Over the Hill*. Nashville: Thomas Nelson, 2007.

Kent, Carol. *A New Kind of Normal*. Nashville: Thomas Nelson, 2007.

Lucado, Jenna. *Redefining Beautiful*. Nashville: Thomas Nelson, 2009.

Meberg, Marilyn. *Choosing the Amusing*. Nashville: Thomas Nelson, 1999.

———. *God at Your Wit's End*. Nashville: Thomas Nelson, 2005.

———. *Love Me Never Leave Me*. Nashville: Thomas Nelson, 2008.

———. *What to Do When the Roof Caves In*. Nashville: Thomas Nelson, 2009.

Patty, Sandi. *Falling Forward*. Nashville: Thomas Nelson, 2007.

———. *Layers*. Nashville: Thomas Nelson, 2008.

———. *Life in the Blender*. Nashville: Thomas Nelson, 2006.

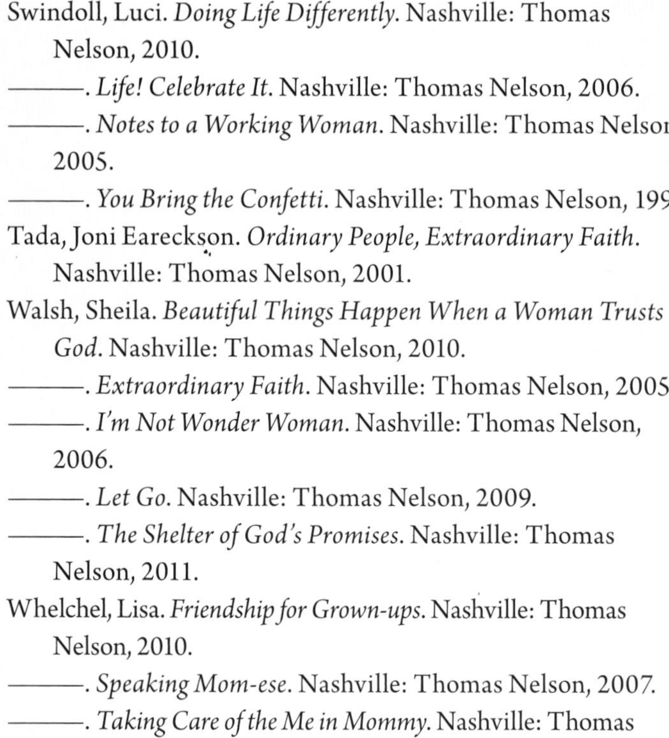

Swindoll, Luci. *Doing Life Differently*. Nashville: Thomas Nelson, 2010.

———. *Life! Celebrate It*. Nashville: Thomas Nelson, 2006.

———. *Notes to a Working Woman*. Nashville: Thomas Nelson, 2005.

———. *You Bring the Confetti*. Nashville: Thomas Nelson, 1997.

Tada, Joni Eareckson. *Ordinary People, Extraordinary Faith*. Nashville: Thomas Nelson, 2001.

Walsh, Sheila. *Beautiful Things Happen When a Woman Trusts God*. Nashville: Thomas Nelson, 2010.

———. *Extraordinary Faith*. Nashville: Thomas Nelson, 2005.

———. *I'm Not Wonder Woman*. Nashville: Thomas Nelson, 2006.

———. *Let Go*. Nashville: Thomas Nelson, 2009.

———. *The Shelter of God's Promises*. Nashville: Thomas Nelson, 2011.

Whelchel, Lisa. *Friendship for Grown-ups*. Nashville: Thomas Nelson, 2010.

———. *Speaking Mom-ese*. Nashville: Thomas Nelson, 2007.

———. *Taking Care of the Me in Mommy*. Nashville: Thomas Nelson, 2006.

About the Contributors

After a lifetime of emotional struggles, bad habit patterns, and the inability to break free from a painful past, Lana Bateman knew there had to be a "bridge" between her difficulties and the victorious Christian life. The freedom she eventually found led her to establish Philippian Ministries and go on to help hundreds of women, men, and couples experience emotional healing. Lana serves as prayer warrior at Women of Faith events, praying behind the scenes for speakers and audience alike.

Daughter of best-selling author Max Lucado, Jenna Lucado Bishop has realized that she has a passion for writing and speaking just like her dad. She is currently a part of the Revolve Tour, an event for teen girls that includes Christian artists like Hawk Nelson, Chad Eastham, and many more.

An original Women of Faith speaker, Patsy Clairmont's quick wit and depth of biblical knowledge combine in a powerful pint-size package. A recovering agoraphobic with a pronounced funny bone, Patsy speaks to women from all walks of life. Patsy and her husband live in Tennessee.

Mary Graham is president of Women of Faith, a division of Thomas Nelson, Inc., which hosts America's largest women's conference. Since 1996, over three million women have attended Women of Faith conferences in eighty cities. Mary serves as host for the conference and works closely with speakers and musicians. In the Women of Faith offices, she directs seventy-five employees and supervises all phases of the ministry, including Women of Faith publishing and recording. Prior to joining Women of Faith, Mary was director of international ministries for Insight for Living. She also invested twenty-two years with Campus Crusade for Christ International. Her work has taken her to every continent, and she has lived in many parts of the United States. She now lives in Texas.

Natalie Grant is a two-time Female Vocalist of the Year Dove Award winner and one of the most powerful voices in both Christian and mainstream music. However, it is Natalie's deepest desire to communicate the heart of Christ to her audience. Author of *The Real Me,* she performs at approximately 150 events across America each year and is a regular speaker at Women of Faith and Revolve conferences. She and her husband Bernie Herms live in Tennessee.

Lisa Harper is a gifted communicator whose writing and speaking overflow with colorful, pop-culture references that connect the dots between the Bible era and modern life. For six years Lisa was the national women's ministry director at Focus on the Family, followed by six years as the women's ministry director at a large church. The author of nine books, with a Masters of Theological Studies from Covenant Seminary, Lisa is a featured speaker with Women of Faith.

Barbara Johnson guided millions of hurting women through the tunnel of despair with her best-selling books including *Plant a Geranium in Your Cranium, Living Somewhere Between Estrogen and Death,* and *Stick a Geranium in Your Hat and Be Happy.* A member of the original Women of Faith speaker team, Barbara delivered her comforting, humor-filled message of love across the country at Women of Faith conferences for six years before illness forced her to leave the tour and continue her ministry of encouragement from home. Lovingly known as "The Geranium Lady," Barbara and husband founded the nonprofit Spatula Ministries, an organization tailored to help parents in crisis. She died of cancer in 2007 at the age of 79.

Carol Kent is hilariously funny, biblically sound, and heartbreakingly transparent in person and in print. Founder and president of Speak Up for Hope (a prison ministry) and Speak Up Speaker Services (a speakers bureau), Carol is an expert on public speaking, writing, and evangelism. She sits on the advisory boards of MOPS International and the Advanced Writers and Speakers Association. She travels the world speaking to tens of thousands each year at various events.

Marilyn Meberg speaks each year to 350,000 women at the Women of Faith conferences and is the author of several books. Never one to avoid the hard questions of life, Marilyn Meberg shares the wisdom she's gained from two master's degrees and a private counseling practice.

Sandi Patty has amassed more awards than any other female vocalist in contemporary Christian music history. She's been inducted into the Gospel Music Hall of Fame, received thirty-nine Dove Awards, five Grammy Awards, and three RIAA-certified platinum and five gold recordings. It is Sandi's down-to-earth style that has endeared her to Women of Faith audiences. Sandi is the author of seven books, including *The Edge of the Divine*. Sandi and her family live in Oklahoma City.

Lori Robertson's "day job" is director of programming at Women of Faith. Stepping from behind the scenes and onto the stage to serve as event emcee is an unexpected career move and certainly not where she anticipated her degrees (BS, MBA) to take her. Now in her eighth year at Women of Faith, Lori lives with her husband and son in Texas.

Luci Swindoll is an author of many books, Women of Faith speaker to over 350,000 women a year, photographer, musician, artist, and world traveler. She loves to share her joy of life with everyone she encounters. Her most recent book has the title of *Simple Secrets to a Happy Life*. Luci lives in Texas.

Kim Cash Tate is the author of *Faithful, Heavenly Places,* and the memoir *More Christian than African American.* A former practicing attorney, she has spoken at Women of Faith events and is also the founder of Colored in Christ Ministries. She and her husband have two children and live in the St. Louis area.

Joni Eareckson Tada has known the grace of God in the midst of the bruising reality of quadriplegia for more than thirty years. Joni is president of JAF Ministries, an organization that accelerates Christian ministry among people with disabilities. She is also host of *Joni and Friends,* a daily radio program. Joni is the author of more than twenty books. She and her husband live in Southern California.

Donna VanLiere is the *New York Times* and *USA Today* best-selling author of *The Christmas Shoes, The Angels of Morgan Hill, Finding Grace,* and other titles. Four of her novels have been turned into made-for-TV movies. She is a gifted conference speaker. She lives in Tennessee with her husband and three children.

Sheila Walsh is a powerful communicator, Bible teacher, and best-selling author with more than four million books sold. A featured speaker with Women of Faith, Sheila has reached more than 3.5 million women by artistically combining honesty, vulnerability, and humor with God's Word. Sheila lives in Texas with her husband and son.

Lisa Whelchel, whose first appearance on *The New Mickey Mouse Club* launched her acting career, is best known for her role as Blair on the perennial hit TV show *The Facts of Life*. She is the author of *Friendship for Grown-Ups, Creative Correction, The Facts of Life (and Other Lessons My Father Taught Me),* and *The ADVENTure of Christmas.* Lisa and her husband live in Texas with their three children.

WOMEN OF FAITH®

Get Fresh . . .
Enthusiasm, Inspiration, Strength at a Women of Faith weekend event!

At Women of Faith, thousands of women come together for two days to laugh, cry, worship, share, and draw strength from each other and from God. Messages, music, and more combine for a one-of-a-kind event designed by women for women.

"I'm always energized for months after attending these events!" –Angie G.

Join us at an event near you!

See details and sign up at **womenoffaith.com** or call 888-49-FAITH (888-493-2484).

"God's presence was felt the very first moment we walked in the door and never left!" –Kellye H.

Don't Wait! Seats are Going Fast.

Bring your friends, bring your family, or just bring yourself . . . but whatever you do, don't miss this opportunity. Register today!

womenoffaith.com | 888.49.FAITH (888.493.2484)

Follow us on facebook twitter

Women of Faith® is a division of Thomas Nelson.

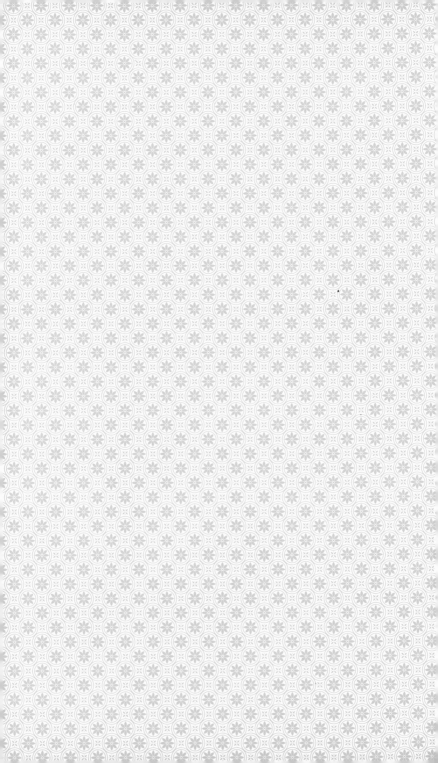